DRAWING THE LINE IN MISSISSIPPI

# HOLT COLLIER

*His Life,
His Roosevelt Hunts,
and
The Origin of the
Teddy Bear*

MINOR FERRIS BUCHANAN

CENTENNIAL PRESS
Jackson, Mississippi

*For* my wife and our children.

To the nimrods of my youth.

---

Copyright © 2002
Centennial Press of Mississippi, Inc.

All rights reserved. No part of this book may be reproduced in any form or by any electronic, photographic, or mechanical means, including information storage and retrieval systems, without permission in writing from the publisher, except by a reviewer, who may quote brief passages in a review.

Front of jacket art: Portrait of Holt Collier by Sam Beibers, Jackson, Mississippi.

Back of jacket and page ii: This cartoon, according to Wallace Dailey, curator of The Theodore Roosevelt Collection, Harvard College Library, was the second published version. One version hung in the National Press Club, Washington, D.C., "since lost or stolen."

Maps by Sam Beibers.
Printed in the United States of America

9 8 7 6 5 4 3 2

Library of Congress Cataloging-in-Publication Data

Buchanan, Minor Ferris, 1951-
   Holt Collier : his life, his Roosevelt hunts, and the origin of the teddy bear / Minor Ferris Buchanan.
     p. cm.
Includes bibliographical references (p. ) and index.
   ISBN 1-893062-37-6
1. Collier, Holt. 2. African Americans--Biography. 3. Roosevelt, Theodore, 1858-1919--Friends and associates. 4. African American hunters—Mississippi—Delta (Region)—Biography. 5. African American soldiers—Biography. 6. Teddy bears--History. 7. Bear hunting—Mississippi—History—20th century. 8. Bear hunting—Louisiana—History—20th century. 9. Mississippi—Biography. 10. Hinds family. I. Title.
   E185.97.C66 B83 2002
   973.91'1'092--dc21

2002073757

## Centennial Press of Mississippi, Inc.
P. O. Box 12974 • Jackson, MS 39236-2974
601-957-9095

# CONTENTS

Preface .................................................. vi
Acknowledgments ...................................... viii

PROLOGUE ............................................. xiii

PART ONE
*Holt Collier and The Hinds Family of Mississippi*

    Chapter 1    A Southern Aristocracy,
                      Green-Hinds-Jackson-Davis ................ 3
    Chapter 2    Cameron Howell Hinds .................... 17
    Chapter 3    A Primeval Wilderness .................... 26
    Chapter 4    From Greenville to Pittsburg Landing ........ 37
    Chapter 5    Ninth Texas Cavalry ...................... 57
    Chapter 6    Boots and Saddles ....................... 72
    Chapter 7    Vicksburg ............................... 81
    Chapter 8    Delta Rangers ........................... 89
    Chapter 9    Occupation and Court-Martial ............ 103

PART TWO
*Holt Collier, Theodore Roosevelt and the Origin of the Teddy Bear*

    Chapter 10   To Texas and a Distant Farewell ............ 121
    Chapter 11   The Hunter ............................. 133
    Chapter 12   The Great White Hunter ................. 151
    Chapter 13   The "Picnic" ........................... 165
    Chapter 14   In the Louisiana Canebrakes .............. 184
    Chapter 15   Pensioner .............................. 198
    Chapter 16   End of the Hunt ........................ 211

EPILOGUE ............................................. 215
Notes and Sources ..................................... 221
Index .................................................. 246

# Preface

On a blustery fall day in 1989 my wife and I took our children on a field trip to the Memphis Zoo. It was a typical family excursion. We finished the bear exhibit when one of our young daughters protested our leaving without seeing a real Teddy bear. I did not know what to do. It was obvious that she thought a Teddy bear was real, much I suppose as she would have believed in the Easter Bunny or Santa Claus.

When I told her that there was no real Teddy bear, that it was just a child's toy, she cried inconsolably. After regaining her composure, she asked very simply: "If it is not real, then where did it come from?" Little did I know that this innocent question would propel me on a decade-long journey that would take me to archival collections over much of this country.

I remembered from some occasional human interest stories that the Teddy bear had origins in Mississippi, though I was not aware of any authoritative work on the subject. After promising my daughter that I would find out an answer to her question, I visited the Mississippi Department of Archives and History. There I found a subject file on Theodore Roosevelt, and from this I found enough details to answer my daughter's question.

As I read the file and reconstructed the story from old newspaper accounts my attention was drawn to a name I had never heard before–Holt Collier. He was the Mississippian most responsible for what happened in those wilderness swamps a hundred years ago. Only the slightest of information was readily available on Collier. What little information I could find was impressive. He was born a slave in Mississippi, had fought for the Confederacy and had killed white men and gone unpunished. It appeared that he had killed more wild bear than Davy Crockett and Daniel Boone combined (three thousand according to Theodore Roosevelt). Roosevelt, a hunter and conservationist of legendary status, is said to have called him the greatest hunter and guide he had ever seen. Of course, his participation in the famous 1902 hunt directly resulted in the creation of the Teddy bear, perhaps the most enduring and beloved child's toy in the world.

Collier was born into one of the first families of the South, and though archival reference specific to him is rare, his childhood and upbringing can be understood by studying the family of General Thomas Hinds and Home Hill Plantation, where Collier was born. In fact, to define Holt Collier and the man he became, a thorough study of the Hinds family dynasty of Mississippi had to be made.

Several exciting accounts of Collier's contributions to the Confederacy survive. A history of his company is provided so that we may know of his day-to-day involvement in the conflict. He saw action in Mississippi, Alabama, and Tennessee and served in many capacities. We know he was a sharpshooter, a scout, and at one time–on Island 76 in the Mississippi River–a spy.

His postwar exploits are no less amazing than his war experiences. During Reconstruction he is known to have killed a white Union captain for which he was tried and acquitted by a military court-martial. He also killed a notorious white Louisiana deputy in what has become known as the "gunfight at Washburn's Ferry," but he was not prosecuted.

These stories and many more, including a detailed account of the celebrated 1902 Roosevelt bear hunt, are combined in this work to provide the reader with a thorough picture of the life of a truly amazing Mississippian. Perhaps with this biography, Collier's life can be rediscovered by a new generation and celebrated by those who will appreciate his individual spirit.

*Minor Ferris Buchanan*

# Acknowledgments

It is difficult to recount all of the aid and assistance received over many long years of research and writing. My failings and lapses of effort were made less painful and less permanent by those who individually and collectively helped me regroup and refocus to bring this project to a conclusion. To all who have helped me along the way, I express my deep appreciation.

My initial recognition goes to those in and around Greenville, Mississippi, who knew the significance of this biography and supported it wholeheartedly. Clinton Bagley was my first contact there. He gave me several leads over the years and led me to several sources for the material used in this book. His unfailing encouragement and assistance was essential to my efforts from beginning to the very end. To Katherine Clements Branton, a lovely Delta lady who provided the first leads on the details of the death of Captain King, I owe a great debt. Those who gave oral histories and provided some of the photographs in this volume include Jane Metcalfe Weathers; Harley Metcalfe, III; Albert G. Metcalfe, Jr.; Leila Clark Wynn; Hank Burdine; Frank Robertshaw; Eddie LaFoe; John Adams; Peter Johnson; Luella Anderson; Nathan Wilson; Charlie Lundy; Anne Marie Parker; Frederick Smith; and Princella Nowell.

I would be remiss not to recognize Elbert Hilliard, director of the Mississippi Department of Archives and History for permission to use and quote from the papers of Harris Dickson. Recognition must be given to the individual staff members who helped me over such a long period of time. Nancy Bounds, Hank Holmes, and Ann Lipscomb were of considerable assistance. Recently, H. Grady Howell and Joyce Dixon have been very helpful. I especially recognize De'Niecechsi Layton for her pleasant attention when it was most needed.

At the Louisiana State Archives, I was fortunate to have Lewis Morris and Faye Phillips work with me. Also, in Oak Grove, Louisiana, local historian Pauline Mobley gave invaluable assistance. All were instrumental in leading me to information on the murder of the Lott brothers.

Wallace Dailey, curator of the Harvard University Roosevelt Collection, was most kind and patient with me in my pursuit of several images and photographs of the 1902 hunt. DeAnne Blanton at the National Archives assisted me in locating individual service records from the Civil War. Ernest J. Emrich at the Library of Congress gave valuable assistance in my use of the Theodore Roosevelt Papers. Harry G. Heiss at the Library of Congress provided useful references and material on the papers of George Cortelyou. Jane F. Vidrine and the staff at the University of Southwestern Louisiana assisted with the John M. Parker papers. Nancy Butler at the Harriette Person Library in Port Gibson, Mississippi, graciously allowed my use of the Hinds-Green History.

For the information on the James A. King background material used in this work, I am indebted to the following: Becky S. Jordan, Iowa State University; Randal B. Caldwell, Esq., Newton, Iowa; Rosie Springer, State Historical Society of Iowa; and Beverly Brown, Jasper County Genealogical Society. The information each of them provided was instrumental in developing one of the most critical chapters of the life of Holt Collier.

Lynda L. Crist, editor of the Papers of Jefferson Davis at Rice University, was generous in her assistance with the Davis-Hinds correspondence. Steven Niven with the Southern Historical Collection at the University of North Carolina, Chapel Hill, helped immeasurably in identifying and providing material for my use from the Clive Metcalfe Papers.

I must recognize Charlie Brenner at the Eudora Welty Library who on several occasions was my information supply line to the outside world. Georgie Blanton Cooper of La Habra, California, opened more doors than she could have known by generously sharing much of her family history. Sarah Doxey Tate, my fourth grade teacher from whom I had not heard in thirty five years, gave me useful information on Clifford Berryman.

Helpful in providing me with criticisms and assessments were Gordon Cotton, curator of the Old Courthouse Museum in Vicksburg, Carol Mead and Ginger Tucker at the University of Mississippi Research and Development Center. Their guidance has been most valuable. Eugene Ham of Fayetteville, Tennessee and

Zeke Downey of Jackson, Mississippi, both intellectuals with many hidden talents, helped define the depth of the characters in their review of this work. The final review of this work was made by Brenda M. Eagles, serving as copy editor, who was instrumental in bringing it up to proper standard.

Alma Carpenter of Natchez offered me the first recognition that the life of Holt Collier merited a serious scholarly study. Her subtle intervention and assistance at the conclusion of this work was invaluable.

My deepest gratitude is to my friend David Sansing, Professor Emeritus at the University of Mississippi, for the contagious inspiration of his lectures so many years ago and for his continued encouragement of this project.

Finally, Shelby Foote, a native of Greenville, and one of the last generation to remember Holt Collier, who opened his doors and his archival collection to me, I feel deeply in his debt.

*He was a man of sixty and could neither read nor write, but he had all the dignity of an African chief, and for half a century he had been a bear hunter, having killed or assisted in killing over three thousand bears. He had been born a slave on the Hinds plantation, his father, an old man when he was born, having been the body-servant and cook of "old General Hinds," as he called him, when the latter fought under Jackson at New Orleans. When ten years old Holt had been taken on the horse behind his young master, the Hinds of that day, on a bear hunt, when he killed his first bear.*

—Theodore Roosevelt, 1908

*...the old man of seventy who had been a negro for two generations now but whose face and bearing were still those of the Chickasaw chief who had been his father....And he was glad...He was old. He had no children, no people, none of his blood anywhere above earth that he would ever meet again. And even if he were to, he could not have touched it, spoken to it, because for seventy years now he had had to be a negro. It was almost over now and he was glad....but still the woods would be his mistress and his wife.*

—William Faulkner, *The Bear*

*HOLT COLLIER, with the 1886 45-70 Winchester, a gift from President Theodore Roosevelt, circa 1922.*

# PROLOGUE

The now famous Mississippi bear hunt involving President Theodore Roosevelt and a hunting party of old friends and hunting comrades officially began on November 13, 1902, at Smedes Plantation in Sharkey County, Mississippi. Though the hunt had been planned at high corporate and governmental levels for months, its success was wholly dependent upon the skill and performance of Holt Collier, a fifty-six-year-old former slave. The extraordinary efforts of Collier to make that hunt a success by single-handedly capturing a large wild black bear is alone worthy of considerable attention. The fact that the popular president was in the hunting party and that it was widely reported in the national press made the event no less impressive.

Almost forgotten now, Holt Collier was a remarkable figure in the history of the Delta region of Mississippi, and he was recognized nationally during his lifetime. From the perspective of many, including modern African Americans and possibly his own contemporaries, Collier's loyalties and his life story must be baffling and difficult to accept. In these more enlightened times his values and motives seem difficult to fathom.

On the plantation of Cameron Howell Hinds in Jefferson County, Mississippi, Holt Collier was born to a life of servitude. But for the Civil War and the emancipation it brought, Collier would have lived a lifetime of bondage. His family members were house servants who had for generations been intimately involved with the aristocratic Hinds family. The Colliers enjoyed an elevated social status and became in their own way extensions of the very masters they served.

To understand the aristocratic Hinds legacy is to understand Holt Collier. Because the Hinds family held prominent positions in society and consorted with people of importance, it was natural that Collier felt comfortable with national figures. Like his master before him, Holt Collier was ever his own man and was never intimidated. It was to men of noble worth he most responded. Among the gentry, whether soldiers, cowboys, businessmen, national leaders, or presidents, Collier saw and appreciated qualities of individualism and self-reliance.

Until his death, Collier remained loyal to Cameron Howell Hinds and his son Thomas. He was raised and taught by them in the skill of the hunt, the accuracy of the shot, the sport of the race, and the honor of the gentleman. Like Fields Cook, another well known privileged slave from Virginia, Holt Collier probably "never knew what the yoke of oppression was in the early part of [his] life." Like Cook, Holt Collier "was very proud when a boy, although [he] had nothing to be proud of."[1] Slave honor and pride are attributes often clouded from view by the overall barbarity of the institution and the legacy it has left our society. However, as in the life of Holt Collier, while "bondage limited slaves' ability to preserve their dignity, it also heightened honor's importance, making any distinction all the more precious."[2]

Collier's treatment as an extension of the Hinds family, his achievements as an expert marksman at an early age, and his service in the Confederate Army as a teenager instilled in him a deep sense of pride and honor that remained with him throughout his life. His pride and standing as a man not to be trifled with or crossed is clearly seen in his postwar dealings with Captain James A. King and Dr. Orville M. Blanton. The deep respect bestowed upon him by his contemporaries is evident from the intimate relationship he had with the Helm, Percy and Metcalfe families.

Taken into military service to be a body servant to Howell and Thomas Hinds, Collier quickly became an armed combatant with his own weapons and mount. The quality of his service to the Hinds family and to the Confederacy is unquestionable. His military service can only be truly appreciated by considering the prohibition then existing against men of color serving in the Confederacy. At the outbreak of hostilities in 1861, many affluent Confederates took body servants with them into military service, but as fighting grew desperate and conditions became unbearable, the soldiers came to realize that war was not a medieval romance, and that "there was no place for body servants on the field of battle."[3] One writer observed that "[i]t was one thing to have Negroes performing all types of work, even with the army, and quite another to put weapons of war in their hands."[4] The prohibition against military service was based most heavily on the proposition that allowing non-whites to serve would be an acknowledgment of their equality with whites. In this racial atmosphere of prejudice and doubt, Holt Collier earned the respect and friendship of regular soldiers.

His training as a young man by Howell Hinds and his chosen profession of hunter afforded Holt Collier respect among prominent men. The South, for generations preeminent as a hunter's paradise, had many geographical advantages over the northern states. The region's vast coastal and river swamps and extensive wilderness areas provided the best sort of cover for game of all kinds. The South was sparsely populated, and the Delta region of Mississippi in the latter half of the nineteenth century was a primeval wilderness, explored first by pioneers like Holt Collier.

Prior to the war southern planters like Howell Hinds indulged "more than any other Americans in the wild sports of the forest and prairie."[5] In the South were found "gentlemen of the land, not pent up in cities, but dwelling on their estates; there we find hunters...and packs of hounds maintained regularly, and hunted with all legitimate accompaniments of well-blown bugle and well-whooped halloo; with mounted cavaliers, fearlessly riding through brush, through briar, over flood, over mire...as desperately, for the first blood, or the kill...."[6]

Social ranks and taboos of caste and class were suspended on the hunt, especially in such interior and frontier regions as the Mississippi Delta. At least temporarily, a man's skill and courage were the only criterion for acceptance. In this gentleman's pursuit Holt Collier was able to earn the respect of others and establish his own reputation as a giant among men. He earned honor as a hunter and guide irrespective of race. "Though the South had its gentlemen hunters like Wade Hampton, all down the line of its social ranks it had devotees of the sport. The small farmer, the frontiersman, the poor white—and frequently the Negro—all were hunters....In many localities certain Negroes or Indians were numbered among the expert nimrods of the community, and their society was at times apparently courted. Long before the advent of Jack Johnson and Willie Mays, hunting was a factor which promoted integration."[7] In the Mississippi Delta and perhaps throughout the entire South, no hunter was equal in skill or courage to Holt Collier.

The bear hunt in the jungle swamps of Mississippi that November day in 1902, newsworthy though it was at the time, is but one episode in the larger context of Holt Collier's life. The Roosevelt hunt merely draws us into the larger picture that is the remarkable life of this legendary figure. This is his story.

# PART ONE

*HOLT COLLIER
AND
THE HINDS FAMILY
OF MISSISSIPPI*

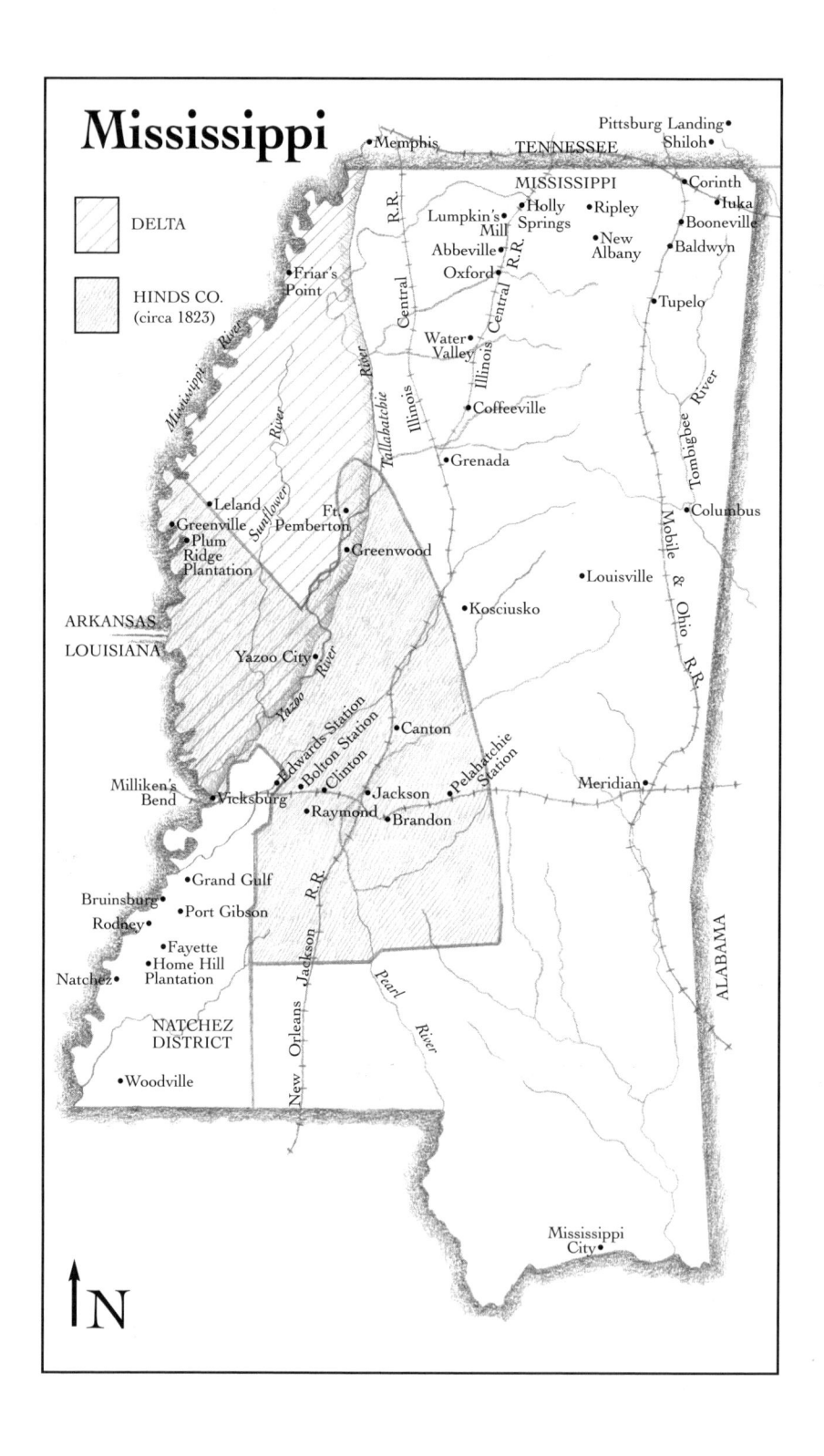

# Mississippi

DELTA

HINDS CO.
(circa 1823)

Memphis • Pittsburg Landing •
TENNESSEE Shiloh •
MISSISSIPPI • Corinth
Lumpkin's • Holly • Ripley • Iuka
Mill Springs • Booneville
Abbeville • • New
Oxford • Albany • Baldwyn
Friar's
Point
Water • Tupelo
Valley
• Coffeeville
• Grenada
• Columbus
Leland • Ft.
Greenville • Pemberton
Plum • Greenwood
Ridge
Plantation • Louisville
• Kosciusko
ARKANSAS
LOUISIANA
Yazoo City •
Edwards Station
Bolton Station • Canton
Clinton • Pelahatchie
Milliken's • Jackson Station • Meridian
Bend • Vicksburg Raymond •
• Brandon

• Grand Gulf
Bruinsburg • • Port Gibson
Rodney •
• Fayette
Natchez • • Home Hill
Plantation
NATCHEZ
DISTRICT
• Woodville

Mississippi
City •

ALABAMA

N

CHAPTER 1

# A SOUTHERN ARISTOCRACY
## Green-Hinds-Jackson-Davis

*"They were the pride of one army,
and the admiration of the other."*
— Andrew Jackson

Among the earliest and most prestigious families of the lower South was that of Colonel Thomas Green, an early settler in the Old Natchez District and a veteran of the American Revolution. Green migrated from James City County, Virginia, to the Natchez District when it was under Spanish rule. A leader in unsuccessful attempts to 'Americanize' the west, he and his son Thomas Green Jr. resisted the Spanish authority and were often jailed for their efforts. One confrontation with the Spanish authorities occurred when, with the colonel's support, the noted pioneer George Rogers Clark was solicited to raise a force sufficient to overthrow the Spaniards. Little came of it other than the landing of a flatboat carrying a small group of scouts on Bayou Pierre.[1]

Green's influence in the area was significant, and he was tireless in his efforts to end the Spanish rule by any devise at his disposal. He once petitioned the Georgia Assembly to lay claim to the Natchez region in defiance of the Spanish authority, an act which could have led to war. His petition failed, but his tenacity outlasted the Spanish, who ceded their authority over the vast area with the Pinckney Treaty of 1795. When the Spanish evacuated their final military station in 1798, Green and his son took their place as members of the new aristocracy on America's western frontier. Colonel Green enjoyed his prestige for only a few years. In 1805, at the age of eighty two, he died leaving behind ten children, the oldest being his namesake, Thomas Green Jr.

Thomas Green Jr. was born in Virginia in 1758 and was considered a distinguished gentleman worthy of respect in his own right. He served in the first General Assembly of the Territory of Mississippi and was the second person to represent the territory in the Congress of the United States. His brother, Abner Green, was territorial treasurer of Mississippi. Cato West, his brother-in-law, served as governor of the Mississippi Territory from 1803 to 1805 and as a delegate to the Mississippi Constitutional Convention of 1817.[2] In the history of the area Thomas Green Jr. is best remembered as the builder and owner of Springfield mansion, the Green ancestral home, located about seventeen miles north of Natchez. Solidly built just before the turn of the century, it looks much the same today as when it was built.[3]

• • •

The history of the Hinds family and their migration deep into the valley of the Mississippi River typifies the pioneer stock that gambled everything for a future in a territory inhabited largely by Indians and wild beasts. The family had been on the continent for five generations when John Hinds migrated into the Natchez District. When he came to Natchez, branches of his family were in New York, New Jersey, Maine, Pennsylvania, Virginia, and Kentucky, and his lineage can be traced directly to James Hinds, who came to Salem, Massachusetts, from Bedfordshire, England, in 1637.[4] A native of Berkeley County, Virginia, and a veteran of the Revolutionary War, John Hinds moved to Bourbon County, Kentucky, about 1780. From there his work as a flatboat captain in the Cumberland-Natchez trade brought him down the Mississippi River into the Natchez District about 1791 to seek his fortune.[5] In the rugged but aristocratic class of pioneers, John Hinds was considered an educated and successful man. He possessed sufficient knowledge of the English language for his time and had enough wealth to make substantial investments far from his home.

One of the first friendships established by Hinds after his arrival was with Andrew Jackson who lived in the Natchez District at the time. For several years Jackson was a friend and counsel who handled legal matters for Hinds in his absence.[6] Hinds was frequently in transit between Kentucky and Mississippi. His friendship with Jackson allowed him to invest in property, post bonds, and maintain litigation.[7]

Before his move to the Natchez District, Hinds sold five tracts of land near the Cumberland River. The transactions, which conveyed a total of 3,920 acres to several buyers, evidenced Hinds's considerable wealth and influence, and served as a reliable indication that the move south was to be permanent. The total sale price was eight thousand dollars.[8] On September 15, 1801 he sold another parcel of Bourbon County property and described himself as being "late of Bourbon County, Kentucky," clearly indicating his intentions to permanently relocate.[9]

Hinds's considerable wealth and investment in Mississippi property immediately placed him and his family among the social elite. He found good land in the rolling hills near the Natchez Trace about a half-day's journey northeast of Natchez. The land he purchased would become his permanent residence and the Hinds's ancestral home. He named it Home Hill Plantation.[10] The property was located near what is now referred to as "Old" Greenville, a governmental center and later the county seat of Jefferson County. Nothing of that community remains today.

Thomas Hinds, John's son, was born in 1780 and was about twenty-years-old when the family made the move into the Mississippi Territory.[11] Four months after John Hinds's death in 1807, the twenty-seven-year-old Thomas Hinds married Leminda Green from nearby Springfield Plantation. She was the sixteen-year-old daughter of the influential Thomas Green Jr. This association and membership with one of the most prestigious families of the area provided Thomas Hinds a secure and prosperous future.[12]

Both the Green and Hinds families owned slaves. It is believed that Leminda brought into the marital estate Allen Collier and his family. Collier was a well respected servant who would ultimately become the personal valet and confidant to Leminda's husband. Although the relationship was one of master and slave, this passing of the Collier name into the servant ranks of the Hinds family began a loyal familial relationship that would survive the Civil War and endure for more than sixty years.[13]

Following the custom of the southern gentry, Thomas Hinds built a comfortable existence for himself and his family on the banks of

Platners Fork between "Old" Greenville and Springfield Plantation. He was gifted and talented in many areas and described in social settings "as a youth of prepossessing appearance, with dark, flashing eyes, slender, graceful figure and good address, coupled with a certain mastery of speech and confidence of manner that arose not only from temperament but from his having been acquainted with the best social customs of an older civilization."[14] It is recorded that Thomas Hinds was "very popular in the new community, and the fact that after only a few years residence in the place he won the heart and hand of the daughter of Thomas M. Green is proof of his having become a social favorite." One result of his pedigreed marriage was the strengthening of what had for several years been a warm attachment between himself and Andrew Jackson. In future years they would be in close contact with each other in some of the most thrilling episodes in the history of Mississippi and of the United States.[15] Hinds's association with the Green family and his friendship with Andrew Jackson also opened up many opportunities for military and civil service, all of which were accepted when offered.[16]

• • •

The first real opportunity for Thomas Hinds to earn his mettle and establish a name for himself came in the early part of the nineteenth century when the young nation struggled against European intervention in its internal affairs. In January 1807 Aaron Burr, the former vice president of the United States under Thomas Jefferson, was in command of a small flotilla that landed near Bruinsburg on the Mississippi River. It was rumored that he was preparing to take control of the area and by doing so dismember the Union. It was also speculated that England had encouraged and perhaps financed his expedition. Hinds and other political leaders of the district hastily organized 250 volunteer dragoons and a large number of minutemen to repel Burr's incursion. The invaders voluntarily surrendered after receiving assurances that Burr would receive a hearing in the territory. Burr was not without friends in the Natchez District and was quickly absolved by a grand jury at a well-attended hearing in Washington, the territorial capital.[17]

*A Southern Aristocracy* • 7

The following year Thomas Hinds and Leminda had their only child, a son they named Cameron Howell. In 1811 Thomas Hinds received a commission from the territorial governor, David Holmes, to become the chief justice of the Orphan's Court of Jefferson County. With the prestige of a judge's office, he was well established in his life as a planter-aristocrat. For the remainder of his life Thomas enjoyed a long and distinguished career in civil and military service, most significantly during the War of 1812.[18]

• • •

The Natchez District and the territories of the Southwest were not unscathed during the War of 1812. In the summer of 1813 there was an escalation of skirmishes with the Creek Indians who were allies of the British. Georgian General Thomas Flournoy launched an attack against the Indians at Burnt Corn Creek in present day Alabama. The Indians turned the poorly planned ambush into a rout, forcing the Americans to retreat and separate.

In retaliation of the ambush, the Indians attacked Fort Mims on August 30, 1813. Fort Mims was a hastily built stockade with little protection, and in the surprise attack, more than five hundred men, women, and children were killed. Known as the Fort Mims Massacre, it quickly transformed localized Indian skirmishes into a theater of war between the Creek Nation and the United States.[19]

In response to public outcry, Governor Holmes ordered Major Thomas Hinds, then with the state militia, to leave his wife and four-year-old son and take command of a volunteer force of two hundred cavalry. Although ill-equipped with provisions and ordnance, they were ordered to report to Fort Stoddert. By mid-October the militia had grown to a sizable force of five companies of infantry and four companies of cavalry, known as the Hinds Mississippi Dragoons.[20]

This volunteer army was placed under orders not to engage the enemy, but to serve as rangers for the protection of the settlers in gathering their crops. Police service was not what the soldiers expected when they voluntarily left their comfortable homes; they had come for battle and glory, not to be employed as lowly constabularies or lonely scouts, traveling through swamp and canebrakes and keeping weary watch over isolated corn-fields and log cabins.

Hinds's men strongly protested their service as not conforming to established notions of military propriety.[21]

Major Thomas Hinds, described in battle as "a small, square-built, swarthy-complexioned, black-eyed man, moving rapidly, speaking imperatively, beloved by his troops, and one of the most intrepid men that ever lived," took up the cause of his troops and complained of the assignment only to be summarily rebuffed by General Flournoy. The entire troop was humiliatingly dismissed by the general as "not disposed to co-operate with us in defense of their country." The general wrote regarding Hinds's Dragoons, "I have consequently returned them to governor Holmes, to be disposed of as he may think proper. You will, therefore, give them no orders, and they are not to be considered a part of our force. You will take care to get their arms when they leave. They will have no use for them where they are going, and we shall want them for men who are willing to remain on the frontier and defend the inhabitants."[22]

The effect of General Flournoy's order on Major Hinds and his command is unknown, but from their later service it is clear that they were not disarmed. All militia in the territory were serving under the command of the territorial governor, who at the time was very sympathetic to Hinds and extremely displeased that Flournoy and the regular army had abandoned the eastern territory.

By the end of October General Andrew Jackson and his army of volunteers had defeated the Creeks in a battle near Talladega and, after suffering serious deprivations through the winter, had finally defeated the entire Creek Nation on March 27, 1813, at the Battle of Horseshoe Bend. With the loss of their Creek allies, the British turned their attention to the western front and moved toward Mobile and New Orleans. Jackson immediately sent for his old friend Major Thomas Hinds and placed the Mississippi Dragoons in direct action against the British. When the British advance was halted near Mobile, Hinds proceeded to New Orleans under orders to "capture and kill every man within the range of their guns." The troops under Major Thomas Hinds remained on the front lines until the defeat of the British early in 1815.

Hinds's Dragoons were involved both in the initial action of the Battle of New Orleans at Villeré Plantation on December 23 and in the final decisive action on January 8, 1815, which ended in a British

*OFFICIAL STATE PORTRAIT OF GENERAL THOMAS HINDS.*

disaster. Hinds, in his zealous pursuit of the retreating redcoats, earned a sterling reputation before being ordered by General Jackson to stand down.[23] His company distinguished itself and earned the special compliments of General Jackson, who said in his general orders of the affair, "They were the pride of one army, and the admiration of the other."[24]

This widely reported statement by the hero of New Orleans had the effect of nullifying General Flournoy's earlier rebuke and propelled Hinds into almost instant celebrity. Only four months after the victory in New Orleans, on April 11, 1815, Hinds received a recommendation from the office of the governor to the United States secretary of war to receive the president's appointment as brigadier general of the Mississippi Territory militia, a commission he received after confirmation by the United States Senate.[25] Upon receipt of his commission, no person enjoyed more respect and renown in popular sentiment in the entire territory than General Thomas Hinds.

• • •

At the same time there was perhaps no single person who better symbolized the aristocracy of the deep south than Joseph E. Davis, a respected landowner, planter, and lawyer. Davis was a friend and neighbor of Thomas Hinds, and he owned some of the largest working plantations in the territory. He was a close friend with the governor, who had appointed him justice of the peace, a position that held considerable esteem. When the call to arms was made after the Fort Mims massacre, Joseph Davis and his brother Samuel joined the dragoons under Hinds's command. His military career ended two months later when General Flournoy sent the troops back to Natchez. Davis recognized military service as an acceptable means to achieve prominence in the local aristocracy, but, being an attorney and successful businessman in his own right, he chose not to subordinate himself to a superior officer. When Colonel Hinds reassembled his volunteers for the defense of New Orleans, he took Joseph's brothers Samuel and Isaac with him, but Joseph remained behind.

Davis's father was a native Georgian who had spent years in Kentucky prior to locating the family in Wilkinson County, south of Natchez. In 1808, while Joseph was reading for the law in Hopkinsville, Kentucky, at the age of twenty three, his mother gave birth to her tenth child, a fifth son. The boy was named Jefferson, after the contemporary President whom his father Samuel greatly admired. Hoping that this would be his final child, Samuel gave Jefferson the middle name of Finis.[26]

In 1815, just a few months following the victory over the British, when young Jefferson Finis Davis was seven-years-old, his father decided to return him to Springfield, Kentucky, to be educated at St. Thomas Boy's School, run by Dominican friars. Joseph learned that General Hinds was planning a trip to Kentucky and asked his friend to allow Jefferson to accompany Hinds and his son of the same age, Cameron Howell.

Cameron Howell Hinds and Jefferson Finis Davis were the best of childhood friends and considered splendid companions on the trip. The party consisted of the two boys, Thomas Hinds, Leminda Hinds, "a sister-in-law, a niece, a Negro maidservant, and a Negro manservant in charge of the pack mules, loaded with supplies and equipment for camping out." The overland journey was long and difficult, described as a "seven-hundred-mile journey on horseback through Indian territory where scarcely a white settlement existed."[27] Although it was certainly a hardship, to the boys the trip was very much an adventure, and both remembered it all their lives.

It took several weeks to reach Nashville. Jefferson Davis's biographer wrote of the trip, "Deer bounded through the forest. Wild turkeys roosted on the tree branches. The Major's [Hinds's] rifle provided all the game they could eat, and sometimes in north Mississippi it protected the party from panthers." The climax of the adventure came at Nashville, Tennessee, "where the party was received by Andrew Jackson, hero of the day. As commander of the battalion of Mississippi dragoons, Major Hinds had fought beside the General through the magnificent engagement of New Orleans the previous January. Jackson had returned only a few months earlier from the battlefield to his estate, called the 'Hermitage.' The mansion that was to become famous was yet a dream. In 1815 the commodious dwelling was built of logs."[28]

The general was "very gentle and considerate" to the boys. Not once during their stay did they hear Jackson curse, though he was notorious for using vivid profanity. The future president encouraged young Jeff Davis, Howell Hinds, and his adopted son Andrew Jr. to contests of running and jumping and pony races, but he discouraged them from wrestling. "To allow hands to be put on another," he said, "might lead to a fight." Rachel and General Jackson made the Hinds party so welcome that the entire group remained at the Hermitage for two weeks.[29]

It is highly probable that Harrison Collier was the manservant mentioned on the 1815 trip to Nashville, considering his age, ability, and his enduring association with Thomas and Howell Hinds. Allen Collier and Harrison Collier were Thomas Hinds's only known body servants. Harrison was born about 1792, and would have been twenty-three-years-old at the time of the journey. He is known to have accompanied Thomas Hinds during the Battle of New Orleans while in the immediate service of General Andrew Jackson.[30]

The purpose of the Kentucky trip for the Hinds party is unknown. Although we know little of Howell's formative years, it is probable that he, like Davis, also received some schooling there. Kentucky was a source of goods and supplies not readily available downriver, and for that reason trips to Kentucky and other northern states became a yearly pilgrimage for the Hinds family. Howell Hinds traveled the Mississippi River in later years for family, schooling, supplies, horses, shopping, races, and gambling purposes, and nothing suggests that his father's era was any different.

Thomas Hinds was often away from home as he continued his busy military career, always linked with and often in the service of Andrew Jackson. Mississippi achieved statehood in 1817, and the following year, under the first adopted militia statute of the state, Hinds's rank of major-general was renewed.

On June 29, 1819, at the age of twenty eight, Leminda Green Hinds died.[31] At the tender age of eleven, Cameron Howell Hinds was left to be raised into manhood and taught the sport of gentlemen by Harrison Collier and Harrison's wife, Daphne. Thomas Hinds resigned his commission soon after the death of his wife but his presence at home was limited. The following year he embarked on a campaign for the office of governor of Mississippi.

Although popular, General Thomas Hinds was defeated in the 1820 governor's race by a vote of almost two-to-one. The race was considered a campaign of personalities, as both candidates were "thought of in the minds of voters as friends of Jackson and were Jeffersonian Republicans."[32]

The absence of Thomas Hinds from Home Hill Plantation was extended that year when he was named a joint commissioner under the command of General Jackson to make a treaty with the Choctaws in the central portion of the state. Their efforts were successful beyond all expectations. After much debate a treaty was negotiated with the famous Choctaw chief Pushmataha at Doak's Stand. The parties jousted, competed in games on the field, and neutralized a combination of white men and "half-breed" Choctaws who had formed a group to prevent the treaty. The Treaty of Doak's Stand took almost twenty days of negotiations. When finalized on October 18, 1820, the treaty conveyed land west of the Mississippi River and fifty four sections within the state to the Choctaws, and provisions were made for the education of the entire Choctaw Nation. The treaty brought to the southern frontier a much-desired peace, and the area ceded to Mississippi was the western half of the middle third of the state, a parcel estimated at five and a half million acres.[33]

Hinds was the one person other than Andrew Jackson most credited with the acquisition of these vast lands for settlement. The Mississippi General Assembly on February 12, 1821, rewarded their native son by naming the entire region Hinds County in his honor. Immediately, they passed an act establishing a county government for what was commonly known as the "mother of counties" because of its vast size.[34]

That same day, because Natchez and nearby Washington, the original seats of district and territorial government, were so remotely located, the General Assembly voted to establish a commission to locate a site for a new capital city. General Thomas Hinds, James Patton, and William Lattimore were appointed to this commission. The legislative directive required them to find a site within twenty miles of the geographic center of the state.

They recommended Le Fleur's Bluff, on the west bank of the Pearl River about ten miles from the Choctaw Agency. At this site the French Canadian Louis Le Fleur and his French Choctaw wife, Rebecca Cravat, had maintained a trading post since well before the turn of the century. Later that year the assembly accepted the recommendations of the commission and named the new capital Jackson in honor of his service during the War of 1812 and for his efforts in acquiring the land from the Choctaws.

Thomas Hinds, William Lattimore, and Peter A. Van Dorn were next appointed to design the overall layout of the new capital city. In the next few years they built a community house for the assembly, employed surveyors, managed public timber, granted lots for building, constructed a courthouse, and founded a college.[35]

Thomas Hinds served a term in the Mississippi General Assembly in 1823. The following year he earnestly sought Jackson's support in a second bid for the governorship. Because it

14 • Holt Collier

EAGLE HEAD PRESENTATION SWORD. Gold, silver & ivory inscribed: "Presented by the Legislature of the Mississippi Territory to Brig. Gen. Thos. Hinds for his service in the defense of New Orleans."

was thought that Hinds could not be elected, Jackson threw his support elsewhere. It was a major disappointment to Hinds, and although in politics Hinds was known to be "characteristically headstrong and stubborn," he publicly announced that he would honor Jackson's wishes. Hinds never forgave Jackson for his interference in that election and often referred to it as a conspiracy. After losing his bid for the governorship, Hinds eschewed public life for a few years, remaining with his son Howell at Home Hill Plantation.

In 1828 Hinds conducted a campaign for the U. S. House of Representatives, again relying heavily on his friendship and prior service with Jackson, who was making his run for the presidency that same year. Hinds was helped immeasurably by Jackson's visit to Natchez and Vicksburg. At public engagements Jackson spoke well of his old friend, and as a direct result Hinds was elected to Congress, where he served under President Andrew Jackson.[36]

• • •

Thomas Hinds's career in what was then referred to as Washington City was short and undistinguished. He resigned in March of 1831 and returned to Home Hill. He was involved in a few political races after his return, but none successfully. In 1833 he sought but did not receive an appointment as United States marshal for the Southern District of Mississippi, an appointment that would have originated from his friend in the White House. His early retirement from Congress and his failed appointment as U. S. marshal indicated a serious chill in his relationship with Jackson. In 1835 a group of influential Mississippians encouraged him to run for the U. S. Senate, but he declined.[37]

When former President Jackson visited Mississippi in 1840, he had a bittersweet final meeting with his old friend. On his return upriver from New Orleans, General Jackson and his entourage stopped at Vicksburg. They were entertained at the home of Dr. William M. Gwin, who used the occasion to entertain a large crowd including General Hinds. Hinds had too much to drink and began to talk loudly to General Jackson about the perceived 1824 conspiracy to defeat Hinds for governor. To avoid a potentially embarrassing scene, Jackson quickly approached his old comrade, "put his hand on his shoulder and said, 'Hinds it is time you should go to bed,' which

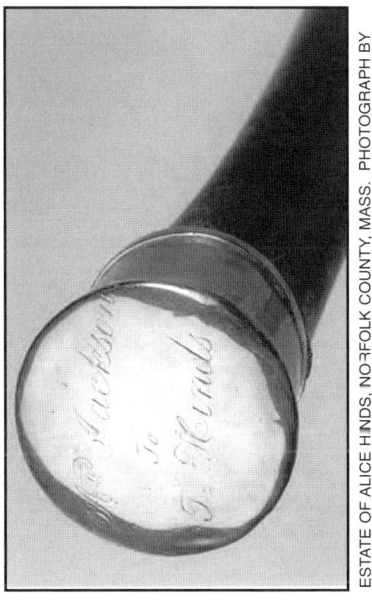

"AND. JACKSON TO T. HINDS"
*Gold and hickory presentation cane from President Andrew Jackson to General Thomas Hinds.*

he [Hinds] immediately did." This would be one of the last public appearances for General Thomas Hinds. He died of a ruptured blood vessel at Home Hill Plantation on August 23, 1840.[38]

His death prompted a third commendation from the Mississippi General Assembly for a lifetime of devotion and dedication to the people of the state. In death he was described as "a warm partisan, he enjoyed the unbounded confidence of all parties, and it is believed that he died without leaving a personal enemy." His obituary in the Jackson *Mississippian,* the state's largest newspaper, recounted his service to the state. "Eulogy upon this truly good and brave man is unnecessary from us. It is well known that he was with Jackson throughout his last campaign against the British and that during the whole of the late war he rendered his country great service and gained for himself distinguished honors. In short, his life was devoted to the common good and all those who revere bravery will mourn his loss."[39]

Harrison Collier was about forty-eight-years-old when General Thomas Hinds died. He and his wife Daphne had been heavily relied upon for the operation of Home Hill Plantation and for the upbringing of the general's only child. With the passing of Thomas Hinds, Harrison and Daphne and all of their children became the chattel property of thirty-two-year-old Cameron Howell Hinds.

CHAPTER 2

# CAMERON HOWELL HINDS

*"Then there was Mr. Howell Hinds—
he sho' was one fine young man....
Gen'l Hinds owned my father and my mother both,
and of co'se he owned me."*
—Holt Collier

With the death of his father, the Green and Hinds legacy fell to Cameron Howell Hinds. At thirty-two years of age Howell Hinds was an only son raised to be a southern gentleman. He was trained and educated for future leadership in a prosperous but doomed aristocratic society. But for his association with young Jefferson Davis, little is known of Howell's early years. From 1842 to 1846 he served as adjutant inspector on the staff of Brigadier General Charles Clark of the Mississippi Militia.[1]

By 1850 Howell was a successful and respected planter with holdings in Jefferson County–Home Hill Plantation–and additional properties in the newly acquired swamp wilderness upriver–Plum Ridge Plantation–on part of the lands ceded by the Choctaws at the Treaty of Doak's Stand.[2] Howell Hinds did not pursue a public life to the extent that his father did, but he did serve one brief term in the Mississippi General Assembly in 1852.

As a result of his mother's early death and his father's lengthy absences, the responsibility for Howell's upbringing had fallen to trusted servants Daphne and Harrison Collier. They were more responsible for raising Howell to adulthood than perhaps any other persons. Because of this close association, Howell was devoted to them.

As house servants, the Colliers were in an entirely different class from ordinary field laborers. A typical house manservant might not know how to read, but he would have better diction than other classes of slaves.  He might not know strict rules of etiquette, but he would certainly know gentlemanly good manners.  Harrison and other house servants probably resided near the main house, far removed from the daily lives of the field hands, whose quarters were some distance from the main buildings.  In addition to their normal duties, house servants would often share or be involved in the idle time enjoyed by the family, thus explaining Harrison's involvement in teaching Howell about guns, horses, and the hunt.  Clearly the Collier family remained inextricably linked to the Green and Hinds families for several generations.  Through these associations, the Colliers developed much of their identity, self-esteem, and self-worth.  They were an integral part of plantation society and were likely considered not mere chattel, but extensions of the Hinds family.  Because the Colliers were privileged house servants, they held elevated status and were often in direct contact with white men of significant position.[3]

• • •

Howell Hinds married Drusilla (Sallie) Cocks of Jefferson County on September 28, 1829.  Of this union two children were born–Thomas Hinds, born on December 23, 1830, and Coleman Hinds, born in December 1840.  Sallie never fully recovered from the second pregnancy.  She died on April 9, 1841, leaving Howell with a young son and a very small baby to raise.  The burdens of family responsibilities may explain his conspicuous lack of a public life.[4]

His second marriage, on Valentine's Day, 1849, would last until his death.  Mary Ann Coleman Lape, of Port Gibson, Mississippi, was a widow of distinguished pedigree.  Ten years his junior, she was born in Lexington, Kentucky, educated at the Sacred Heart Convent in Boston, and was the sister of prominent local citizens Judge John Coleman and Dr. Frank Coleman.  Her first husband was William Lape, a well-respected planter and merchant in Port Gibson.

Along with her respectable background Mary Ann Lape brought into the marriage four young daughters–C. C. Lape, aged eleven; Mary E. Lape, nine; Ellie A. Lape, seven; and Martha W. Lape, five.[5] Howell's marriage to Mary Ann produced four children: Maria Crozier Hinds, born in 1850 and dead by July 10, 1851; Alice Hinds, born in 1853; John Hinds, born in 1855; and Howell Hinds, Jr., born in 1858.[6] At the time Howell's youngest child was born, Thomas, his eldest, was twenty-eight years of age.

Where his father had devoted his time and energies to politics and military affairs, Howell spent his time amassing a small fortune in land and slave holdings. During the years his father was in Washington, Howell took over the farming operations, which included a large tract of land about one hundred miles upriver in what was then known simply as the "swamp" or "wilderness," a vast primeval delta of impenetrable swamps and canebrakes not yet fully explored. Stretching north-to-south almost two hundred miles from Memphis to Vicksburg and east-to-west about seventy miles at its widest point, this Yazoo River basin, known as the Mississippi Delta, was believed by these and other men of vision to conceal a rich alluvial soil that would serve their cotton kingdom aspirations for generations to come.

Howell Hinds's attention was soon directed toward this new investment upriver. A study of his operations reveals a transfer of his priorities from the old plantation to the new. In 1830 forty-six slaves served at Home Hill, but by 1837 this figure had dwindled to thirty-two. In 1838 it was down to fifteen, and in 1840 the slaves at Home Hill numbered only thirteen, probably just enough to keep the place profitable and to serve the family who remained behind. The yet-undeveloped Plum Ridge Plantation in the wilderness swamp upriver enjoyed a contrasting increase in its slave population, from nineteen in 1831 to twenty-five in 1835, twenty-six by 1836, and thirty-four by 1838. Plum Ridge reached a high in slave population of thirty-seven in 1841. The largest number of servants listed for Howell Hinds at any one time was fifty-eight, a small number compared to several other investors in the new region who held slaves totaling in the hundreds and acreage in the tens of thousands.[7]

• • •

Plum Ridge Plantation was located inland, just one mile south of the river town of Greenville (not to be confused with "Old" Greenville in Jefferson County). At its largest, Plum Ridge was just over one thousand acres in size. Situated on the banks of Rattlesnake Bayou, it adjoined several other young but promising like concerns.

Because of its wilderness setting, life at Plum Ridge during the decades of the 1830s, 1840s, and 1850s was quite primitive and unsuitable for women or children. Clearing the land of forest and beast was difficult and extreme work. It would be hard to imagine a frontier home during those years that would remotely provide the comfort that was available to the family at Home Hill. For this reason young Thomas Hinds was sent to Plum Ridge in the early 1850's to manage its daily affairs independently. From all indications, he performed his duties well.

Howell Hinds was known as a man who enjoyed the thrill of gambling, whether on horse races, fox hunts, cards, or trick shooting. He traveled regularly up and down the Mississippi River with Harrison Collier at his side. Personal oversight of Thomas's progress and the development of Plum Ridge was accomplished on those regular river forays.

• • •

When young Thomas moved north to the swamp property Harrison Collier was in his fifties. Daphne, a seamstress, housekeeper, and nurse at Home Hill, was about ten years his junior. The year of the first union of Harrison Collier to Daphne Collier is unknown, but it is certain that by 1850 they had several children, two of whom were Marshall Collier and Holt Collier. Holt was born about 1846. Because Marshall's age varies in the records, it is impossible to determine his age accurately. Several other Colliers known to be the offspring of Harrison and Daphne were Joseph, Amanda, Augusta, Allen, Maria, Mary, Meriamm, a boy, and George.[8] During the early development of Plum Ridge, the entire Collier family remained with Howell Hinds, his wife, and their children at Home Hill in Jefferson County.

• • •

The Hinds family was one of the preeminent first families of Mississippi, and Howell Hinds exerted his influence in the remotest parts of the state. In September 1850 he sent his son Thomas to the state university at Oxford. Thomas traveled upriver to Memphis and proceeded by land route to Holly Springs where he took a room at a roadside tavern owned by Wyatt Epps. At the instruction of Thomas, his trunk and other possessions were to remain with him and were taken by the innkeeper to his room. Before retiring for the night Thomas claimed to have locked his tuition and travel money in his trunk.

As was a common practice in those days, during the night a late arriving guest was placed in the room with Thomas. The late arrival departed very early the next morning, and when Thomas arose he claimed to have discovered his trunk broken into and his money gone. Although others heard Thomas claim a loss of only $80, Howell sued the innkeeper in his own name for a claimed loss of $185. Most people of his position would have avoided litigation at a distance of more than two hundred miles, but not Howell Hinds. Regardless of the fact that the father was an improper party, evidence was conflicting, and the property had, at Thomas's insistence, been his responsibility, the trial court ruled for Hinds and the appeals court affirmed its decision.[9]

• • •

One of the earliest documented events likely to have been witnessed by the young slaves Marshall and Holt Collier was a July 11, 1851, visit by Colonel Jefferson Davis, U. S. senator from Mississippi. He addressed the citizens of Fayette and almost certainly used the occasion to visit his old friend Howell Hinds at Home Hill Plantation. In addition to being a lifelong friend, Jefferson Davis is believed to have been a regular visitor to Home Hill Plantation, described then as a "beautiful country residence."[10]

Another early event very likely to have been witnessed by the Collier brothers was the hanging of Jesse and Albert, two slaves who had murdered their master. The death of W. Killingsworth and the burning of his plantation home at the hands of his slaves on July 20, 1854, ultimately involved everyone in the county. The trial which was held at Fayette on July 26 was widely attended by the surrounding plantation owners, and the male slaves of the area were required to attend the resulting executions.[11]

When the time came to carry out the judgment, Jefferson County planters took all of the male slaves to Fayette to witness the hanging of Jesse and Albert and to learn from the example made by them of the ultimate punishment to be exacted for rebelling against their master. Marshall and Holt Collier, as servants of Howell Hinds, would have had premium seats for the executions, and what they saw would certainly have made a lasting impression on them. At the hanging "Jesse confessed that he done it all, that no one helped to do it." Just before he died Jesse "exhorted his fellow servants to be faithful and do their duty."[12]

• • •

Holt Collier's early childhood was spent almost entirely within the confines of Home Hill Plantation. The Hinds home has been romantically described as being situated "amongst the rolling knobs of Jefferson County, Mississippi...on a hill from which three hundred yards of oak dotted lawn fell away to a fence" with a "whitewashed plantation gate." Beyond the Hinds's large house "stretched another lawn, seventy five acres in orchards, and a twelve acre garden where grew the choicest vegetables. Eggs in plenty came from his hennery, herds of cows supplied the milk; his smoke house overflowed with hams and sides of sausages. Paddock and pasture produced the noble Glencoes that won many a purse upon the track at Saratoga and Brighton Beach. He raised his own sheep, goats, pigs." From interviews with Holt Collier in later years, Harris Dickson wrote that at Home Hill "Howell Hinds owed nothing to the world and the world outside offered little that he needed."[13] As idyllic as life at Home Hill was described, it was not by any means perfect, except perhaps for the Hinds family. It was forever flawed and tarnished by the fact that the entire plantation system was built on the backs and from the blood of slaves.

Howell Hinds was described as a "black-bearded...kind master, an efficient money-making planter, clean, straight, honest. He raised his thoroughbreds and sported like a gentleman. For months on end he never touched a drop, then the conviviality of an occasion might start him on a spree."[14] Though he was totally dependent on slave labor, there is no evidence that Hinds used the whip against his slaves, nor is there any evidence that he was abusive towards them.

If his treatment of the Collier family is any indication, it would appear that Hinds's methods were paternalistic.

While Harrison and Daphne were responsible for the main house, the duty of both Marshall and Holt Collier was to care for the large pack of hunt hounds on the place. Holt would sometimes accompany his father and Howell Hinds on the hunt and into the town of Fayette afterward. On several occasions Holt witnessed both his master and father become heavily intoxicated and fall into the grips of "delirium" from alcohol. Once, Hinds was so intoxicated that he "lay out all night in a hickory thicket until he got sober next morning." Sleeping in the woods alone with a drunk was a frightening experience for the young boy. From these and other similar experiences he grew up with a "hatred for liquor, and to the end of his life...never took a drink."[15]

• • •

About 1856, at the age of ten, Holt Collier was taken upriver to Plum Ridge Plantation to serve as a juvenile valet to young Thomas Hinds. There he would live out the remainder of his eventful life in and about Washington County, Mississippi, in the northwestern edge of the original Hinds County. His departure from Home Hill was described by Dickson from Collier's accounts in later life, "At early morning the middle-aged master and the little slave boy set out together from Home Hill, traveling by surrey twelve miles to Rodney on the river. Holt's big eyes gazed in wonderment at the first steamboat he had ever seen, although his master had told him stories about them, and he could hear their whistle from the plantation, Holt had never seen a steamboat. Now he was actually going to ride on one, for the master took him by the hand and led him across the stageplank. Then he saw Uncle Henry Jones driving the surrey back towards home, and the old life lay behind him."[16]

Collier's own description, given when very aged, reveals a fond memory of his days at Home Hill and the relationships between his family and Howell Hinds: "...ole Gen'l Tom Hinds...was a gen'l in the British war; my father waited on him and Gen'l Jackson at the Battle of New Orleans. After that war was over wid, Gen'l Hinds brought my father back to the plantation in Jefferson County,

Mississippi, an' made 'im free. Leastways that's what everybody said, but it didn't make no difference to him 'bout bein' free. He never left the ole Gen'l, but stayed with 'im' til he died. Then there was Mr. Howell Hinds—he sho' was one fine young man—my father used to carry 'im 'roun' a-straddle on his neck. That's where I was born, down in Jefferson County, a little piece outside of Fayette—'bout four miles. Gen'l Hinds owned my father and my mother both, and of co'se he owned me."[17]

When Holt was sent upriver where the wilderness was being tamed, his parents and family remained behind. To this day, large numbers of Colliers live on the property that once was Home Hill Plantation. Some of their ancestors share burial ground with the Hinds family. In the family plot, located just down from where the main house once stood, are the damaged but legible gravestones of the Hinds and Collier families. The following are some examples with original spelling:

*Sacred to the memory of Gen. Thomas Hinds*
*Born in Berkly County, Va.*
*January 19th, 1780*
*Removed to this State at the Age of 19.*
*He gave promise of the future by the deeds of his youth.*
*Was distinguished for his daring intrepedity in the last war*
*with Great Britain; and verified public expectations*
*by the lofty stand he afterwards assumed and always sustained.*
*In the counsils of his State, He was*
*an incorruptible patriot bold in conception and fearless*
*in execution. Covered with honors and with years,*
*He descended to the grave on the 23rd day of August, 1840;*
*Aged 60 years, 7 months and 4 days.*
*How sleep the brave who sink to rest*
*By all their country's wishes blessed.*

• • •

*Sacred to the Memory of*
*Leminda Wife of Thomas Hinds*
*(and Daughter of Thomas M. Green)*
*who departed this Life the 29th of June 1819*
*in the 28th year of her Age*

*Sacred to the Memory of John Hinds*
*who departed this life the 19th February 1807*
*aged 54 years 4 months 8 days*

*Carrie*
*Daughter of Richard & Edith Hinds*
*Born Mar. 1, 1880*
*Died Dec. 17, 1897*
*Aged 17yrs. 9ms. 16 ds*
*Beautiful (illegible) Sheaves but green*
*A fair bud to earth to blossom in heaven*
*Footstone: C.H.*

• • •

*Richard*
*Husband of Edith Hinds*
*Died Jan. 10, 1898*

*Mary Collier*
*Jan. 5, 1854*
*Mar. 19, 1904*
*Rest Mother, rest in quiet sleep*
*While friends in sorrow o'er thee weep.*

*Elliot Collier*
*Feb. 25, 1880*
*June 18, 1914*
*Beloved one, farewell.*
*Footstone: E.C.[18]*

# CHAPTER 3

# THE PRIMEVAL WILDERNESS

*"Holt continued stabbing the
unfortunate beast until it was dead."*
— Harris Dickson

As the glaciers melted in the last cycle of a worldwide ice age, the level of the Gulf of Mexico rose, swelling sediment-rich rivers and streams great distances inland. Continuous flooding in the lower Mississippi Valley caused the land to be covered with a thick alluvial soil, a rich sediment which had been washed from over forty percent of the land area of what is now the continental United States. One of the flat basins on which these deposits ultimately came to rest was the vast delta of Mississippi, Louisiana, and Arkansas.[1]

The Yazoo-Mississippi Delta is typical of those alluvial flats. It is bordered on the west by the Mississippi River, on the east by the great Yazoo bluffs, some two hundred feet in height. The Mississippi Delta it is said, begins "in the lobby of the Peabody Hotel in Memphis, and ends on Catfish Row in Vicksburg." In area it measures over seven thousand square miles.[2]

The land was "a jungle equal to any in Africa, with dense forests of cane and giant trees from which hung great cling vines of wild grape and muscadine. The density of growth choked off air and held in moisture and a pulsing heat; it was so thick a horse and rider could not penetrate; even on foot one needed to cut one's way through. Only the trees, some one hundred feet high, burst above the choking vines and cane into the sunshine. Stinging flies, gnats, and mosquitoes swarmed around any visitors. One pioneer reported killing fourteen bears in eight days. Another warned of wolves and the fetid alligator, while the panther basks at [the river's] edge in the cane-brakes, almost impervious to man....nearly as large as a young calf. They are the most savage looking animal I ever saw. Their strong sinewy legs with large hooked claws like a cat could tear a man to pieces in a trice if they chose to."[3]

Prior to the appearance of the white man, this wilderness was the largest, most diverse ecosystem on the North American continent. In it the giant virgin cypress forest towered over vast canebrakes and primeval swamps. The red gum and white oak were unsurpassed by any trees of the eastern forests. It was observed that forests like these were "not to be found until we reach the sequoias and redwoods of the Sierras." Among the virgin timbers were "hackberry, thorn, honey locust, tupelo, pecan and ash." The knees of the cypress sloughs measured "two or three feet above the black ooze." An undergrowth of lush palmetto was evident throughout the entire region.

Among the extant fauna were the alligators and garfish. Monstrous snapping turtles, "fearsome brutes of the slime," weighed as much as a man and had huge horny beaks that with a single snap could easily take off a man's hand or foot. The garfish grew to unimaginable length and size, and the black bass and vipers–water moccasins, rattlesnakes, and copperheads–were prevalent. Racoons and opossums were plentiful as were minks, otters, black squirrels, and wood rats. The swamp rabbits were "thoroughly amphibious in their habits, not only swimming but diving, and taking to the water almost as freely as if they were muskrats."

The canopy of the forest provided shelter for many birds, including barred owls, mockingbirds, painted finches, cardinals, winter wrens, thrashers, warblers, vireos, and seven or eight species of woodpeckers, the most notable of which was the ivory-billed woodpecker.[4]

To settle and work in this vast wilderness was extremely hazardous, and many lives were lost to panthers, bears, rattlesnakes and moccasins. Many died from diseases such as yellow fever, malaria, and typhoid fever, which were constant plagues. This was the area of the South feared by slaves upriver, and referred to in such works as *Uncle Tom's Cabin* as the place slaves go to die when sold downriver. To the white landowner, it was "almost worth a man's life to cast his lot in the swamp" because the rich alluvial soils were like gold. The rich earth was ideal for growing cotton, the ultimate cash crop. Elsewhere, topsoil was measured in inches, but in the Mississippi Delta topsoil was tens of feet deep, and could be counted on to produce the highest yields of cotton in the entire country.[5]

The Delta of Mississippi is properly named the Yazoo River Basin. It is a flood plain composed entirely of alluvial deposits, and it appears almost perfectly flat. Upon a close examination it reveals a slight elevation along the banks of the rivers, streams, and bayous. As the inland waterways overflowed, the coarse silt was deposited along those banks, resulting in a slow building of a natural levee slightly higher than the surrounding area.[6]

Howell Hinds developed his Plum Ridge Plantation in a wilderness swamp whose only human inhabitants were Native Americans and fugitives from justice. It was a hard existence for anyone who ventured there. Regardless of the extreme difficulty of clearing this frontier, slowly over the years and by degrees, as the fertility of the alluvial soil became known, wealthy planters lured by the prospect of cheap land purchased great tracts for future development. Investors came from Louisiana, South Carolina, Tennessee, Kentucky and Virginia. Many investors, like Howell Hinds, came upriver from the Old Natchez District.

Planters brought with them armies of slaves whose hard labor cleared the formidable and seemingly impenetrable canebrakes and swamps. They opened arable land and built plantations on the slightly higher ridges along the Mississippi River and inland streams. The area became prosperous quickly and soon developed its own culture and identity. Hardships abounded for the slaves, but the wealthy planters experienced few of the struggles common to the typical American pioneer.

The Washington County plantations that had been settled before the Civil War were located primarily on the Mississippi River or on Lake Washington, connected to the river by Union Bayou, Rattlesnake Bayou, and Williams Bayou. The inland wilderness for thousands of square miles and millions of acres was a virgin forest with hundreds of miles of almost continuous canebrake along the natural levees of the bayous and rivers.

• • •

Into this environment Holt Collier journeyed upriver as a very young boy. Another river traveler who took the same route from

Vicksburg to Greenville about the same time wrote, "Above Vicksburg the country as we saw it from the steamer's deck looked wilder. Trees, cane and vines grew to the edge of the river bank. The clearings were more scattered and the caving of the bank more decided. Occasionally a monarch of the forest would topple, bend and dip its head in the murky stream, or would settle down with top upright."[7]

A description of the landing at Greenville also survives. "The stage plank was shoved out and a few passengers disembarked and we trod on Greenville's soil. It was like landing in the wilderness. Timber was standing. The streets were muddy and not well defined. Planks placed lengthwise served for sidewalks. We were greeted by some of the citizens of the place and the proprietor asked us to the hotel. It was about dinner time and we sat down to the table. There was no bill of fare, but our eyes saw at a glance bear meat, venison and spareribs, sweet potatoes, corn bread, milk and coffee. If the hotel had a name at that time I have forgotten it, but I do not forget the streams of cold air that came through the unbattened cracks. It was winter time and cold."[8]

The town of Greenville was little more than a rustic river landing with a few stores, a primitive boarding house, one church, a courthouse, and ten or twelve residences. Much like any typical pioneer river town of the times, it was described as a "carefree community, everybody bent on having a good time." With no public schools, it was the custom for each household with children to have a private tutor.[9]

Greenville was begun as a crudely planned community when in 1838 Samuel Reed Dunn bought eighty acres of land, divided it into lots, and sold them. The town was named in honor of General Nathaniel Green, an officer with General George Washington, for whom the county was named. The original county seat was Princeton, located a few miles downstream. When Princeton caved into the river and disappeared, Greenville became the county seat. After selling off all lots, Dunn moved to his Glenbar Plantation on Deer Creek, which in later years would become the property of Clive Metcalfe.[10]

As a river town, Greenville was of little commercial importance except to serve as a point of arrival and departure for the few elite who lived in the vicinity. In the fall cotton grown in the young but producing plantations was shipped from the port. The original site of river town was precariously situated and by 1858 was lost to the river by erosion and what little remained of the town was burned by the Union forces during the Civil War.[11]

• • •

From the river landing, Howell Hinds, Holt Collier, and a small entourage traveled a mud path south of town along the bank of a deep slough called Boggy Bayou until they reached Rattlesnake Bayou. The road through dense cane and cypress forests in time became an outlet to the "extensive and rich planters on that bayou, the Montgomerys, Mr. Alec and Mr. Pinckney, Major McAllister, the Plum Ridge Plantation and others."[12]

W. W. Stone, one of the early settlers of Washington County, described Plum Ridge Plantation as a large well improved plantation estate which Hinds populated with a large number of slaves. Stone also described Howell Hinds as "much given to sports of the race course and of hunting large game."[13]

At Plum Ridge wildlife of all species, especially bear, were plentiful. The indigenous flora and fauna were ideal habitat for a cunning animal. "The fact that a hunter could go out before breakfast and kill two or three deer, and that bear was as abundant, while exceedingly pleasant to the hunter, did not bring joy to the heart of the careful housekeeper as well, nor to a planter who was not a hunter." The bears were known to invade the yard of a settler. They would "come at night, when all were asleep, and overturn and drink up a full churn of cream for the next day's churning," and it was not uncommon for planters to post a slave outside "whose business it was to watch the hog pens all night, to keep the bears from killing and carrying off the hogs."[14]

Mrs. H. B. Theobald, well known around the town because she sold the property upon which the modern city of Greenville now stands, considered the bears to be a pestilence. "Bears were plentiful, and were counted on in the planting as unwelcome pensioners upon the settlers." She described seeing a bear walking off with arms full of yellow grain. Theobald described how occasionally the bruin would meet "a worthy foe." She described how "a neighbor woman, heroic and muscular, saw a bear raiding her hen coop. She took a hand spike, and with five blows killed the brute at the gate."[15]

The huge stands of cane in this untouched wilderness were a primary habitat for the bear and other wild game. The standing cane along the swamp area near Plum Ridge and the Greenville landing was as much as three miles wide and thirty miles long. Except in brief stretches of clearings, the canebrake was unbroken. Bodies of water were alive with many varieties of fish. There were many paths through the cane leading in all directions. They were made by and belonged to the master of the wilderness swamps, the great black bear.[16]

• • •

Upon young Holt's arrival in Greenville, he was immediately put to work providing meat for the workers of the plantation. Often he killed an abundance of game and provided for the neighbors as well. He was given a pony to ride and a twelve gauge Scott shotgun. Hinds stationed him on the porch of a cabin in the slave quarters with instructions to shoot all the pigeons, robins, and other birds he could. When his right shoulder was so sore that he couldn't fire from it any longer, he was required to use his left shoulder. From the experience Collier quickly became an accomplished marksman. At an early age he learned to shoot equally well from his left and right shoulders.[17]

As his talents grew, the young slave boy became a useful and profitable property for Howell Hinds. Quail matches among wealthy planters were very popular in the years leading up to the Civil War and were frequently held at prominent plantations up and down the river. Hinds challenged his talented young nimrod against the unsuspecting marksmen and won substantial sums in the process. "At various times Colonel Hinds pitted his man, Holt, against..." some of the most noted sportsmen between Mississippi and Kentucky. Holt is known to have competed against Major Keep of Mayersville, Mississippi, as well as Jeff Brown and Major Lawrence of Louisville, Kentucky. One noted marksman, Mr. Lomax Anderson, of Lake Village, Arkansas, lost a match to the young slave boy, which provided winnings to Colonel Hinds described as "a purse of one thousand dollars in gold."[18] It is no wonder that Holt Collier, an accomplished marksman at an early age, was valued by Howell Hinds. The benefits he realized for his services were commensurate with his value. He was dressed in fine clothes, provided suitable accommodations, and treated with special affection. In his later years Holt Collier often described his standard of living as a boy to have been far better than at any other time in his life.

In interviews with Holt Collier after the turn of the century, he described Howell Hinds, young Thomas Hinds, Plum Ridge Plantation, and journeys up and down river. He fondly recalled: "Gen'l he had another big plantation up here in Washington County, and the two young gentlemen—Mr. Tom and Mr. Howell—they brought me up here with 'em. They raised me; my mother stayed on the old plantation. Befo' the war we used to travel a whole lot—us three. They certainly was spry young men, fond of ladies and frolickin' and horses; jes' liked to have a whoopin' good time. I warn't nothin' but a little boy, but wherever they went they carried me—all over the United States. They carried me to Niagara Falls when I was a little bit of a chap—New York and Brighton Beach, Saratoga and Long Beach. They wouldn't hardly step foot off the front gallery 'thout I went along. When I got big I wore finer clothes than they did. I had to go amongst white folks and they kept me up in fine style."[19]

In an interview about 1930, Holt Collier described those early days to a reporter from the *New York Herald Tribune*. He was eighty-four-years-old, but suffering no apparent loss of faculties. An account from those interviews provides additional confirmation of his life as a child: "He says his shooting apprenticeship began when he was ten years old. His master bought him a fine shotgun—a twelve-gauge Scott, costing $215.00—and stationed him on the porch of a cabin in the slave quarters. It was winter time, and several clumps of chinaberry trees near by were swarming with blackbirds."

"De Cunnel say, 'Holt, you pick dem birds out o'de trees wid dat gun!' So day after day he blazed away at the birds, furnishing the makings for blackbird pie for the table in the 'big house' and enough left over for the neighbors."

"After Holt had learned to shoot a shotgun or rifle from either shoulder with deadly accuracy, Hinds took him on his first bear hunt. They came up Rattlesnake Bayou only a mile or two. There, in the swamps between Plum Ridge Plantation and the Greenville river landing, at the tender age of ten, Holt Collier killed the first bear of a lifetime total that exceeded 3,000."[20]

Holt Collier became a respected plantation huntsman and was given great latitude for a slave. The labor expected of him was limited to the hunt–cleaning the guns, feeding and training the dogs and horses, cleaning the carcasses of game killed, and always scouting the swamps for locations of the most treasured game and favored meat, the black bear.

The swamp plantation at Plum Ridge and the surrounding lands were unexplored virgin territory, and the game was plentiful beyond imagination. According to Collier, it was not unusual for him and Thomas Hinds to "get up at dawn and kill two bear before nine o'clock." Holt was known to have kept the kitchen at Plum Ridge and "all the neighborhood supplied with ducks, geese and squirrels."

The black bear had a reputation for being unthreatening in most encounters with humans. However, when hungry, awakening from hibernation, protecting its young, or being pursued, the black bear could react to a human with great ferocity, sometimes with lethal consequences. On only two occasions during his life was Holt Collier injured by his prey. On a hunt with Howell Hinds when Holt was about fourteen years old, he was careless and allowed a bear to slash him on his left wrist. He carried the scar the remainder of his life. The injury was severe, but it eventually healed. Holt killed the bear that clawed him and was immediately treated by Howell Hinds who, in an effort to administer aid, "tore off his own shirt, made a strong bandage and stopped the blood while Holt continued stabbing the unfortunate beast until it was dead."[21]

• • •

To avoid the sweltering heat of Mississippi summers as well as yearly encounters with yellow fever, the Hinds family and many other plantation families made annual summer pilgrimages north into Kentucky. The trips began in May of each year and the returns would occur in October. The return trips always brought needed provisions for the remote plantation and its inhabitants. Substantial amounts of dry goods and supplies–including flour, sugar, molasses, coffee and whiskey—were necessary for a work force as large as that at Plum Ridge. Typically, a planter maintained lists of clothing measurements and shoe sizes.

Trips by the landed gentry, although common, were only as elaborate as finances would allow. By the standards of neighboring plantations, Howell Hinds was a planter of means, but certainly not in the class of those who owned hundreds of slaves and thousands of acres. On the trips north the more privileged travelers would carry entire families, several personal servants, horses and carriages.

Sam Worthington, whose family was among the first to settle in Washington County, wrote a romanticized passage describing the regular journeys upriver by an entire elite planter family. "When I first appeared on the scene, it was the invariable custom of the planters to go North May 10th and return to Mississippi October 10th. They carried their families with them and always several slaves. This I know was the case in my father's family; we never traveled with less than five, and he always carried his own carriage and horses with him. The planters went North by steamboat to Louisville, Kentucky, scattering to the various watering places and seaside resorts; but go where they might, the "pregnant hinges of the knee" were bent to them everywhere. Bear in mind that I am writing now of a time when the Washington County planters owned from one hundred and fifty to one thousand slaves, and made annually from one thousand to eight thousand bales of cotton. There were practically no poor white people in Washington County then, and few white people who worked, and the line was sharply drawn against those who did....When the planters returned to Mississippi in October, the usual fall and winter plans for hunting were laid."[22]

Worthington's observation that few white people worked is corroborated by the statistics. By 1850 the average white family in Washington County owned more than 80 slaves. Over the entire Mississippi Delta, slaves outnumbered whites by 5 to 1.[23]

Holt Collier served as a juvenile valet and, until the nation was divided by war, annually accompanied Howell and Thomas Hinds on their excursions upriver to such destinations as Memphis, St. Louis, Lexington, Cincinnati, and, according to Holt, Saratoga and Brighton Beach. While Holt enjoyed these trips, he was no doubt annoyed by all the attention he attracted in the free states of the North. Dressed in the best broadcloth, felt hat, and shiny morocco boots, he would be urged by the free blacks to escape.

Holt laughed about it in later years. "They would say all sorts of things to me just because I was a boy. But not to the boss. The boss would fight in a minute, an' those folks knew it. One time at Cincinnati I thought I would have to put the boss in trouble. Those people were deviling me so hot to stay up there that I got pestered and told the boss."

"All right, Holt," he said, "this is a free state. You can stay up here if you want to."

"But," I told him, "there isn't nothin' up here for me. When you go home I'm goin' with you, or die."[24]

On those trips Holt's responsibilities were to groom and keep Hinds's racehorse. He would sleep in the stalls with the animals and bet his money on them, frequently winning. When Holt was twelve years of age, Hinds visited his cousin Alice Crozier near Bardstown, Kentucky, where the boy's aunt served as cook. He was left with the Crozier children, and an effort was made to give him some rudimentary education. Hinds made this attempt to see that Holt at least learned to read and write, but as quickly as the boy had proven himself with gun and trap and race horse, he showed no inclination whatever to take up "book learning." It has been said that the gun led him astray. At night he would hide his gun in the spring house, a deep cleft among the rocks where Mrs. Crozier kept her milk and butter. There the icy water gushed in and drained out, and there the young boy hid his gun until the morning when he would conspire with the young white boys to skip school and go to the woods to hunt.

Holt would sneak to the spring house, get his gun, and stay all day in the woods, shooting rabbits and the white-mouth brown squirrel. This daily exercise would have been a happy arrangement if Holt's aunt had not interfered. His Aunt Frances was Alice Crozier's cook, and she felt somewhat responsible for her nephew's education.

"Miss Alice," she said, "I aims to tan the hide off o'dat boy an' make him go to school."

"No Frances," Mrs. Crozier stopped her, "Cousin Howell will not whip Holt himself, or allow anybody else to touch him. If the boy doesn't want to go to school you can't help it."[25]

In later years Holt's lack of formal education was often commented on by those who knew him. One writer observed: "Though Mr. Hinds never succeeded in having the boy educated in books, he, however, trained Holt to be honorable, truthful and trustworthy, and this training was evident throughout his life."[26]

• • •

The pigeons of Plum Ridge were no luckier than the game in the Kentucky backwoods. They were killed by Holt in great numbers. Howell Hinds made a habit of bringing from his old home in Jefferson County large quantities of pine knots to be used for out-of-door lighting and for night hunting. These lightwood knots were also used to blind the pigeons on their roost. Holt would accompany Tom Hinds to a pigeon roost and beat the birds from the low branches with fishing poles. In a very short time they would have a buggy full of birds. The pigeons would perch so thickly on the tree limbs that often a good sized limb would be broken by their weight. So ruthlessly were these birds slaughtered that today they are extinct.[27] With their long, gracefully tapered tails these birds were known decades later as passenger pigeons *(Ectopistes migratorius)*. The torch and pole method of mass slaughter of pigeons was not limited to the Mississippi Delta, but was common over the entire United States and well known on the European continent.

Years later Collier often spoke of Plum Ridge and how Hinds had raised cotton on the broad acres of that plantation–so much cotton that they hauled the bales to the river landing in wagons drawn by sixteen horses. Holt spoke of the servants singing as they worked and of how Howell Hinds loved good horses, rode from dawn until dark for business or pleasure, and how the work horses were finer and more spirited than those used by others to drive their carriages.[28]

CHAPTER 4

# FROM GREENVILLE TO PITTSBURG LANDING

*"There I laid like a rabbit in a brier-patch
until we got clean up to Memphis."*
— Holt Collier

When Abraham Lincoln was elected President in 1860, southern leaders panicked. Throughout the South representatives were selected to attend secession conventions in state capitals. Little meaningful effort was made by either side of the slavery issue to contain the coming conflagration. The secessionists believed themselves to be on solid constitutional grounds, relying on the writings and work of the Founding Fathers. Political rhetoric took on an air of emotionalism and celebration, particularly in the deep South.

Southerners had felt victimized by recent developments in national politics, and secession provided a means for redress. Parades, fireworks, speeches, and celebrations accompanied each secession convention. South Carolina was the first to secede on December 20, 1860, with a unanimous legislative vote of 169 to 0. Mississippi followed suit on January 9, 1861, with a vote of 85 to 15.[1]

On February 4, 1861, delegates from the seceded states met in Montgomery, Alabama, to elect leaders and write a constitution. The convention elected Howell Hinds's lifelong friend Jefferson Davis president of the Confederate States of America. Davis, aged fifty-three, was a graduate of the United States Military Academy at West Point, a veteran of the Black Hawk and Mexican Wars, a former U. S. representative, and secretary of war in the administration of President Franklin Pierce (1853-57). He was serving in the U. S. Senate when Mississippi seceded. Davis was a compromise candidate who had declined to attend the convention, learning about his election while pruning rose bushes at his Mississippi home.[2]

Inspired by the prevailing radical emotions, South Carolina Confederates fired on Fort Sumter on April 12, 1861. The first volleys, with the victory that followed, gave the new Confederate States of America a feeling of overconfidence that would ultimately be crushed by a military force never before seen in war.

With the exception of those families who moved north or traveled abroad, the conflict would be devastating to almost all Southerners. While states' rights might have been the announced reason for leaving the Union, the articles of secession passed by the individual states rarely mentioned any reason other than the need to preserve the institution of slavery. In Mississippi, there was no question of the reasons for leaving the union. A declaration of the causes for secession stated that the most prominent reasons for secession were "thoroughly identified with the institution of slavery," stated by the secessionists as being the "the greatest material interest of the world."[3]

• • •

The mood in Jefferson County following secession was one of reserved excitement. Men were eager to join the war effort but were not sure what sacrifice would ultimately be demanded of them. The initial term of service was only one year, and almost all units were mustered into Confederate service by the authority of the state, not by the newly formed Confederate government in Montgomery. Skepticism about the war existed among many of the gentry. Some initially avoided military service but made generous contributions of horses and cotton for the cause. Others traveled north to be with family, and some traveled abroad.

Most of the companies formed in Jefferson County were raised with significant popular support. One such company was the Jefferson Flying Artillery, which Howell Hinds joined and of which he was elected lieutenant.[4] In Washington County things were much the same. Thomas Hinds joined Ed Byrnes's Artillery Company, also as a lieutenant.[5]

Soon after the election of Lincoln, Holt Collier had begun to hear "white folks talking about war." Because the Hinds women only visited the Mississippi Delta in the autumn season, there were only men at Plum Ridge Plantation for Holt to make a pretense of waiting on. In the days following secession and the establishment of the Confederacy, Howell Hinds rode every morning to town, gathered all the news, and returned home. Holt listened to every word of what the gentlemen said. The young slave described "soldiers marching everywhere...kept busy drilling." According to Collier, on a nightly basis "the white folks were holding meetings, making speeches, and couriers dashing around on horseback."[6]

Many years later Holt described the excitement in the air, when the war broke out, "we couldn't hear nothin' but fightin' and soldiers, an' gittin' up companies an' drillin'. Cunnel Howell Hinds, of co'se, an' his son, they was amongst the fust to stir around an' git ready to go. Everybody sho' was busy, ridin' back and forth, holdin' meetin's an' gittin' up companies, an' makin' clothes. I was into it big as anybody, 'cause I thought I was goin' jes' like the others; never dreamed o' nothin' else."[7]

• • •

The activity of the local men and the rumors about Lincoln freeing the slaves resulted in a plan of insurrection among many Jefferson County slaves, including some belonging to Howell Hinds. The plot, made possible by the decreased number of white males in the area and emerging factions of emboldened slaves, was not successful. Nonetheless, several local slaves were executed during the summer of 1861. By July of the following year, forty slaves had been executed and at least that many put in irons in what would be later known as the Second Creek Massacre.[8] Additionally, with many whites lacking funds to hire overseers to control the large population of slaves, the servants began to take liberties–harboring runaways, killing stock, stealing, and being a general nuisance to the white population.

Howell Hinds, concerned at the state of affairs and torn between protecting the local citizens and the call of military duty, reflected on the difficulty of the times when he wrote of the insurrection in a letter to his friend, Mississippi Governor J. J. Pettus: "On my return from Jackson I found...an organization by the negros for the purpos of riseing on the 4th of July next at which time they had been induced to believe Lincons troops would be here for the purpos of freeing them all....each one was to kill his master and that they would later (have) the fine houses and the white women....the citizens of Jefferson are not willing any more companys should leave the county."[9]

• • •

With great excitement and fanfare the Jefferson Flying Artillery was mustered into state service at Fayette and entered Confederate service soon thereafter. Captains were William L. Harper and Putnam Darden, who was promoted after Shiloh. First lieutenants were Howell Hinds and A. J. Cameron. Edward W. Crozier, possibly a cousin of Hinds, was later promoted to second lieutenant. The company, originally organized as a cavalry unit, was soon afterward equipped with artillery.

Before departing with his unit, Howell Hinds transacted several personal matters in Washington County, presumably in an effort to settle any question of his estate should he be killed in service. He conveyed several slaves by gift to his son Thomas "for love and affection & in consideration of his services as manager on Plum Ridge Plantation." The slaves given to Thomas were: "John, Knight, Myra & their 2 children Toby & Shields, Young, Freeman, Richmond, the two latter children of Caroline, Edward & Anna, children of Augusta, Quitman, Mary, Ann, child & Lark."[10] Of particular interest to Thomas Hinds was the conveyance of ownership of Augusta and her children, Anna and Edward. Augusta was Holt Collier's sister. She and her children would remain with or close to Thomas for the remainder of his life.

Hinds's company remained in Jefferson County stationed at Cane Ridge Church and Camp Dunbar until July 1861, when it was moved to Mississippi City opposite Ship Island. There it was assigned to protect the coast and the entries to New Orleans and Mobile. The coastal area was the only portion of Mississippi to experience troop movement of significance in 1861. A fort on Ship Island, then under construction by the U. S. Engineers, had been occupied by state troops.

Like his father before him, Howell Hinds did not like his assigned duties, nor was he content to accept them. It was his desire to be in Virginia or Missouri, where significant exchanges with the enemy were expected to occur. After suffering through a month of incessant drills and mundane camp life in the coastal heat, Hinds arrogantly wrote to his old friend President Jefferson Davis making his demands known.

*August 24, 1861*
*Jackson, Miss.*

*To: Jeff Davis*

*This dispatch is sent at my instance. Order us to Missouri or Virginia. Answer immediately.*

*Howell Hinds*[11]

It is not known if this message had any effect. However, all troops in the area, including the Jefferson Flying Artillery, were evacuated from the coastal region by September 17. They withdrew from their stations without seeing a northern soldier or firing a shot. They were ordered to Virginia, going by way of New Orleans upriver to Memphis, where they were to bivouac for a week before proceeding further.[12] This movement was in concert with the army's strategy to protect Kentucky from an early investment by the enemy. On December 3 Ship Island was reoccupied by Union forces.

En route north to Memphis, Hinds managed a brief stop at Plum Ridge where he was greeted by his wife and all of the children, who were visiting from Jefferson County. The furlough for Hinds was short, as troops were rapidly deploying to Memphis for further orders. This short visit to Plum Ridge was cause for a hasty celebration. Along with drilling and parading in Greenville, considerable festivities were held throughout the area. All of the military pomp and pageantry impressed Holt, who remembered: "all this drilling of soldiers and marching at the brass band," and the "big house rang with music." "Young men galloped up to dance with the girls. They had parties and festivals. The piano never stopped a minute."[13]

Holt Collier was fourteen years of age and desperately wanted to join both Howell and Thomas on their assignment to Memphis, but Howell would not consider it. The young Holt would not surrender easily. He was persistent in his efforts to accompany Howell Hinds into battle, just as his father, Harrison Collier, had accompanied General Thomas Hinds a generation earlier.

Both Howell Hinds and the younger Thomas Hinds had declined Holt's pleadings. The scene was described by Harris Dickson from Holt's recollections. "The lower edge of Plum Ridge lawn was then surrounded by a high rail fence. Father and son rode out of the little gate, turning west towards the river. Until that moment Holt had not believed that they really meant to leave him. He was a big boy now and thought himself almost a man, yet he began to blubber and to run, racing down to the fence where they must pass him. There he sat on the top rail bellowing, didn't care who heard him, while Marse Tom and the boss rode by.

"'Boss,' he yelled, 'I'm jest obleeged to go with you.'

"'No, Holt, that's settled.' The master checked his horse. 'You might get killed.'

"'But, boss, you say you don't know whether you's comin' back. If you don't come back I wants to be where you is. Then I'll know what becomes of you.'

"'I cannot take you Holt,' Marse Howell answered firmly. 'Go back to the house and look after Ole Miss.'

"The black boy sat on Plum Ridge fence bellowing and calling after his master until long after the two gray uniforms had vanished around a turn in the road. The boss had gone to war. And Holt was left behind."[14]

In another account of the event compiled from interviews of Holt Collier, "Holt tells us that at the time when the Civil War began, he was living on Plum Ridge, the Hinds's plantation, south of the present city of Greenville. Mr. Howell Hinds, later Colonel Hinds and always spoken of by Holt as 'The Old Colonel', and his son, Tom, were making ready to join the Confederate forces. When Holt Collier, then only fourteen years of age, learned of his master's preparations for departing, he asked to go with them. To Holt's great disappointment, however, his master and Tom agreed that the little colored boy was too young to enter the army."

"'I begged like a dog, but they stuck to it—'You are too young!,' Holt relates.

"'When my Old Col. left to join the army, he left me sitting on the fence crying and begging him to let me go with him.'

"'He said, 'No, you might get killed.'

"'I said I've got as good a chance as you. He left me sitting there watching him go across the fields to Old Greenville to catch the boat.'"[15]

Collier elaborated on his separation from Howell Hinds several times in later years: "One night I hear old Cunnel say, 'No, siree; Holt can't go. We ain't got no right to git him kilt.' I never let on I heerd 'im, but I kept up a mighty lot o' thinkin'. All this time the soldiers was gatherin' down at ole Greenville, four miles below here— that's all caved into the river long ago, an' washed away. It was nearly dark one evening when they all rode away from the plantation, lookin' mighty fine on their high-steppin' horses. I warn't nothin' but a boy, an' I hadn't never parted from them two young men in all my life. They was goin' away, an' I didn't know whether they would live or git killed. I jes' nacherly couldn't stan' it, so I set on the fence an' busted out in a big cry after they rode off through the swamp. It 'peared like my heart would break, but ole marster had tole me, 'No, Holt, you **got** to stay home."[16]

It would be the only time in his life that Holt Collier willfully disobeyed Howell Hinds. That night, after Hinds left the plantation for the river landing and the transports awaiting him, the young boy did the unthinkable. He overcame his grief, collected a few personal items in his budget and quietly departed without telling a soul. "Slipping like a shadow, making himself very small, very silent, and attracting no attention," young Holt Collier stole away from Plum Ridge.

Between the plantation and the river was "a tangle of lakes and swamps, of bayous and morasses" that Holt would have to cross in the darkness of night. He walked along a rickety causeway, only to fall into the lake where he waded about in water amongst the cypress knees and crawled out again to continue his journey.[17] On foot and in the dark of night the fourteen year old found his way to the river, embarking on a journey from which he could not turn back, a journey that would define him as a man and earn for him a lifetime of great respect and admiration.

Collier reached the Greenville landing where he could hear the stir and bustle aboard six steamboats that were tied up beside the levee. He hid in a store near the water's edge owned by a Jewish merchant named Ross. He watched for hours as men in gray passed across the gangplanks by the light of torches, loading their steamers with cannon and munitions of war. Nobody noticed the small slave boy who carried a bundle.[18]

He confided in a cook on the steamer *Vernon* who filled Holt's stomach, then showed him how to slip aboard on the boat on which the youngster had already seen his master. Holt was successful at making his passage across the gangplank after which he "dropped like a rat into the hatchway." Holt remained in the hull undisturbed for two nights and a day. On the second morning all the boat whistles blew in chorus. They had arrived in Memphis.[19]

When he emerged from hiding Holt saw the bluffs of the river city where there were amassed hundreds of soldiers, cannon, provisions and cavalry horses. At the top of the bank Holt later described seeing Howell and Thomas Hinds mixing with other officers. Among them were Lieutenant Colonel Nathan Bedford Forrest, Generals James Chalmers, John C. Breckinridge, former Vice President in the Buchanan administration, and Charles Clark, who would become the wartime governor of Mississippi in 1863. Collier claimed to have also seen two other Confederate leaders on the occasion, General Braxton Bragg and cavalry commander Colonel Wirt Adams. He collected his budget and marched off the boat to confront his master.

When Thomas first saw Holt approaching he called out to his father to take notice.

Howell observed the young man walking up the hill towards them. He took off his hat, rubbed back his hair and stated bluntly, "If we are going to hell we'll have to take that boy."[20]

Hinds, exasperated at the boy's persistence, told the other officers: "Gentlemen, I raised that boy in my house and he's following me." The officers laughed, "gave him money and treated him nice." They joked with him saying: "Don't you know you are going to the graveyard?"[21]

Holt responded confidently: "I got as good a chance as you."

No more was said of Holt's youth, and he went into training at Camp Boone in Tennessee. His initial service would be as a bodyservant to Lieutenants Howell and Thomas Hinds.[22]

In later years Holt described his experience of going off to war. "Down to ole Greenville the boats was all tied up, a-takin' soldiers on board. The young men was laughin' and talkin' like thay was goin' to a picnic; and the young ladies was givin' 'em flags and pinnin' flowers on their coats. But the old men looked kinder solemn when they didn't think anybody was watchin' them. I heerd Cunnel Howell Hinds say one night, 'Fightin' in a war with a man's own flesh and blood is a serious thing.' But the ole Cunnel was done into it then, and if you ever knowed 'im you wouldn't never 'spect 'im to be a-quittin' or a-turnin' back."

"I hid in the woods and watched 'em loadin' the boats—co'se nobody didn't pay 'tention to a little darky like me. After a while the negroes commenced puttin' the old Cunnel's horses, and Mr. Tom's and Mr. Howell's horses on board the *Vicksburg*. I knowed their baggage jes' same as I knowed my every-day breeches. I watched for a chance, and when none of 'em wasn't lookin' I picked up a bundle and sneaked on board the boat. I hid 'way back in a dark corner, right beside a lot of saddles that belonged to Mr. Tom Hinds. There I laid like a rabbit in a brier-patch until we got clean up to Memphis. I didn't raise my head 'til we got to Memphis—but I sho' was one hungry boy, 'cause I hadn't had a bite to eat nor a mouth ful o' water. After we had done stopped a little while I heerd 'em beginning to unload the boat, an' I sneaked out. I was so weak I couldn't hardly walk, and powerful scared o' what Cunnel Hinds was goin' to do to me."

"I hadn't no mor'n walked out on the guards befo' I saw Mr. Tom Hinds and his father standin' up on the deck amongst the soldiers. Nobody paid me no mind, an' I was fixin' to sneak across the stage-plank when Mr. Tom said, 'Father, look yonder.'"

"'What is it, Tom?'"

"Cunnel Hinds looked up an' saw me an' busted out in a big laugh. 'Well, Tom, it *do* look like we got to take that boy everywhere we go. 'Tain't no use trying to leave *him*—he jes' ain't a-goin' to stay behind."

"Of co'se, I knew 'twas all right after Cunnel Hinds done broke out an' laughed, so I went to waitin' on 'em same I always done. That was how I happened to go with the army in the Confederate War."[23]

• • •

Howell and Thomas were in separate units but were assigned to the same field corps. Both the Jefferson Flying Artillery and Byrne's Artillery were assigned to Hardee's division in the army of General Albert Sidney Johnston, widely considered the finest and most experienced officer in the Confederacy. With young Holt Collier in their service, the unit departed Memphis destined for Virginia, as demanded by Hinds in his earlier correspondence to Jefferson Davis. In Chattanooga, however, a change of orders was received, and Johnston's entire command moved north to Kentucky.[24]

Kentuckian Albert Sidney Johnston graduated eighth in his West Point class of 1826. His roommate and close friend at the Point had been Leonidas Polk, later to become Episcopal bishop of Louisiana and fellow general in the Confederate army. Jefferson Davis, also a classmate, but two years his junior, idolized Johnston. He was fifty-eight years of age, experienced from his leadership in the Black Hawk War and the war with Mexico, and well respected in both the North and the South.

When war erupted, Johnston was offered a high command with the Union army. He refused, preferring to remain loyal to his adopted state of Texas. Stationed at the time with the U. S. Army in California, he immediately surrendered his commission and traveled under guard to Richmond, where by September 1861 he was given command of all operations in the west (Texas, Louisiana, Mississippi, Tennessee, Alabama, Missouri and Kentucky). During the entire term of his active service he was the highest ranking Confederate general in the field.[25]

• • •

The strategy necessary to protect the western theater of war in January and February 1862 required shielding Nashville from any threat, particularly from the Union forces amassing in Kentucky. Johnston immediately ordered Bowling Green occupied as part of a 430-mile line of defense which extended from the Cumberland Gap into Missouri. Having only five thousand troops at Bowling Green, most of them poorly equipped, the Confederates attempted to create the impression of superior numbers. They engaged the enemy frequently in raiding campaigns that winter but were unable to raise the numbers of men in the field sufficient to confront the increasing Union forces at Cairo and St. Louis.[26]

Two commanders of the Union forces in the west were to significantly affect Johnston's efforts. They were Naval Flag Officer Andrew Hull Foote and General Ulysses S. Grant. Additionally, by the end of the winter of 1861-62 Union forces in Kentucky were greatly strengthened in numbers, and the southern army was clearly not sufficient to halt their advance.

Howell Hinds and the Jefferson Flying Artillery, accompanied by Holt Collier, arrived in Bowling Green on October 13, 1861. On October 29, 1861, a reorganization of all units officially mustered the men from state service into the service of the Confederate States of America.[27]

• • •

Brigadier General Charles Clark of Mississippi was well known to Howell Hinds. They had been friends and served together in the state militia before the war.[28] Clark, who as governor later surrendered Mississippi to Union forces, commanded the First Division, First Corps, Army of the Mississippi. Under the military reorganization Hinds was reassigned to Clark's staff and spent much time at Camp Boone outside Nashville. He resigned his rank with the Jefferson Artillery and was replaced there by his friend Putnam Darden. By April, 1862, Howell held the rank of major and assistant adjutant-general to Clark.[29]

Holt Collier was considered a personal servant to Howell and Thomas Hinds. He had much time to familiarize himself with camp life and the idleness endemic there. He frequently labored as a camp servant with general duties. His role changed drastically one day when a train was derailed near the Green River Bridge. A skirmish with Union troops followed. At the time of the incident Holt was serving as an orderly tending to a wounded man named Dunbar. With his patient's gun and ammunition, Holt took a place on the firing line near the bridge. He was discovered when Lieutenant Thomas Hinds approached the line. The officer found much humor in the scene. This brief action and the boy's demeanor under fire was the end of his service as a camp servant and the beginning of his service as an unofficial soldier for the Confederate army. He proved himself by being "a dead shot, utterly fearless, firing a gun from either shoulder or a pistol from either hand."[30]

Collier provided his own account of that incident to several correspondents in later years.

"When the soldiers got unloaded they went out to Camp Boone, Tennessee. Mr. Tom Hinds was first lieutenant of Burns's Artillery, and Cunell Howell Hinds was lieutenant of Cap'n Put Darden's company. The ole gentleman afterward got promoted to be a cunnel.

"They drilled a heap at Camp Boone, and officers was sent there to teach 'em how. It didn't take those young men long to get to be tol'able good drill hands.

"One night about ten o'clock we had double-quick orders to go to Mulvilhill, Kentucky, close to Elizabethtown. We traveled all that night, and at nearly day-light we took the train and got as far as Bowling Green.

"I never will forget seeing a lieutenant climb up on the top of the depot an' pull down the Union flag—it was about noon-time. All the young soldiers cheered and cheered, but I saw two or three old soldiers that looked mighty curious about it.

"We sho' was in a hurry; I heard 'em say we was tryin' to beat Gen'l Rousseau—he was the Federal general of the Yankee army we was tryin' to beat him to Mulvihill. But we hadn't got more'n a piece of the way from Bowling Green befo' our train got wrecked. The track was tore up mighty bad by some of the Union people, and by that kind o' trick the Yankees beat us to Mulvihill. So we camped at Bowling Green River Bridge—and stayed there quite a while. The Yankees advanced down and the first fight we had was on the big hill to the right of the bridge at Green River.

"After that was all over the Yankees fell back to Mulvihill, and we moved down to Bowling Green and went into winter quarters.

"When the fight broke out that time they all went away and left me in camp by myself and I was a mighty little darky. Somebody had left a musket an' a sack full of cartridges. So I jes' buckled on the cartridge belt, an' follered along 'til I got to where the shootin' was goin' on. All the men was a-pluggin' away, so I got in a place where I could see real good, an' commenced a-shootin', too.

"'Twarn't long until I heerd some one bust out in a big laugh behine me, and there was Mr. Tom Hinds a-settin' up mighty straight on his hoss.

"'Look here, boy, ain't you scared you'll git kilt?' Mr. Tom said, an' he looked so peculiar I couldn't help but laugh.

"Dunno, sir; ain't my chances mighty nigh as good as yours?

"He jes' laughed an' laughed, then rode off a-hollerin' at some men. Co'se he was my master, an' if he didn't say nothin' it warn't nobody else's business, so I kept on a-shootin'. When everybody said the fightin' was done over with I come on back to camp with the rest of 'em, and the men all laughed at me and my big musket.

"'Where you reckon that big gun is a-goin' wid that little bit o'nigger?' one of 'em said.

"'You let that nigger alone, another one assured 'im, right brief. 'That nigger's a soldier.' I sholy did feel proud when he said that. Then we fell back to our winter quarters in Bowling Green."[31]

In time Howell Hinds would give Collier an iron gray gelding thoroughbred named Medock which Holt rode until the end of the war. He also wore a Confederate gray uniform and a short jacket with braided edges.[32] So early in the war it could not have been suspected that this young slave would ultimately experience more combat and serve with far more distinction than either of his masters.

During the winter months of 1861-62 the Union army under the command of General Ulysses Grant continued to grow and gain strength. In the early days of February General Grant and Admiral Foote moved against Fort Henry on the Tennessee River and Fort Donelson on the Cumberland River. The massive land and naval forces took the garrison at Fort Henry with such ease that Johnston was convinced that his army should retreat into Tennessee. A valiant but ineffectual defense of Donelson resulted in Bowling Green falling into Union hands on February 14, 1862. Donelson, subject to Grant's demands of "unconditional surrender," fell on February 16, and the strategically vital city of Nashville soon fell to the Union forces.

Johnston's command retreated to Murfreesboro, Tennessee, where they bivouacked from February 23 until April 2. Howell Hinds spent some of this time at Shelbyville about twenty-five miles south of the command. With battle imminent, Thomas Hinds was having second thoughts and did not wish to return to his regiment seeking instead to return home for the stated purpose of raising his own company. In an effort to make it possible for Thomas to avoid almost certain action in battle, Howell Hinds attempted to exert his once considerable influence by writing to Mississippi Governor Pettus and President Davis.

*Near Shelbyville*
*March 6, 1862*

*Dear Friend*

*My son Thomas who is in Byrne's Artillery from Washington County, Miss. & is 1st Luet. of the company desires to raise an artillery company of his own & asked me to write to you to authorize him to do so. He is as well drilled as any one you will find with the experience he has had which has been since July last. He would be pleased to hear from you at your earliest convenience. I know not to what point you could communicate to him as we are ignorant of our destination but presume you know where we will remain long enough for a letter to reach him. Our disaster at Donaldson is a severe blow to us & consequently dispirits our soldiers very miserably. The effect is terrible on the trainees and many have left & returned home & others say they will not go beyond their homes. If however they could have assurances that we would concentrate a sufficient force to drive the enemy back I have no doubt they would remain true to us. Why such a force was surrendered at Donaldson without an attempt to get out is to me inescapable & I think it will be very difficult to satisfy you of the policy of this counsel. Hoping you will reply favourably to Tho's request I remain as ever your friend.*

*Howell Hinds*[33]

Reorganization of individual units in Johnston's army took place while at Murfreesboro. Colonel Nathan Bedford Forrest served directly under General Clark and proved himself a forceful and independent leader in Kentucky and at Fort Donelson. His cavalry command became principally responsible for scouting and reporting on the movements of the enemy. His reports and those of others indicated that General Don Carlos Buell was moving to Pittsburg Landing on the Tennessee River for the probable purpose of reinforcing General Grant in his move on Corinth, a strategic railroad crossing. Grant, it appeared, had taken no respite after his victory over Donelson.[34]

It was immediately apparent that to halt the rapid penetration into the deep South by the Federal army, an attack on Grant would have to be made before Buell could reinforce him. Johnston ordered all units to move with dispatch toward the landing, located on the Tennessee River less than three miles below a small primitive log church known as the Shiloh Meeting House.

• • •

Johnston's original plan was to attack Grant on April 4, but General P. G. T. Beauregard, his second-in-command, consumed valuable time arguing for a more intricate and difficult plan of attack. General Beauregard was the hero of Fort Sumter, having been in command in Charleston at the time. He was a vain and flashy French Louisianian known to quarrel with his superiors, including President Davis.

On the evening of April 4 rain began to fall, contributing further to the difficulties of implementing Johnston's plan of attack. There were other command problems that haunted Johnston. For unknown reasons General William Hardee refused to march without written orders. Bishop Leonidas Polk's men were mired down by the heavy rains and were unable to advance. General Bragg, commanding General Clark's unit which included Howell Hinds and Holt Collier, had become lost among the unmarked roads and swollen creeks. General Earl Van Dorn, fully briefed of the urgency of the situation, had not yet arrived with his troops from the west. Van Dorn started his movement on March 17, 1862, at Van Buren, Arkansas, but did not arrive in Corinth until April 30, 1862, far too late to be of any assistance to Johnston.

After delays and discord among his corps commanders who also included Generals Leonidas Polk and John C. Breckenridge, Johnston's army was positioned late on April 5, 1862, for an assault on the Union forces at Pittsburg Landing. The Rebels slept that night in such proximity to the Federal tents that the music from their camps could be distinctly heard.[35]

Johnston had been harshly criticized for the loss of Kentucky and much of Tennessee. He had made strategic retreats in those campaigns, and his cautious judgment had allowed his army to survive to make this stand against Grant. With the objectives clearly drawn and the consequences of a defeat obvious, Johnston made brilliant preparations for an attack against Grant's forces. Positioning his armies between and across the Corinth roads, with Owl Creek on his left and Lick Creek on his right, he effectively cut off any flanking option the Union armies might attempt. With the Tennessee River at Grant's back, retreat was impossible.[36]

On April 5, 1862, Federal pickets observed and reported Confederate troop movement. Grant, with his friend General William Tecumseh Sherman at his side, discounted the reports. The Union command in the field believed the Confederate army was amassed in Corinth to defend the railroad crossing. The rebels seen and heard near Shiloh were assumed to be pickets and scouts.

Early Sunday morning, April 6, 1862, a Union reconnaissance force engaged the Third Mississippi Infantry Battalion. The report from the muskets set off a chain reaction along the Rebel lines which could not be halted. At Johnston's headquarters, Beauregard took command of the central position to direct the Confederate forces. Johnston could not contain his excitement. He immediately rode to the front where the troops were engaged.[37]

The ground chosen for battle by Johnston was undulating and heavily timbered with scattered clearings and woods giving some protection to troops on both sides. There was also considerable underbrush. The Confederate onslaughts were made with such disregard for casualties that the first Union line of tents quickly fell into their hands. As many as five thousand panic-stricken Union stragglers were soon lying under cover of the river bluff at the Union rear.[38] The Confederates maintained their attack until late in the afternoon when the Union line was all of a mile behind the position it had occupied that morning. Johnston's plans were carried out as intended, and a major Confederate victory was at hand.

On the first day of battle the Confederates routed the Union forces, who were caught almost totally unawares. The division of General Benjamin M. Prentiss was overrun, a Confederate cavalry regiment passing almost unimpeded through its ranks. About three thousand of Grant's army surrendered from Prentiss's division alone. General Bragg observed that "the enemy was found utterly unprepared, many being surprised and captured in their tents, and others, though on the outside, in costumes better fitted to the bedchamber than to the battle-field."[39]

Howell Hinds and Holt Collier served with the ill-fated General Charles Clark. He received an order from Bragg to assault an enfilading battery to his left. The assault was gallantly made but was repulsed with severe loss from shot and canister and the musket fire of heavy infantry support. Clark's entire brigade charged and helped to drive the enemy back five hundred yards. His opponent on the field was none other than General William T. Sherman, whose route of retreat was marked by the "thick-strewn corpses of his soldiers."[40]

When General Clark fell severely wounded, Howell Hinds was nearby. He immediately exposed himself to the thick enemy fire and carried his commander from the field. Clark commended Hinds in his official report of the action. "To my staff my thanks are due for their gallantry and good conduct....Major Hinds was by my side and assisted me from the field."[41]

Not far down the line of battle a Tennessee regiment, in the thick of much of the fight, became demoralized. With certain victory at hand and showing no sign of halting the advance, General Albert Sidney Johnston rode out in front, in full view of his troops. His order to charge was persuasive, encouraging, and compelling. He was inviting men to death, and they seemed willing to obey.[42]

As the men moved forward there came from the Union line a sheet of flame and a roar of cannon and musketry laden with iron hail. Johnston, though erect in the saddle, was visibly affected by the sudden barrage of fire. His horse was shot in four places but remained standing. His clothes were pierced, and a boot sole was cut and torn. He did not leave the field in time to avoid the next volley. With it came a minié ball which struck Johnston in the right leg and tore an artery. He died shortly afterward.

Holt Collier was standing nearby and witnessed the scene of Johnston's death. He gave accounts later describing in detail how "a bullet struck him in the thigh, severing an artery." Collier recalled that "six soldiers carried him to the shade of a tree where he died in a short while."[43]

Collier's vivid description of the scene leaves little doubt that he witnessed the momentous event. The details he provides in his recollections are consistent with regimental histories and other documented records. "At the battle of Shiloh I was on the battlefield with Gen'l Albert Sydney Johnston. He was shot in the thigh and bled to death. We run smack over the Yankees and drove 'em into the river, took their encampment and captured everything. But after Gen'l Beauregard was put in command...he laid over Sunday to fight Monday. Monday they had, I think, thirty thousand reenforcements on us, and tore the army all to pieces."[44]

At the time of Johnston's death–mid-afternoon on the first day–the Confederates were gaining ground and steadily advancing. The vacuum in command caused by Johnston's death resulted in a lost opportunity that reverberated throughout the Confederacy. In almost eleven hours of continuous assault the butternut troops had driven Grant back to within sight of the landing. With more than an hour of daylight remaining, and to the amazement of most of his command, General Beauregard issued the order to withdraw all forces beyond the enemy's fire.[45]

General Buell arrived at the river landing with reinforcements for Grant just after the noon hour and made every effort to bring his troops into action. When hostilities ceased on April 6 he had been successful in transporting fewer than five thousand men into position. Through a night burdened by a heavy rain, the navy labored to put Buell's remaining men and provisions ashore. By the morning of April 7 Buell had reinforced Grant with more than twenty-five thousand fresh and ready troops, fully armed and provisioned. The Federals took the offensive on the second day, routing the enemy, and forcing the Confederates from the field.

Byrnes's Artillery, with whom Thomas Hinds saw action, aided the Kentucky Brigade on both days. The artillery units for both the Union and Confederates reportedly won the admiration of officers and soldiers alike by the skill and gallantry with which they plunged into the thick of the fight. Men on both sides of the fray died at their guns. One historian wrote that "Byrne's battery rendered not less useful service on Sunday, and again on Monday, to the Kentucky

Brigade. When Byrne called on the Sixth Kentucky Regiment for a detail, 'No detail,' cried John Spurrier, springing from the ranks, 'but all the volunteers you want!'"[46]

• • •

The devastation and carnage at Shiloh was the worst seen thus far in the war. The Confederate forces totaled 40,335 on the first day and suffered over 10,000 casualties (1,728 killed, 8,012 wounded, 959 missing or captured), a stunning twenty-five per cent. The Federal troops fared little better. The official count put 44,895 Federals in the field (approximately 58,000 after the arrival of Buell), of which there were 13,000 casualties (1,754 killed, 8,404 wounded, and 2,885 captured or missing).[47]

The gilded vision of the southern gentlemen that the war would be a gallant and honorable matter was left on the battlefield in the wake of a horrible slaughter. Good friends and comrades lay stranded and abandoned on the field, dead or suffering. Mangled and disfigured bodies lay where they fell. The Shiloh Church had been converted into a makeshift Confederate hospital where amputated arms and legs were heaped in large piles outside. Blood ran in the roads an inch thick at places. A pond turned red from the blood of troops from both sides. Corpses were grubbed by feral hogs. Grant later recounted that the field of battle was "so covered with dead that it would have been possible to walk across the clearing, in any direction, stepping on dead bodies, without a foot touching the ground."[48]

The soldiers of the Confederate army, who had the day before anticipated a great victory, were now defeated, dispirited, and weary of battle. In retreat they formed a ragged column that extended several miles south toward Corinth. A cold rain began at the end of the second day and lasted through the night. Roads became quagmires. Wounded and dying Confederates were crowded into wagons, cold and wet. The rain turned into a hailstorm. Most of the retreating men had nothing to protect them from the elements except the clothes on their backs.

After the Battle of Shiloh, Corinth, a small Mississippi town across the Tennessee border, became a charnel house for the dead and the dying. Soldiers were laid out in homes and businesses across the town.

The Tishomingo Hotel became a makeshift hospital where another mound of amputated arms and legs was evident in its yard. Infection and gangrene were common. Conditions were unspeakable.[49]

Reaction to the wholesale slaughter was the same on both sides of the conflict. Shock and outrage at the number of losses were voiced loudly. Grant was briefly removed as field commander and criticized widely for being ill prepared and exposing his army needlessly in an indefensible position. Beauregard was also the object of debate and ridicule but remained in command for another month.[50]

• • •

Although there is no evidence that young Thomas Hinds was wounded or physically impaired, Shiloh was for all purposes the end of his military career. By the end of April 1862 he began an aggressive letter-writing campaign to be relieved from duty. He wrote that month to General Breckenridge that "I am suffering" and "unfit for duty." He was given a leave of absence, but failed to return when it expired.[51]

He wrote Breckenridge on May 22, 1862, claiming to be anxious to return but asserting that his doctor "says that if I go back in my present condition it will only be to suffer a relapse of my disease." Having claimed his inability to serve, Thomas paradoxically requested that if "the Government will furnish the money I can get horses enough for the Battery and as to men there will be no difficulty."[52]

Thomas Hinds acquired no government money, but he did receive an extension of his furlough, and later sent General Breckenridge a certificate from his physician attesting again to his "inability for duty." Though neither he nor his father would ever admit it, Thomas had become a deserter. He tried to meet General Breckenridge on several occasions, and on July 6, 1862, after his original one-year term of service had officially expired, he tendered a letter of resignation of his commission, claiming again his ill health.[53] Breckenridge never replied to his letters, and because Thomas was never sure whether or not he had been relieved, he forwarded additional statements by his physician attesting to the condition of his health.

# CHAPTER 5

# NINTH TEXAS CAVALRY

> *"I said I will go with Capt. Evans' cavalry.*
> *I was in Gen. Ross' Brigade, Col. Dudley Jones*
> *Regiment and Capt. Perry Evans' Company"*
> — Holt Collier

The attack on Grant's forces at Shiloh had been a part of the Confederate strategy to halt the Union advance into the southern heartland. One important element of that strategy that never materialized was the reinforcement of General Albert Sidney Johnston's army by soldiers of the Trans-Mississippi District under the command of General Earl Van Dorn. Van Dorn was the son of Peter A. Van Dorn, a native of Port Gibson, Mississippi, and a West Point graduate. He was considered a great asset for the South, and had been initially assigned to serve with Joseph E. Johnston, James Longstreet, and Thomas Jonathan Jackson in Virginia. However, because of his jealousy of command, he was reassigned and by January 1862 was in command of the Confederate forces west of the Mississippi River, comprised primarily of Texans and Missourians.

It is apparent that Van Dorn's appearance and demeanor did not instill confidence in his troops. A contemporary said of him that he "looked to me more like a dandy than the general of an army. He was small, curley or kinkey headed, exquisitely dressed, was riding a beautiful bay horse, evidently groomed with as much care as his rider, who was small looking and frenchy....[H]is hair is what, in a lady, you would call auburn, but in a soldier and gentleman, sandy. He wears it flowing and uncut, and his beard full, though not bushy or neglected. His complexion is soft and blonde, almost like that of a woman, and I was told he could, and at times actually did blush."[1]

Van Dorn had seen battle in March, at Elkhorn Tavern (Pea Ridge). In that battle with a force of sixteen thousand he was defeated by a force of only ten thousand. From Van Buren, Arkansas, he was ordered to Tennessee to reinforce Johnston. He departed on March 17, 1862, for Memphis, but did not arrive there until April 18, 1862, ten days after the Battle of Shiloh. He finally arrived in Corinth on April 30, 1862. He blamed his slow and agonizing movement on the bad weather, poor roads, illness of his troops, and shortage of supplies. Regardless of the actual causes of his slow advance, Van Dorn, already branded by his earlier loss at Pea Ridge, became a scapegoat for the loss at Shiloh, receiving blame from both Beauregard and President Jefferson Davis.[2]

Assigned to Van Dorn's army was Whitfield's Texas Brigade, organized for state service at Brogden's Springs, Texas, in late summer and mustered into Confederate service on October 2, 1861. The brigade would become known as Ross's Texas Brigade in December 1863, when General Whitfield retired due to ill health and Brigadier General Lawrence Sullivan "Sul" Ross took command. Consisting of the Third, Sixth, Ninth, and Twenty-seventh cavalry regiments–all from Texas–Ross's Texas Brigade saw some of the hottest action of any of the mounted Texas regiments during the Civil War.[3]

The Ninth Texas Cavalry, organized in Grayson County, included several companies of young men from neighboring counties of northeast Texas. Company B was from Red River and Hunt Counties, C from Grayson, D from Titus, E from Red River, F from Cass, G & K from Hopkins, H from Lamar, and I from Titus and Grayson counties.[4] At Corinth a reorganization resulted in the election of Dudley Jones as colonel of the Ninth Texas Cavalry, a position he would hold almost continuously until the end of hostilities in 1865. Holt Collier was introduced to the wild young Texans upon their arrival at Corinth, and he was much impressed by what he saw. They had no equal in marksmanship or in equestrian talents.

Dudley Jones was probably a native Texan. He was eighteen years of age at the commencement of the war and was studying to become a lawyer at Maury Institute in Columbia, Tennessee. In 1860, at the age of seventeen, Jones owned twenty-two slaves and property valued at twenty-six thousand dollars, all in his own name.[5] He withdrew from Maury Institute to join the Confederate army as a private soldier. Elected Colonel by the men of the Ninth Texas Cavalry, he was known as the "boy colonel," and according to those who knew him, he was a worthy "recipient of this very high honor...based on personal observation." Losses to his regiment were unusually severe, nine out of ten by the end of the war. Jones was described as being "of light complexion, with dark hair and brown eyes, slim and of good height, was by habit scrupulously neat, and very precise in all his communication as well as dress, 'a great ladies man,' and much of his diary is given to his enjoyment with them when not on duty. He was always studious, and... established a library for the 9th and it contained many valuable volumes." Following the war, Jones was so highly esteemed by his fellow Texans that he was elected to serve in the state's postwar constitutional convention and was chosen over all others to lead the ceremonial delegation to return Albert Sidney Johnston's remains to his home state.[6]

• • •

Company I of the Ninth Texas Cavalry was known as the Titus Grays. It was a close-knit unit of one hundred and fourteen young men and boys from the frontier who sought glory and honor in the service of the South. Though the officers of the Ninth had wealth and many owned slaves, the common soldiers were not part of the slave-holding aristocracy. They were farm boys and cowboys from the vast open southern plains seeking the glory that action in battle could provide. The Texas troops, with their own war for independence a not-too-distant memory, were fighting for states' rights and freedom from centralized government. It was with this company of young sharpshooting cowboys that Holt Collier would serve as a combatant for the remainder of the war.

When the Titus Grays arrived in Corinth, James N. English was captain. Under reorganization Perry Evans was named captain and remained in that position until January 1864, when he was detached for independent ranger service in the Mississippi Delta.

Perry Evans was the youngest son in a family of eleven children. Born in Breathitt County, Kentucky, in 1837, he had lived since 1851 on his mother's cattle ranch just north of Mt. Pleasant, Texas. One of his men described him as a "true type of the pioneer stockman, he was medium in size and of dark complexion, dark hair and eyes, had a slow soft voice, and a modest or retired appearance, never spoke loud or became excited and his nature was kind when he was not mad, but when he became mad his reason became lost or dethroned and he was fierce as a tiger and would act as in desperation. He was usually cool and said but little, and was always brave and ready for service, he alone kept his counsels and had few confidants, as a Captain he performed his duty without a word and...his face always wore that cold expression that neither was susceptible to love or hatred...."[7]

The men of Company I were equipped rudely with only the basics for service. They earned a reputation for the use of their Bowie knives, fast horses, high boots, upturned hats, and wild behavior. They had rifles, both flint and steel, but many of them were full stock muzzle-loaders that had been used for killing bear, deer and other wild game. Double-barrel shot guns were favorites, and there were many different stamps, from the "London twist" to the malleable cast barrel. Several pistols were in the command, all in great demand by the officers, who needed them as sidearms. Most noticeable and unique of the weapons carried by all of the young men of the Titus Grays was a huge knife, made from an old mill file, made by a blacksmith and ground sharp according to the desires of the owner. The horses were Texas mustangs, and several were believed to have strains of noted blood in their veins. The clothing of the men was light and not suited for hard service. Almost all the men wore long boots made of Texas tanned leather with a large flap at the front of the leg to protect the knee. Blankets were pieces of carpets taken from home to be used as bedding. The company uniform of the Titus Grays had a blue stripe on the shoulders of the jacket.[8] The uniform and attire of these Texans was soon adopted by Holt Collier and would be his trademark appearance for much of his life.

• • •

At Corinth Company I and the Ninth Texas Cavalry were immediately pressed into service as scouts and rangers checking Federal movement from Shiloh. Except for skirmishes–near Iuka, Booneville, Sharp's Mill and Farmington–and constant artillery fire from the Union positions there was little direct action with the enemy. The four-hour battle at Farmington resulted only in the capture of an abundance of "Yankee trinkets." The only casualty for the Ninth Texas was the death of Mat Swan, a boy only thirteen years old.[9] Eventually, under the constant pressure from the advancing Union army, Beauregard abandoned Corinth on May 30, 1862.

The fall of Corinth was a more serious blow to the Confederacy than the loss at Shiloh. By early summer, under pressure from a disheartened public, Jefferson Davis summoned Beauregard to Richmond and replaced him with General Braxton Bragg. Van Dorn was reassigned to command the Department of Southern Mississippi and was ordered to Jackson for the preparation of a defense against Grant's planned attack on Vicksburg. Bragg remained in command of all forces in Northeast Mississippi.[10]

Until June, 1862, Van Dorn, Forrest, Howell Hinds, Byrne's Artillery, the Ninth Texas Cavalry, and Holt Collier served together in Northeast Mississippi under the command of General Beauregard. During the summer after the change in command, Forrest was headquartered with Bragg, and he conducted raids and reconnaissance in Tennessee.[11]

The summer of 1862 provided little action as Union forces settled in at Corinth and Grant began to plan his Vicksburg campaign. The Texans began their duty under newly elected acting Brigadier General Sul Ross, and the Ninth Texas Cavalry adjusted to the leadership of Colonel Dudley Jones. The Ninth Texas spent the entire month of July 1862 in camp at Mooreville drilling in formal parade fashion and participating in routine duty. In August they moved to Tupelo and remained there until they marched on Iuka in early September.[12]

• • •

In August 1862 President Jefferson Davis authorized Howell Hinds to return to Jefferson County for the purpose of raising another company of troops. Hinds had written Davis in his typically demanding style to ask for authority to raise a company of his own. He loosely interpreted the reply as an order in the affirmative. No one questioned his interpretation of a telegram received directly from the president.

> *Received at Richmond, August 26, 1862*
> *By telegraph from Fayette, (August) 25*
>
> *To Pres't Davis*
>
> *Will you give me authority to raise an artillery company.*
>
> *Howell Hinds*
>
> *Ans. The law does not permit the organization of men subject to conscription into new companies. Do you wish to form a company of men over thirty five years of age?*
>
> *J. D.*[13]

Hinds had the greatest of expectations but was dreadfully unsuccessful in his mission. He reported to President Davis. "All the chivalry of our country had gone off as I found out after you gave me authority to raise an artillery company. I could get but eight men to join."[14] Hinds was not required by his old friend or by the demands of his rank to return to the field of battle. In September, only two weeks after being authorized to raise his company, Hinds was appointed Provost Marshall for Jefferson County, "to preserve order among military persons, and to prevent improper intercourse with the enemy, by either citizens or soldiers."[15]

• • •

Soon after their arrival at Corinth, Holt Collier had become acquainted with the youthful Texans of Perry Evans's company. He rode on some of their missions and competed with them in their equestrian contests. They quickly established a reputation for horsemanship, marksmanship, and high spirits. Though Collier would not drink, Perry Evans's company of Texans had several men who enjoyed intoxicants whenever and wherever they could find them. The liquor "had to be very scarce if they did not find it." Wherever they went, if alcohol was to be found, the Texans "were liable to have a drunk man at any hour."[16]

The Texans also had a reputation of racing their horses against other companies, frustrating them on every occasion with the superior breeding and fleetness of their horses and the talent of their riders. A typical race on any given Saturday would involve many wagers and be held on a sandbar measured for distance with soldiers lined up on each side of the track "by thousands." One regimental history of the Ninth Texas Cavalry refers to the competing rider for Company I as an "Indian boy."[17]

By the time Hinds received his orders to return to Jefferson County, Holt had earned the respect and admiration of the Texans and wished to remain in their service rather than return to Mississippi. General Forrest requested of Hinds that Holt be allowed to serve directly under his command. Rather than turn the boy over to Forrest summarily, Hinds gave the young slave the options to return to Home Hill or to remain and fight with the Texans or with Forrest. Holt chose to remain with the Texans, and from that point forward he was considered a soldier in the company.

Holt Collier described the scene several times in his later years, providing additional details at each telling. "Because of my being an expert with a gun and a horse and my knowledge of the woods, Gen. Forrest talked with Capt. Evans to whose company I had been assigned...about my enlisting as a soldier. They asked permission of my Old Colonel and he called me to him and told me to choose for myself. I said 'I will go with Capt. Evans' cavalry. I loved horses and felt at home in the saddle. I was in Gen. Ross' Brigade, Col. Dudley Jones Regiment and Capt. Perry Evans Co. 9th Texas Regt. My Old Col. gave me a horse, one of three fine race horses he had brought from Plum Ridge. He was a beauty, iron-gray and named Medock...it was a long time until I saw my old Colonel again."[18]

In another account Collier described the events that led to his enlistment. "They enrolled me jes' like they did the white men. Gen'l Forrest wanted me, and Cap'n Perry Evans from Texas, he wanted me. Both of 'em went to Cunnel Howell Hinds, and he said, 'All right; I tried to leave that boy at home, but he wouldn't stay.' The Cunnel give me one of his throughbreds to ride and I went in for a soldier. I went with the Texas soldiers, Gen'l Ross' Brigade, Cunnel

Dudley Jones' regiment. Cap'n Perry Evans was my cap'n. I was the only colored man in the whole entire regiment that was a sho'-nuff soldier. All my white friends was good to me. I was a boy, but I was a fine shot and a fine rider. The company used to practice a heap shootin' and ridin'."

One unusual technique called belting was implemented by the Texans who would hone their skills as marksmen and horsemen with one exercise. The riders would circle a tree at full gallop while firing at it. Holt said, "We used to gallop around and belt a tree—that is, galloping the horses around in a circle, shootin' six-shooters into a tree and beltin' it, same as you would belt it with an axe. Those men could gallop around a tree fast as the horses could go, and shoot so many bullets into a tree that they would kill it. That was our practice."[19]

For the remainder of the war Holt Collier rode with the men of Company I, Ninth Texas Cavalry. His orders during the next three years consisted of daily reveille with early commands to "boots and saddles." He was involved in the defense of Vicksburg, a continuous action across Tennessee and Alabama, several battles of note including Corinth and Holly Springs, and for more than a year he served in detached ranger duty along the river counties of Northwest and Central Mississippi.

• • •

On September 14, 1862, the Confederates advanced on the railroad town of Iuka, Mississippi, near the Alabama border, and took the town after light skirmishing. In addition to taking one hundred prisoners, provisions abandoned by the Union forces and much needed by the Rebels were general quartermaster stores and luxuries valued at over one million dollars. On September 19 after several days of picket duty and enemy shelling, General William S. Rosecrans's Union army advanced and re-captured Iuka, but not without much destruction. The Battle of Iuka cost the Confederates about three hundred casualties.[20] Holt Collier and the Titus Grays participated in the taking of the town and in its defense afterward.

From September 21 through October 2 Holt's company fell back to Baldwin and Carrollville. On October 28, they moved to Ripley to rejoin General Van Dorn who had left his position in defense of Vicksburg and combined his forces with those of General Sterling Price in hopes of retaking Corinth. Bragg had left in July to defend a new advance by Buell on Chattanooga. Van Dorn, along with Price, who had been left in command at Tupelo, now had two military objectives, the defense of Vicksburg and the protection of Bragg's rear flank.

The importance of Corinth was never in question by either side. It was known as the "crossroads of the south." At Corinth the Memphis and Charleston Railroad, running east to west, crossed the Mobile and Ohio, running north to south. The Mississippi Central Railroad from Jackson, Tennessee, to Jackson, Mississippi, passed only a few miles to the west. It was a primary rail hub for the transportation of goods, supplies, and men to the entire Confederacy.

On September 29, 1862, the Ninth Texas Cavalry and all of its units, including Company I, joined Van Dorn for the retaking of Corinth. Following orders the soldiers were unaware that Van Dorn was repeating the same errors which had caused his loss at the battle of Pea Ridge. He was sending his troops into battle without the benefit of proper reconnaissance of the opposing forces. He committed his forces without advising his ranking officers of the details of his strategy, which left them uninformed and resentful. The army moved steadily from Ripley for four days, entering Tennessee with a plan to circle Corinth and attack from the north.[21]

On the night of October 2 the Texans were in the advance and engaged in skirmishing all evening. The two-day battle of Corinth began in earnest on October 3. Company I and the Ninth Texas Cavalry were actively involved and experienced the brunt of the battle from beginning to end. It was Holt Collier's first battle experience without the company of either Howell or Thomas Hinds.[22]

The Confederate attempt to retake Corinth began with skirmishing along the lines. They succeeded in making advances, losing many men and capturing about three hundred Union soldiers in the first wave. The fighting witnessed by Holt continued all day and was described as "most galling" and "the slaughter of the enemy was terrible." By the afternoon of the first day the Confederates occupied a bloody battle ground covered with the dead soldiers killed by the "unerring aim" of the Confederate muskets. That night Collier and the men of Company I ate a hearty supper of rations taken from Federal haversacks found on the field. On the second day, the artillery and musket fire was very intense, shaking the very earth and cutting the trees all around. The Texans were under fire of grape and canister from artillery, and they encountered "the most terrible fire of small arms conceivable." Company I gained the enemy's breast works only to be ordered to fall back as they were cut to pieces. The Ninth Texas Cavalry "bore the brunt of this battle and suffered most terribly—Lt. Col. Jones losing his horse and we so many of our best men." The small regiment suffered ninety-three casualties.[23]

While in retreat a detail of thirty men under a flag of truce returned to the field to bury the dead. When Van Dorn reached the Hatchie Bridge he encountered a fresh corps of Union troops under General Edward Ord advancing from Bolivar, Tennessee. A battle ensued, and Van Dorn found himself in a very precarious situation, backed up to the Hatchie River with Ord at his front and no line of retreat. Leaving the entire Ninth Texas Cavalry at his rear to engage Ord, he managed to make his escape upstream, retreating a total of twenty five miles that day. For the next several days, the Confederates retreated, discouraged and without sufficient provisions. By October 12, 1862, they were bivouacked at Lumpkin's Mill on the Mississippi Central Railroad about seven miles south of Holly Springs. Cold weather and rain set in. They had no blankets and insufficient clothing. Conditions were miserable.[24]

On October 20 Union General Rosecrans sent a message to Van Dorn under a flag of truce assuring him that the Confederate wounded at Corinth had been properly cared for and the dead buried with a proper tribute. Rosecrans' message to Van Dorn complimented the Confederates and "all who fought & died ... bravely." One soldier in the Ninth Texas wrote that it was "quite a new feature in the war for our enemy to compliment us."[25]

While at Lumpkin's Mills, Ross reorganized his brigade to include only Texas units. This change made Holt Collier's service unusual in two respects. Not only was he a non-white in an all-white army, he was a non-Texan in Ross's Texas Brigade.

The North Mississippi weather was severely cold and harsh for several weeks. Even though the men had inadequate clothing and too few tents for shelter, they were required to continue participation in drills and parades. On November 8, the regiment was ordered to retreat further south across the Tallahatchie River to Abbeville, where the Texans took charge of the post, which was the northern terminus of Confederate railway travel in Mississippi. The Texans remained in camp and had guard duty which included the regular transporting of prisoners to Jackson twice a week. They participated in spirited competitions with horses and guns and made every effort to regain their earlier strength.[26]

• • •

On November 15, 1862, while Holt and his adopted Texans were serving police duty at Abbeville, they witnessed a most unusual military trial, the court-martial of a general officer, their commander, Earl Van Dorn. Charges against the general were the direct result of his action at Corinth–failing to provide his officers with proper maps, eschewing engineer services, being negligent in reconnoitering, marching with insufficient supplies, marching in a hasty and disorderly manner, and disastrously delaying an attack on the eve of the first day of battle. Charges of drunkenness, which had been publicly bruited against him, were also made an issue. The court was presided over by Generals Sterling Price, Dabney Maury, and Lloyd Tilghman. It was weighted in favor of Van Dorn, and after two full days of testimony and deliberation he was acquitted of all charges. Regardless of the outcome of the trial, Van Dorn's reputation was permanently damaged, and the effect of the court martial on his Texas troops could not be ignored. Van Dorn's fitness and character had been debated since early in the struggle.[27]

James Phelan, one of Mississippi's two senators in the Confederate Congress, was disgusted with the image and military record of Van Dorn, and wrote to President Davis that the atmosphere in Mississippi was "dense with horrid narratives of his negligence, whoring, and drunkenness" and that "an acquittal by a court-martial of angels would not relieve him of the charge."[28] Davis had to act. He demoted Van Dorn and assigned the District of Mississippi to General John Pemberton.

The fall of 1862 was a difficult time for the Confederacy. Lee had been repulsed at Sharpsburg. Bragg, without Van Dorn's reinforcements, had been forced to retreat from Kentucky. Corinth was irretrievably lost. Grant was advancing slowly but surely into Mississippi with naval incursions into the Yazoo River basin. The Federals were mobilizing thousands of troops and tons of supplies, and they had sufficient strength for an early advance on Vicksburg, their primary objective.

The Ninth Texas Cavalry remained in Abbeville until December 2, 1862, when they retreated to Oxford. Union troops under General Grant occupied Holly Springs only thirty miles to the north. Holt and the Texans served as rear guard, destroying the Abbeville depot and all government stores as they evacuated. While the retreating forces camped in the streets of Oxford, Grant's skirmishers were advancing through Abbeville. The retreat with the Texans in the rear continued through Water Valley, Coffeeville, and Grenada, where on the night of the December 7, 1862, they camped a mile south of town. They stayed south of Grenada for a week, drilling and resting.[29]

A few days later, the Texans paraded for Confederate President Jefferson Davis, who was making a visit to the front to inspire his men. The units were consolidated in block formation to listen to him speak from his horse. He was described on that occasion as "tall and thin," with "bony hands and long fingers...high cheek bones and high forehead," with "blue eyes, a sharp nose, thin lips and an appearance of bad health from dyspepsia or nervousness." He was neatly dressed in Confederate gray with no indication of rank. He reminded the troops that "he too was a Mississippian, his home, his all was there, and if the State fell into the hands of the enemy he would suffer in common with them." Davis finished by telling the assembled soldiers "that the fight would continue until our independence was gained or our last resource exhausted." One observer wrote after hearing the speech, "somehow I got it into my head that if all the States east of the Mississippi River were taken, we would continue the fight in the West and Mexico, and only end when driven into the Pacific Ocean."[30]

It is unlikely that Holt Collier participated in the presidential parade, considering Davis' standing order against any Negro serving as anything other than a servant or laborer in the Confederate army.

Some Confederates thought that by advancing toward Grenada, ninety miles from his closest base at Holly Springs, Grant had overextended his ever-lengthening supply and communication lines. General Van Dorn was eager to polish his tarnished image, and so promoted to Davis an attack suited only for cavalry. The move, if successful, would destroy Grant's headquarters in Holly Springs and capture all the provisions stored there. The secret plan, born of desperation, was approved by President Davis as a necessary measure, as Grant had done immeasurable damage on his deep penetration into the heart of the South. On December 15 the Texans found themselves again under the direct command of General Van Dorn.

Van Dorn's rapidly deployed Holly Springs campaign included Collier's Texas company as well as all companies of the Ninth Texas Cavalry. From Grenada, the march north was extreme in all respects. It was the dead of winter and the weather was bitterly cold. On December 16, 1862, the troops moved out before dawn and rode until midnight, a total of forty five miles. Leaving at sunrise on the seventeenth, they kept a northeasterly course all day, traveling another thirty eight miles. The next day they advanced thirty three miles, slowed only by the affectionate outpouring of the citizens of Pontotoc. "Passing through the beautiful town of Pontotoc, the hungry troopers were enthusiastically welcomed by the noble and patriotic citizens of the place; and trays, dishes, and baskets of the choicest edibles were offered on all sides, and pitchers of wine and milk as well. No halt was allowed, and the men pursued their mysterious way munching the welcomed 'grub' dispensed by the fair hands of Pontotoc's good, and beautiful, and noble heroines."[31]

That night they passed through New Albany and camped outside of town. At sunrise on December 19 they again mounted to the call of "boots and saddles" and proceeded twenty seven miles to camp. That night they camped five and one half miles south of Holly Springs. In disregard of the extremely cold temperature the order that night was silence and no fire.

At 3:00 a. m. on December 20, 1862, Van Dorn's troops silently took the road to Holly Springs. The Ninth Texas Cavalry rode in the front center position commanded by Colonel John S. Griffith. Van Dorn had dispatched a spy, well acquainted with the town, to determine the number and position of the enemy and to accurately locate the picket on the Ripley road. Once committed, the command proceeded at a brisk pace to go around the town, away from their target hoping to elude Federal scouts that had been hanging on their rear guard. When scouts returned and reported that the Federals had taken the bait, a countermarch was made toward Holly Springs.

The spy discovered prior to launching the assault that the Federal troops had been preparing for a grand ball and were off their guard. The Rebels, "grimy...poor, ragged, half-starved fellows" moved toward the town by "columns of fours, and guns uncapped." They moved silently, placing guards at all the houses in the immediate vicinity of the line of attack. They captured the picket, without so much disturbance as the discharge of a gun. The attack on Holly Springs was made with three brigades, a center, right, and left flank. Holt Collier and the Texans took the center and were at the head of the charge.[32]

As the outskirts of the town were reached, the air was filled with the "bugle's shrill, harsh blast...upon the crisp morning air and shouting, yelling rebels." The swift action caught the entire Union garrison unawares. Several Federal officers emerged from their tents only to be informed by the ragged Confederates that they were prisoners of war, and the women of the town were described as "beautiful young ladies—some still in *dishabille*—throng the square; all rejoicing, all excited." An account of the raid described the reaction of the citizens, "Tears of joy gush forth from many an eye, and manly voices grow husky from emotion. O, that entry into Holly Springs was the incident of a life-time." The only Federal troops to resist were a group of Iowans who were outnumbered and quickly dispersed by a "headlong charge" led by Colonel Jones and the men from the Ninth Texas Cavalry.[33]

The Confederates captured property of considerable monetary value, including immense quantities of bacon, pork, flour, hard bread, and coffee, all found at the depot stacked in piles as high as a man's head and in rows a quarter of a mile long. Great quantities of arms and ammunition were also found. It was unusual to see such a beleaguered army undergo such a rapid and complete transformation in external appearances as did the Confederates at Holly Springs. They had arrived with threadbare uniforms and inadequate supplies. After taking Holly Springs one of the transformed soldiers was seen wearing "the uniform-coat of a Federal colonel on his back, a plumed hat on his head, and his feet and legs [were] encased in patent-leather cavalry-boots." The provisions taken were not retrieved entirely from Federal warehouses. Civilian stores and supply houses fell victim to an indiscriminate pillage by Missouri troops who were quickly followed by Tennesseans, Mississippians and Texans. Stored in the courthouse at the center of the square was the magazine which contained an immense quantity of ordnance, bombshells, powder, and weapons. It was all set afire as Van Dorn's army left the city. The exploding pieces from the burning magazine sounded to the fleeing Confederates as if a battle were in progress to their rear.[34]

Accounts of the raid at Holly Springs place the value of the provisions destroyed between five million dollars and ten to twelve million dollars, including over two thousand bales of cotton, one thousand bushels of wheat and corn, all of which were "consigned to the flames." Under orders the Texans destroyed much property, but according to the regimental histories, they did not participate in the pillage of the town. The courthouse which served as Grant's magazine was blown up about 3:00 p. m., the effect of which shook "the earth for miles" with shells reportedly continuing to explode for twenty-four hours more. The Confederates withdrew quickly and left Holly Springs by the Salem road and camped ten miles out.[35]

The southern victory at Holly Springs had a significant impact on the progress of the war. With it, north Mississippi lost its strategic importance for Grant. He was forced to abandon his land assault on Vicksburg in favor of an amphibious campaign.

CHAPTER 6

# BOOTS AND SADDLES

*"In the spring the union forces drove us back to Iuka.
We retreated through Tennessee into
Alabama fighting every step of the way."*
—Holt Collier

Van Dorn's raid on Holly Springs had been planned and made in conjunction with a sweep by General Nathan Bedford Forrest through west Tennessee. The success of both cavalry actions had immediate repercussions for Grant's Vicksburg campaign. Anticipating the movements of Van Dorn and having received scouting reports of a large Rebel contingent moving north, Grant telegraphed the Union headquarters at Holly Springs and ordered the Federal cavalry to intercept the Rebels at Rocky Ford. The commanding officer at Holly Springs, Colonel Robert C. Murphy, did not know the location of Rocky Ford and allowed his men to retire for the night with orders to move at first light, a failure to act which assured the success of Van Dorn's expedition.

The Confederates were not discriminating in their destruction of provisions or of the town. They burned trains, depot buildings, warehouses, an armory that had been used as a hospital, the courthouse, and half the buildings on the square. The unchecked success of Van Dorn angered General Grant. Not only was he embarrassed, he was deprived of necessary supplies for the winter. The Union's successful advance through Kentucky, Tennessee, and one hundred miles into Mississippi had been brought to a sudden halt.

By mid-morning on December 21 Grant's troops had retaken Holly Springs. The next day Union Colonel Benjamin Grierson's cavalry rode out of Holly Springs en route to Grand Junction, Tennessee, with orders to follow Van Dorn "until he was caught or

West Tennessee was so completely exhausted as to render it impossible to support an army."[1] It was to be a long hard pursuit.

Captain Perry Evans, Holt Collier, and the Titus Grays had led the Confederate center charge and remained on duty at all times during the brief occupation of Holly Springs. Leaving the town and traveling north, they were deep behind enemy lines assigned to rear guard duty. They traveled ten miles on the evening of the December 20, and the next day they engaged a strong Union position at Davis's Mill on the Hatchie River, again leading the center of the charge. At Davis's Mill the Texans lost about "twenty dead upon the field, and twice that number wounded."[2] That day they traveled seventeen miles.

December 22, 1862, was a day of rapid movement for the Ninth Texas Cavalry. They left destruction and mayhem in their wake, burning bridges and destroying tracks through several towns in West Tennessee. The jaded Confederates burned several bridges and railroad trestles at Moscow, Locks Mills, and Somerville. They traveled twenty-nine difficult miles that day.

They encountered Federal pickets on December 23, and traveled another twenty-five miles to a camp outside Bolivar, Tennessee. On December 24 the Texans arose to the daily orders of boots and saddles at 3:00 a. m. and engaged the Bolivar pickets. They charged the town, captured thirty men and destroyed the railroad and telegraph lines. Stockades and winter quarters were burned by the Rebels who dismounted and were ordered to the front, where they fought a large body of skirmishers. They fought for two and one-half hours without support, suffering nine wounded and four missing. On retreat south the Texans passed Grand Junction and heard the sound of drums beating a long roll in their pursuit. They moved ten more miles to camp without fires, having traveled that day forty-seven grueling miles.[3]

With Grierson's cavalry in hot pursuit, the Texans continued to serve as the rear guard on Christmas Day. The Federals put significant pressure on them at Ripley, Mississippi, and chased them to New Albany, skirmishing the entire distance. There were two bridges to cross at New Albany, and Van Dorn's army was able to delay the enemy's advance with three companies taking the front. That day they covered thirty-three miles. On the day after Christmas, under continuous pressure, Van Dorn and his men hastily retreated another forty-seven miles. Finally, on December 27, Van

Dorn and the Texans crossed the Confederate lines at Grenada, and the troops were allowed a rest. The distance traveled on the final day of the brief but strenuous campaign was thirty-two miles.

The Holly Springs campaign was one of the high water marks for the Ninth Texas Cavalry. From the time they departed Grenada on December 16 until their return December 27, Holt Collier and the Texas cavalrymen traveled on horseback in freezing weather approximately five hundred miles, taking the fighting position in every battle. Van Dorn evaded or outfought several of Grant's superior divisions that pursued him from surrounding positions. Those Union forces were led by such able Union officers as Benjamin Grierson and James B. McPherson.[4]

The successful raid on Holly Springs by the Confederates was a stinging setback to Grant's strategy. Van Dorn's destruction of Union supplies at Holly Springs and Forrest's raids along the Mobile & Ohio Railroad delayed the fall of Vicksburg as much as six months. If Vicksburg had fallen in late 1862 or early 1863, the war likely would have ended many months sooner. General Grant's anger was soundly felt by the garrison commander at Holly Springs. When the time came for him to find a scapegoat for the Holly Springs debacle, Grant did not have far to look. On January 8 a general order was issued by General Grant dismissing Colonel Murphy from the service of the U. S. Army. The order was retroactive, taking effect from December 20, 1862, the date of what Grant described as "his cowardly and disgraceful conduct."[5]

• • •

As General Grant revised his plans for the assault on Vicksburg, the Ninth Texas Cavalry remained in camp at Grenada recuperating from their long ordeal. On January 2, 1863, they were ordered mounted and moved to the defense of Vicksburg. They made it only as far as Lexington, Mississippi, before being ordered to countermarch to Grenada for an anticipated campaign into Tennessee.

During the entire month of January, Holt Collier and the Texans were engaged in a second winter march suffering through torrential rains and snow with no tents and insufficient protection. Conditions were extreme, and human endurance was at its limit. Movements were laborious for man and beast. On February 1, 1863, Holt Collier and his adopted Texans were again en route to Tennessee, advancing through Pontotoc to be cheered again lustily by the women and children who displayed Confederate flags and sang patriotic songs.[6]

With Grant weakened in his move against Vicksburg, Confederate strategy turned to Central Tennessee where General Braxton Bragg held a tenuous position just south of Nashville. Van Dorn was put in charge of all calvary units in Mississippi and ordered into Tennessee to reinforce Bragg's exposed left flank. The movement deprived Pemberton's defense of Vicksburg of much-needed protection and would be widely debated after the fall of the city.

Van Dorn assembled his newly reinvigorated cavalry in Tupelo and proceeded across the northwest corner of Alabama toward Tennessee in what continued to be onerous weather conditions. It rained and snowed through January and the first half of February. Rivers and creeks were hazardously swollen. The long and fatiguing march to Tennessee was described as "seemingly interminable," and was wearisome in the extreme, "utterly devoid of interesting incident."[7]

The progression went from Tupelo across the Alabama line near Bear Creek at Burleson to the old dilapidated town of Russellville, through La Grange, to Florence, where they crossed a dangerous Tennessee River on February 16, 1863. The next day they proceeded through Masonville and Lexington, Alabama, only to be halted by the swollen Sugar Creek where they encountered a battalion of Union sharpshooters who were successful in harassing their targets. The Confederates burned important bridges and threw roadblocks into expected pathways of invading troops. These actions forced wearisome and time-consuming delays. To make matters worse, unionist bushwhackers offered a constant threat to lead units and stragglers. The enthusiasm of the Texans, so prominent only two weeks earlier at Tupelo, faded as horses struggled in mud up to their haunches, and men sat in their saddles, cold, wet, and disgusted.[8]

Van Dorn and his army received a hero's welcome at Pulaski, Tennessee, where they were cheered by citizens, young and old. The women of the town brought the beleaguered troops the first flowers of the season and made every attempt to show them a pleasant welcome. They passed through Lynnville on February 20 and proceeded to Columbia the following day. The common soldiers had limited protection from the weather, which was horridly cold. One soldier wrote that "it has been raining hard all day & very cold—are perfectly saturated & perfectly benumbed with cold & suffer more intently than heretofore at any time."[9]

From February 22 through March 4 the command remained bivouacked south of Nashville in and around Williamsport, Spring Hill, and Santa Fe. Bragg placed Van Dorn and General "Fighting" Joe Wheeler in charge of a total of five thousand troops. Forrest joined this command, bringing the effective strength to about sixty-five hundred. The area of operation extended from Columbia to Spring Hill. Van Dorn's objective was to prevent the Union force on his front from moving against Bragg.

• • •

Thompson's Station in 1863 was little more than a whistle stop on the Nashville and Decatur Railroad. Completely surrounded by small irregular hills, it consisted of a depot, a school, and several undistinguished buildings, all along the railroad and just three hundred yards from the main road. At 8:00 a.m. on the morning of March 5 orders came for the Ninth Texas Cavalry to form a line of battle on the left of the brigade. A position was taken behind a stone fence south of town to await the enemy's advance. The Confederate position was set in a prominent line of hills, traversed at a right angle by the Columbia Pike. To the east were the Federal positions with their sharpshooters in sight. The Battle of Thompson's Station was a hard-fought action with Holt Collier and the Texans at front and center in the attack. The large Union force consisted of three thousand infantry, a battery of artillery, and about five hundred cavalry. The Federals advanced first, only to be driven back. After a Confederate charge was repulsed, the Federals retook the field and were driven back again. The final charge, made almost five hours after the contest began, was by the Texans. It resulted in a total victory only because General Forrest and his cavalry arrived in the final moments to provide the necessary push. "The Texans made charge after charge, upon the line of the enemy....Outnumbered, surrounded, and being attacked by the impetuous charges of the Texans every moment, [they] finally raised the white flag."[10]

The Confederates' desperation was evident from their behavior following the surrender. It had become standard procedure for the under-equipped Confederates to loot and pillage in such situations. Shoes, guns, belts, knives and other small articles were prizes too valuable for the destitute army to resist. One Federal officer remarked, "It was a sad and revolting sight to witness the barbarity of the inhuman demons stripping our noble dead."[11]

Thompson's Station by any standard was not an important battle for the fate of Tennessee, nor was it significant for tactical reasons. Van Dorn reported 367 casualties. Northern casualties totaled 378. It was, however, an indicator of a new type of horse warfare that in the early months of 1863 was becoming more popular among the Confederate troops. Beginning with the successful raid on Holly Springs, the cavalry and mounted infantry was proving itself a valuable weapon in disrupting Union objectives. Van Dorn and Forrest, along with John Hunt Morgan and Joe Wheeler, all independent men, were skillfully using these rapid attack tactics to great effect.

From March 6 through March 14 Van Dorn kept his troops moving daily with early morning orders of "boots and saddles." They traveled with no particular objective other than to avoid the large Union forces that continued to pursue them. After burying those killed at Thompson's Station they proceeded through Bethesda, Spring Hill, Taylor's Springs, Farmington, Lewisburg, Columbia, and Mount Pleasant. They rested in camp near Mount Pleasant, Tennessee, for five days and proceeded to Spring Hill on March 20. There they remained for twenty days, playing cat and mouse games with the Union forces which were daily in their sights. The only significant action during this episode was a skirmish at Kennard's Bridge, where the Texans lost nine men to capture.[12]

A surreal atmosphere enveloped both armies in Tennessee as Confederate General Bragg and Union General Rosecrans settled comfortably into their respective positions. In the ranks the men grumbled, wrote unexciting letters home, and wished for the end of the conflict.

For the regular soldier duty in Tennessee that spring was less than inspiring. "Sickness was prevalent in every camp; men were saddle-sore from long hours of patrolling the extensive defense line; forage for horses was scarce. Shortages from rations and ammunition were prevalent in every command, but it was the lack of plain food that drew the most considerable complaint from the ranks....All along the Confederate Tennessee front troops pilfered food, stole horses, and bickered with their fellow soldiers. Many took absence without leave. Others deserted outright. Constant and aggressive conscription was necessary to keep troop units even at minimum strength."

Regardless of the hardships encountered, the Confederate cavalry seemed to enjoy their duty. Units reconnoitered enemy positions and attacked any weak spot they could find. "Only the cavalry seemed to be interested in engaging the enemy....Tennessee was in the full bloom of spring, and the cavalry in Bragg's army was in its finest hour."[13]

After Thompson's Station, Forrest, who had held his command as an independent unit, allowed himself to come under Van Dorn's authority. The two brigades were combined on April 10, 1863, for an ill-fated attack on Franklin, just a few miles up the road from Spring Hill, where the Union soldiers had armed themselves with new Burnside breech-loading carbines. Forrest had enjoyed some success in an earlier raid on Brentwood, inside the Union lines. A jealous Van Dorn, who was outnumbered three-to-one, desired some glory for himself.

His efforts against the well-fortified Union position at Franklin failed miserably. After entering the town briefly, his army was overwhelmed and repulsed. Few casualties resulted, but the ease with which Van Dorn was turned away and the personal differences inherent between the West Pointer and the scrappy Forrest led to a rift between the two commanders that never healed. The defeat at Franklin also put the Rebels on edge fearing the Union commander had gained enough confidence to attempt a move against their headquarters at Spring Hill. The next month saw little action other than parties for the officers and daily drilling for the men. Holt Collier and the Texans participated in every aspect of the limited Tennessee campaign. Van Dorn remarked on April 23, 1863, that "the Ninth Texas Cavalry were the best horsemen in the world and were inferior to none in drill."[14]

• • •

At Spring Hill, General Van Dorn, true to his reputation, became romantically involved with the wife of a respected local physician, Dr. George B. Peters. The general was described as "a horrible rake," and it was said in Spring Hill that Van Dorn could often be seen "at times with some fine looking ladies driving about in his splendid four-horse ambulance." It was readily apparent that Van Dorn had paid undue attention to Mrs. Peters for an extended period of time, but that Dr. Peters "was unaware of the extent of the general's attentions."

When Dr. Peters caught "a servant delivering a note from Van Dorn" to his wife, he finally confronted Van Dorn with an ultimatum that he "would blow his brains out if he ever entered the premise again." Soon thereafter, following a trip out of town, Peters discovered that Van Dorn had disregarded the warning. The cuckolded husband set a trap, and on the morning of May 6, he finally caught Van Dorn precisely where he "expected to find him" in a most compromising position. The general, confronted again, promised to provide the doctor with a written statement "exonerating his wife of any guilt in exchange for his [Van Dorn's] freedom."

On the morning of May 7, 1863, when Dr. Peters called at the general's headquarters demanding that he produce the document, Van Dorn answered that he had changed his mind because it would hurt the "cause" and his own reputation. Peters was then treated indignantly and Van Dorn called him a "damned cowardly dog." Dr. Peters was not a man to be so humiliated. He immediately drew his pistol and aimed the gun so as to shoot Van Dorn in the forehead. When Van Dorn made a convulsive movement Peters fired, and the shot struck the left side of Van Dorn's head just above the ear. The Confederate general was killed instantly.

Peters escaped on horseback but a year later was captured in Bolivar County, Mississippi, just north of Greenville. He was transported to Meridian where he was acquitted after a military trial. He subsequently forgave his wife, remarried her, and settled again in Spring Hill after the war.[15]

Though it was the end of a shameful career, Van Dorn's death cast a universal gloom over his troops. William H. Jackson took temporary command of the cavalry. Picketing, foraging, and skirmishing resumed soon after Van Dorn's burial in Columbia, Tennessee.

• • •

While the Ninth Texas Cavalry was bivouacked in middle Tennessee with nothing but time on its hands, Grant was finalizing his plans for the Vicksburg campaign. At that stage of the war Vicksburg was considered the most important objective for both armies. If Vicksburg were lost to the South, Richmond would be cut off from the Trans-Mississippi Department, which had become important in the supply of men and provisions from across the river in Arkansas, Louisiana, and Texas. For the Union cause, opening the waterway to New Orleans would mean no further impediment or harassment from Confederate land batteries, and it would allow the Union navy free travel and unlimited access to the southern ports.

The Ninth Texas Cavalry, Perry Evans's Company I, and Holt Collier were ordered back to Mississippi to face the coming Union juggernaut. For the Texans it was another long and difficult march south returning over much of the same difficult Tennessee and North Alabama terrain they had traversed a few months earlier. On May 29, 1863, they received a generous welcome from the citizens of Columbus, Mississippi. They passed through Louisville, the Old Choctaw Agency, Kosciusko, and Thomastown, and arrived at Canton, Mississippi, on June 3, 1863. There they rested for two days and were reviewed by General Joseph E. Johnston, who complimented them for their appearance after a fatiguing march of 375 miles in fourteen days.[16]

To the west a distance of sixty miles lay Vicksburg, a city under siege. There were reports and rumors of a huge buildup of Union troops and entrenchments that had been dug in preparation for an assault. Grant had taken only nineteen days to secure a position behind the city, during which he had easily defeated the Confederates at every engagement. The obvious Union strength was an ominous and foreboding indication of the impending fall of Vicksburg and the Union invasion to come.

CHAPTER 7

# VICKSBURG

*"The Federals were thick as hops and I began to get uneasy.
On the fourth night I told my Old Colonel good-bye."*
— Holt Collier

After the loss of his supplies at Holly Springs General Grant dedicated all of his resources to an assault on Vicksburg by way of the Mississippi River. When he failed in his attempts to penetrate the area north of the city by direct frontal attack at Chickasaw Bluffs and a naval river campaign through the Yazoo River basin, he decided to risk a running of the Vicksburg, Warrenton, and Grand Gulf river batteries to make a landing south of the bluff city. Grant's successful landing at Bruinsburg, south of Vicksburg, infused forty-three thousand troops with full support of artillery and supplies into the heart of Mississippi. By July 4, 1863, when the city finally capitulated, the Union force in Mississippi was more than seventy-five thousand strong.[1]

With General Sherman attacking to the north of Vicksburg and Colonel Grierson conducting a cavalry raid through the length of the state, Grant effectively split the Confederate forces in Mississippi. The landing of the Union forces at Bruinsburg on April 30, 1863, sent shock waves through the state. Grant's army moved rapidly, taking Port Gibson on May 1, Raymond on May 12, and Jackson on May 14. The last real effort by the ill-equipped Confederates to stop the advance to Vicksburg was at Champion's Hill on May 16, 1863. The stand made there by the butternut troops was unsuccessful, and by May 18, 1863, the Union advance was skirmishing with the Confederates on the eastern outskirts of Vicksburg.[2]

General Joseph E. Johnston, commander of Confederate forces in Mississippi, had a reserve of almost forty-five thousand men and large supplies of ordnance but refused to send reinforcements to General Pemberton, who was commanding the defense of Vicksburg. Johnston also refused to make a sustained attack on Grant's rear. As a result of Johnston's timidity, the only effort committed to the relief of the city consisted of isolated guerilla cavalry attacks meant to harass and impede what would become a Union saturation of the West Central portion of the state.

During this unsuccessful campaign to relieve Vicksburg, the Ninth Texas Cavalry served in legion with the command of General George B. Cosby, which included Wirt Adams's Mississippi Cavalry.[3] In early June, 1863, Holt Collier and his Texas company moved to Satartia, a small farming community on the Yazoo River about thirty miles northeast of Vicksburg. There they found that the Federals had destroyed all of the gin houses and dwellings and stolen all the horses and slaves in the surrounding area. The Union command in the area was ten thousand strong, far too large a force to engage in battle. On June 10 the Texans were sent to Bolton Station on the Southern Railroad in direct line between Vicksburg and Jackson, where they heard the constant bombardment of Vicksburg, twenty miles to the west. From Bolton Station for the next two weeks Holt and his companions scouted and picketed enemy positions. On June 24 the entire Ninth Texas Cavalry was ordered to Edwards Station, just west of Bolton and seven miles closer to the enemy.[4]

• • •

During the winter of 1862-63, Howell Hinds languished at Home Hill Plantation in Jefferson County unable to raise a company as authorized by President Davis. The artillery company he had promised never materialized. He was successful at enlisting only eight men. Plum Ridge in Washington County was behind enemy lines and beyond his reach. His efforts were limited to maintaining civil authority in a country already depleted of men and wealth.

Upriver in Washington County conditions were not much better. On March 8, 1863, with the Federals patrolling the Mississippi River between Memphis and Vicksburg, an impoverished Thomas Hinds wrote from Plum Ridge Plantation in Washington County that "I would as soon die in the army as out of it." He complained that "the Yankees...have taken away every thing I have. The commissioned officers are with the privates in acts of the most outrageous character. When they visit a planter's house they make the privates keep guard while they plunder and steal."[5] In a letter from Home Hill, Howell Hinds wrote describing the situation near Greenville, "The Yankees are destroying all that country and besides the stealing of negroes and other property."[6]

In April 1863 General Pemberton called upon Howell Hinds to retrieve a cargo of bacon that had been stranded up Choctaw Bayou in Louisiana by Union gunboats patrolling the Red River. The assignment meant going behind enemy lines, as Grant's troop movement across the river in Louisiana was massive. The official request from Pemberton meant that for a brief occasion Hinds would see some action outside the confines of Jefferson County. To be successful he would have to cross through enemy lines at the risk of certain death if captured.

> JACKSON,
> April 18, 1863
>
> Maj. Howell Hinds,
> Fayette, Miss.:
>
> We have a cargo of bacon on a boat in Choctaw Bayou, 4 miles west of Water Proof. It is of vital importance to save it. Can it be transported to the river, and crossed at Rodney, and from thence sent to the railroad? If so, you will undertake the direction of the enterprise. If you can get it across anywhere you will do a great service, for which Lieutenant-General Pemberton will be most grateful. Answer.
>
> W. H. McCARDLE,
> Assistant Adjutant-General[7]

Hinds accepted his orders and performed his duty as directed, almost certainly with difficulty. The fact that men were willing to risk their lives for something as insignificant as a load of bacon is illustrative of the hard times that had befallen the South. In a later report General Pemberton wrote to headquarters of Hinds' efforts.

> *A cargo of bacon, which had been run up Choctaw Bayou on April 18 to avoid the enemy's gunboats on Red River, was by the energetic exertions of Mr. Howell Hinds, of Jefferson County, Mississippi, successfully transported from the bayou across the river to Port Gibson....*[8]

At the time General Grant successfully landed his massive army at Bruinsburg, Howell Hinds was living at Home Hill, only twenty miles away. He continued to serve as provost marshall of Jefferson County, responsible for preserving order among military persons and preventing improper intercourse with the enemy. His orders were to punish those who would relieve the enemy with money, harbor or protect an enemy, correspond with the enemy, or give intelligence to the enemy. Persons found in violation of the law could suffer death at Hinds's discretion.[9]

In all of his endeavors Hinds was known as a man of action. He could not resist the urge to take up arms against the invading armies of the North. When Grant made his landing Howell Hinds left his post as provost marshal and joined the cavalry unit of his young friend Colonel Wirt Adams. Serving nearby in the same division were Holt Collier and the Ninth Texas Cavalry. Riding in Adams's command was Captain William Swann Yerger, an officer who had served with Hinds on the staff of General Charles Clark at Shiloh. Because all commissioned positions were filled, Hinds accepted duty with Adams at the lowly rank of private.

Wirt Adams was well known and much respected for his harassment of the Union armies; his name was often mentioned with other great calvary leaders like Nathan Bedford Forrest, Joe Wheeler, and John Hunt Morgan. Howell Hinds had ridden with him earlier at Bowling Green in 1861 and again at Shiloh in 1862. Adams's cavalry was closely involved in the fighting throughout the river campaign and was at Grant's front from the time the Union troops turned west from Jackson toward Vicksburg. His mounted troops were considered the most valued of Pemberton's advance cavalry.[10]

Adams's was assigned a defense along the Big Black River in Yazoo County. On June 22, 1863 at the plantation of William Hill his unit was engaged in a heated battle with a 130-man detachment from the Fourth Iowa Cavalry. The Iowans were on a fatigue mission with pickets out front for protection. Their mission was to fell timber and obstruct a road to Bush's Ferry on the river. The Confederates charged the pickets and drove them back into the fatigue party, where the Federals took cover behind a rail fence.

At the fence the issue became clear when the Iowans produced a two-pounder gun which quickly became Adams's goal to capture. The ragged unit charged down the road by column of fours within pistol shot of the two-pounder. The cavalry was exposed to the fusillade from the Union position and was ripped by canister and small arms fire. After continued pressure, the Iowans had to regroup. It was a difficult maneuver, and when attempted, the butternut horsemen surged up the road, captured the two-pounder, after which it "was root hog or die as the Iowans scattered to the winds."[11]

In the action at Hill's farm, losses to the Fourth Iowa Cavalry were eight killed, sixteen wounded, and thirty three missing or taken prisoner.[12] Casualties for the two Confederate regiments were five killed, sixteen wounded, one missing, and forty horses killed. Among the seriously wounded commissioned officers was Captain William Swann Yerger, who fell while "gallantly leading his company." Of the seriously wounded enlisted men was private Howell Hinds, shot through the body and left with a wound that must have been considered mortal. The bullet entered the middle of his stomach and came out a half inch to the left of his backbone.[13]

• • •

The Ninth Texas Cavalry was serving along the broken front at nearby Satartia, and word of Hinds's injuries passed through the lines. Captain Perry Evans gave Holt Collier a pass to visit his old mentor and provide whatever assistance he could. He carefully rode in his Texas uniform with upturned hat and high boots through the Federal lines to a house fourteen miles southeast of Yazoo City, where he was met at the home of Howell's cousin Eliza Wilkerson. From Collier's later accounts, Harris Dickson described the scene,

"Holt didn't knock but strode into the room with two big six shooters at his belt, a cavalry rifle and bayonet. The girls were scared sick but Colonel Hinds waved at him from the bed. Holt knelt beside his old master, caught his hand and both of them were crying."[14]

Collier's own version of the incident was recorded years later when he described hearing the news and visiting Hinds, whom he had not seen for months. "News that my old Colonel had been wounded came through the lines.... I got a pass from Capt. Evans and left that night. Riding night and day I reached the home of a relative of the Colonel's. I hid my horse in a cane-brake nearby and slipped up to the house after dark. Miss Eliza, the Colonel's cousin, let me in and showed me where he lay. I went in and when he saw me he waved his hand for everyone to leave the room. I went over and knelt down by his bed and put my arms around him and hugged him close. He began to cry and said, 'Holt, I am badly hurt, but I believe I will pull through.' After awhile the family came in and we talked until daybreak. I was treated like a royal guest by Miss Eliza and the others. She made me a couch beside the Colonel's bed and I slept there during my stay. I never left the house and the family were on guard all the time I was there. The Federals were thick as hops and I began to get uneasy. On the fourth night I told my Old Colonel good-bye."[15]

Holt Collier returned to his company and saw action at Messenger's Ferry near Edward's Depot just prior to receiving the news that Vicksburg had surrendered. With the fall of Vicksburg on July 4, 1863, the Union troops were free to return east toward Jackson in force. This movement led to a steady retreat by Confederate forces, first to Clinton, then to Jackson, and ultimately to Pelahatchie Station on the Southern Railroad.

• • •

Though Grant had taken Jackson prior to his advance on Vicksburg, he had abandoned it back to the Confederates when he turned toward his goal to the west. The Union forces had done limited damage to the city on their first visit. It would not be so fortunate when visited in July 1863 by Union forces under the command of General William T. Sherman. In that siege the capital city of Jackson was pummeled by exploding artillery. The entire countryside was stripped of corn, cattle, hogs, sheep, and poultry. Fields of growing corn were thrown open to pasture the army's livestock. Sherman observed in a communiqué to Grant, "the wholesale destruction to which this country is now being subjected is terrible to contemplate, but it is the scourge of war."[16] In Brandon, a few miles east of Jackson, Sherman halted his eastward advance on July 19. On July 23, 1863, Sherman evacuated Jackson and returned to Vicksburg, assured that General Joseph E. Johnston would not attempt to retake the river city.

Howell Hinds, wounded and behind enemy lines, had surrendered himself as a prisoner of war and was paroled to await exchange. His convalescence took months, after which he wrote again to President Davis describing his recent experiences and circumstances. The letter is telling in his attitude and erroneous reliance on the strength of the southern cause.

*Home Hill,*
*Oct. 11th, 1863*

*To President Davis,*

*My Dear Friend,*

*It has been a long time since I have written you,—not from a disinclination, but knowing you are over burthened (with) business and harassed with all kinds of correspondence, I was disposed to inflict you as little as possible with my dull epistles. Many changes have taken place since I wrote you. All the chivalry of our country had gone off as I found out after you gave me authority to raise an artillery company. I could get but eight men to join, and I joined Col. Wirt Adams' regt. as a private, and remained with it until I was wounded on the 22nd of June last, and from which I have just now recovered and will return to duty so soon as I ascertain I am exchanged. The Yankees pay us an occasional visit in Jefferson but so far have committed but few depredations in this county; have stolen a few horses and mules. A very large am't of cotton has been captured in the vicinity of Natchez belonging to the Confederacy....We are so situated here we get but little news, all our mail facilities having been suspended since Vicksburg fell. I hope Bragg has made his victory complete if he has it will be very difficult for Abe to get more troops from the West....We have been looking anxiously for our Fleet of Gun Boats. I hope they will soon be at work and if you can get all the men in the field who have been called for we will whip all the armies the Yankees can be able to bring against us. If we should need more I hope you will call for all from 16 to 60. You have been one of the best abused men in the Confederacy, and it is what you had a right to expect from the noncombatant crokers and speculators—a race of men who have done more to injure our cause than all else, and I hope to see them exterminated at least they should not be allowed to live in this country. They have been the cause of thousands of good men leaving their post and going home to look after their familys for fear of their being in destitution in consequence of every necessary being put up to starvation prices. I trust there will be some mode adopted to reach those cormorants and meet out to them a just retribution, with my kindest regards to your family and your brothers if there, believe me truly your friend,*

*How. Hinds*

*endorsed: H. Hinds, Home Hill Oct. 11, 1863; with regard to state of affairs in Miss. Recd. Nov. 18.*[17]

Howell Hinds was wrong in his expectations of Confederate strength. One can only speculate that he, like many others of his aristocratic lineage, felt unconquerable and unvanquished. The fact that his letter took more than a month to reach Richmond is itself a clear indication that by the fall of 1863 his was truly a lost cause.

CHAPTER 8

# DELTA RANGERS

*"I verily believe they would have braided the tail
of a cyclone if commanded to do so by Captain Evans.
They usually 'lost' their prisoners going through the cane-brakes.
Going out there once just after them,
I scared the buzzards from three bodies they had 'lost.'"*
— Sam Worthington

Lost to the Confederate cause in the defense of Vicksburg were 31,600 soldiers taken prisoner, 172 cannon, more than 60,000 rifles, and tons of ammunition. The Confederate army had suffered more than 9,000 battle casualties while defending the city. Port Hudson, the last Confederate Mississippi River battery, surrendered its garrison of 6,000 men five days after the fall of Vicksburg.[1] With all river batteries taken, Grant had opened the entire length of the Mississippi River for regular navigation and for the Union to access America's vast interior. President Abraham Lincoln proclaimed, "The Father of Waters again goes unvexed to the sea."[2]

After the surrender of Vicksburg all Confederate hopes for victory over the Union forces would be under the hard terms that could be acquired only from attrition. The northern objective of dividing the South had been realized. The Union army became relentless in its penetration of territory and pillaging of the country to finance and support their war effort while denying the southern armies much needed materials and provisions.

General Grant, who proved himself by always pressing the advantage once it had been gained, alerted Sherman to be prepared to move east against Johnston and his army of forty-three thousand men as soon as Vicksburg was in Federal possession. The objective was to attack Johnston, destroy all bridges, railroads and structures in sight, and to drive the Confederate army out of Central Mississippi. Sherman's move east was harassed and impeded by constant cavalry skirmishes with the Ninth Texas and Adams's Mississippi Cavalry. Battle and skirmish lines were drawn daily over a wide front which moved like a flowing tide ever outward from Vicksburg. Engagements between the Union and Confederate forces were a daily occurrence. Holt Collier and his Texas comrades skirmished with Sherman's army throughout the month of July at Edwards Station, Messinger's Ford, Bolton, Clinton, Jackson, Yazoo City, and Canton.[3]

In August, 1863, Holt Collier and his company of Texans scouted and picketed north of Jackson beyond Canton, engaging the Federal troops and skirmishing with them continually. They moved constantly through Central Mississippi, traveling in wide circles through Yazoo City, Lexington, Benton, settlements along the Big Black and Pearl rivers, Goodman Station, Ratliffe's Ferry, Pelahatchie, Camden, Madison Station, Durant, Vaiden, Duck Hill, and Kosciusko. They returned to Canton at the end of the month.[4]

Near the abandoned town of Vernon, about twelve miles north of Lexington, the Texans bivouacked during most of the month of September, drilling and standing for review by Generals S. D. Lee, Joseph Johnston, and William Hardee. On September 28 and 29, they began a series of hotly contested skirmishes with the Federals from Brownsville in Hinds County to Moore's Bluff and Benton in Yazoo County, with the Federals retreating into Yazoo City. In those two days, direct pursuit of small bands of Federals covered more than eighty miles.

• • •

October 14, 1863, was the Ninth Texas Cavalry's second anniversary of their organization and entry into Confederate service. A casualty list was prepared for the occasion. The list does not include deserters or those dead from sickness. The regiment began with about 1,240 men. After two years of service the casualty rate was roughly twenty percent.[5]

| *Killed in Action* | 58 officers and men |
| *Mortally wounded in Action* | 24 officers and men |

| | |
|---|---|
| *Wounded in Action* | *128 officers and men* |
| *Taken Prisoners* | *64 officers and men* |
| *Making a total of* | *274 officers and men* |

The third year in unbroken service to the Confederacy began with the Ninth Texas Cavalry fighting a swamp and wilderness campaign in Mississippi. It had few objectives and was headquartered wherever it might find its foe. It became the responsibility of these "delta rangers" to protect the general population while engaging the enemy at every opportunity. In consequence of the Union occupation the local civil authorities had lost the ability to enforce the law. The constant penetration by Federal troops and the emboldened slave populations created ever more frequent problems. The Confederate forces available to the region acted as much to police the area as they did to combat the invaders.

Captain Perry Evans and the men of Company I scouted the Yazoo River basin every day that fall. Skirmishing was a regular duty though little would be gained but bragging rights. With a lack of guidance from a higher command, the widely disbursed companies began to act in an autonomous fashion, coordinating their movements only when facing superior forces. Captain Evans and his men encountered the Federals a half-dozen times in mid-October, killing four Union soldiers, once barely escaping a larger force by crossing the Big Black River.

During a bitterly cold December of 1863 the entire regiment was ordered north through the Yazoo River basin swamps to Indian Bayou near Garvin's Ferry on the Sunflower River. Their mission was to transport a shipment of guns through frozen swamp paths to the Mississippi River for use by the Trans-Mississippi Department in Arkansas.[6] Extreme conditions confronted the troops on this long journey. They had to cross the Sunflower River covered with almost two inches of ice. Weather conditions were described as bitterly cold with the smaller streams frozen over. The men were poorly provisioned, thinly clad, and suffered terribly. Roads in the swamp were impassable by wagons, which required the rifles to be taken from the boxes. Each man, from the commanding general on down, was given two guns to carry to the river, where they were ferried across with great difficulty. During the entire exercise of traversing the river, an artillery duel between a gunboat and a Confederate battery was in progress.[7] Because mud for several miles had been frozen and was sharp to the touch, many of Ross's men returned to Benton with their boots cut and worn out. Many suffered from the effects of frostbite."[8]

Because Perry Evans's company ranged widely in the Mississippi Delta vicinity of Thomas and Howell Hinds's Plum Ridge Plantation, the significant responsibility of guiding the regiment through much of the wilderness swamp fell largely on Holt Collier. He led the Texans to Greenville through the familiar swamps of Deer Creek, the Boque Phalia, and Black Bayou which was covered with ice more than four inches thick in early January 1864.

When the main body of the Ninth Texas Cavalry was ordered to return to the vicinity of Yazoo City in mid-January, Holt, along with several soldiers personally selected from the regiment by Captain Perry Evans, reorganized into a detached unit which became known as Evans's Texas Scouts. From January 1864 until the end of the conflict, they served as rangers throughout the Mississippi Delta.[9]

Howell Hinds returned that winter to Plum Ridge Plantation and remained in Washington County in an attempt to protect it from the Federals. In the absence of any organized resistance the Union army quickly earned a reputation for pillage and looting. Evans's Texas Scouts, with the help of Hinds and several other prominent men, took it upon themselves to do what was necessary to protect the property and lives of the local citizenry. In essence Howell Hinds, Holt Collier, and Perry Evans became partisan rangers taking vigilante actions when they deemed them necessary and engaged the enemy in guerilla raids when they were encountered.

• • •

Egypt Plantation was a large operation located in Bolivar County north of Greenville. It was owned and operated by the Lobdell Estate. Prior to the war it was managed by an overseer named Milford Coe. When war broke out Coe joined the Bolivar Troop under the command of then Captain Charles Clark, First Mississippi Cavalry Regiment. At the Battle of Belmont in November 1861, one of the earliest engagements in the west, Coe "demonstrated that he was a constitutional coward," and he left the service.[10]

Coe returned to Bolivar County and obtained employment as the new overseer for Rhodes Estill, who owned a large plantation on Lake Bolivar, three miles from the main Mississippi River landing and just opposite the lower end of Island 76. (The river islands were numbered by boat pilots counting south from the confluence of the Mississippi and Ohio Rivers.) The new employer was old and a chronic invalid, and he desired that no impediment come between him and the Union forces. As the United States fleet made its presence felt inland, Estill sent Coe to the gunboat *Marmore*, stationed near the town of Bolivar, to present gratuities to the officers and to solicit protection for himself and his property.

The influence of the invading forces on Estill's overseer had an unexpected result. Coe found that consorting with the enemy could be very profitable. His selfish motives and his newfound friends induced him to become a renegade against the South, and he deserted to the cause of the North.

By late 1863 Coe had established a hideaway on Island 76, secured from detection and penetration by a natural moat. The island, also known as Goat Island, was about two miles long and one-half mile wide. It was heavily forested with hundreds of acres in which a large body of men could hide.[11] Coe kept a small army of runaway slaves and several renegade whites with him. A tall, powerful slave named Tom, who was well known in the area and had been foreman on the nearby plantation of Colonel Cristopher Fields, acted as his lieutenant. The slaves worked for Coe, supplying him with a large wood yard from which he collected war prices from the Federal gunboat captains.

Occasionally Coe would organize some of his select men and raid the interior, always collecting many fine mules and other stock. He never missed an opportunity to take fugitive slaves. When he returned to his island hideout, Coe would dispose of the loot at his pleasure. During one of these forays he stole everything of value from Estill, his former employer, and abused the invalid with "rancor of a bitter hatred." On that same raid he took the mules and livestock from William Sillers and others. To the locals Coe was the lowest form of criminal. John Crawford Burrus, a contemporary, described Coe and his band of outlaws. "Here on this island, in command of a band of miscreants as evil as himself, ripe for treason, strategem and spoils, this desperate robber dwelt, a perpetual menace to the welfare of our people in a radius of many miles."[12]

In mid-January 1864 Holt Collier, then about seventeen years of age, was sent to Island 76 posing as a runaway slave. Acting with instructions and under the direction of Howell Hinds and Captain Perry Evans, he remained on the island for several days without arousing any suspicion. The plan was to attack the island fortress with as small a contingent as possible. Detailed and precise information of the objective was required. On his return from the island Collier provided full information on the location of the camp and the strength of the garrison. Most important, Holt was able to determine that Coe kept all of the weapons in the house occupied by himself and his white associates for fear that the slaves would revolt against him.

Late on the evening of January 19, 1864, a flat-bottom bateau containing Howell Hinds, Bob Lee, Alf Smith, Jack Estill, and Holt Collier silently passed across the old river channel using muffled oars. It was a night of "darkness and fog." They traveled "silent as a phantom, across the murky waters of the old Mississippi on as gallant and as desperate a mission as was ever undertaken by men who realized the issue to be success or death to every man of that silent group."[13]

They quietly landed on the sandbar below the camp and in single file approached the hut occupied by Coe and his closest companions. With guns drawn and on the ready, the cabin door was forced open, and through the dim light of a single lantern Coe and his comrades were looking into the muzzles of six army Colts while "Hands up. No noise!" was uttered in a near whisper, "the quiet intensity of which was sufficient to make one's hair rise and gooseflesh crinkle one's skin."[14]

The men from the hut were captured, bound, and gagged. Several fugitive slaves were also captured. All prisoners were taken into a clearing in the woods where they were made to wait for first light, threatened with instant death if there were any attempt to flee. At daybreak a Yankee trading boat, the *Sutler*, commanded by a man known only by the name of Booker, landed at the wood yard. Some of the vigilantes disguised themselves with Union overcoats and walked aboard. In less than five minutes they took control of boat and crew. Hinds and his men transported their prisoners across to the

Mississippi side of the old riverbed. Captain Booker paid a substantial sum to Howell Hinds to prevent him from torching the boat.[15]

Howell Hinds and his allies returned the stolen property, including mules and cattle. Estill and Sillers regained most of their stock, and the runaways were instructed to return to their respective owners, a command which most obeyed. Coe was taken as a prisoner to Rhodes Estill where he "demonstrated his cowardice" by making agonized prayers to Mr. Estill pleading that his life be spared. His prayers were to no avail. Coe, one of his white comrades, and the slave Tom, were executed. Their execution was described by John Crawford Burrus as "an easier and more honorable death than they deserved."

The raiders of Island 76, like their prey, were desperate men. With the lone exception of Holt Collier, each participant of that raid would suffer a violent death. Texan Bob Lee returned home after the war, acquired a reputation for killing a number of men, and was himself shot down at an early age. Alf Smith, who had a well earned reputation as an honorable and chivalrous man, was killed in a "personal affair" a few years following the war. Jack Estill, known for leading an adventurous life, was murdered in Texas about 1895.[16]

• • •

Union General William T. Sherman returned to Mississippi in February 1864 on a mission to destroy and burn anything from Vicksburg to Meridian that could be used by the Rebels to prolong the insurrection. It was Sherman's inauguration of his scorched earth policy of war. Of his 1864 Meridian expedition Sherman wrote:

> *My movement to Meridian stampeded all Alabama. Polk retreated across the Tombigbee and left me to break railroads and smash things at pleasure, and I think it is well done....Our loss was trifling, and as we broke absolutely and effectually a full hundred miles of railroad at and around Meridian, no car can pass through that place this campaign. We lived off the country and made a swath of desolation 50 miles broad across the State of Mississippi, which the present generation will not forget.*[17]

In conjunction with the Meridian expedition, Admiral David Porter, who had been in command of Union naval operations during the Vicksburg campaign, made a sizable contingent of vessels available to Sherman's command for an expedition up the Yazoo River into the heart of the Mississippi Delta. This raid was concluded on March 5, 1864, by the repulse of the Federals from Yazoo City. The Confederate forces opposing Porter's Yazoo River campaign included the Ninth Texas Cavalry, which had also served at Sherman's front at the beginning of his Meridian campaign.[18]

Holt Collier and Company I participated with other Texas units in the defense against the Yazoo River expedition, after which Captain Perry Evans, Holt Collier, and the small company of irregular Texans returned north into the Delta counties. Evans and his select group of scouts would from that time forward be permanently detached, never again to serve directly with the Ninth Texas Cavalry.[19]

After defending against Sherman's expedition to Meridian, Ross's Texas Brigade, without Evans and his men, was sent directly to Georgia where it again fought Sherman during the siege of Atlanta. The Ninth Texas Cavalry went on to participate in the battles of Atlanta and Franklin, Tennessee, and engaged the enemy daily during its 1865 retreat into Alabama and back to Mississippi. They were finally surrendered in Citronelle, Alabama, on May 4, 1865, while serving with General Nathan Bedford Forrest's command.

• • •

Captain Perry Evans and his company of scouts served out the remainder of the war as free rangers. They were constantly up and down the river counties of Mississippi, riding to the aid of citizens in distress and engaging the enemy and their sympathizers whenever stealth and good judgment dictated. Hiding in the vast swamp wilderness, they ventured out as needed. To the Federals, they were nothing better than common guerilla outlaws. The southern civilians occasionally voiced concern at their brutal methods, but were nonetheless pleased to have them in their service. Because Holt Collier was thoroughly familiar with the area, his service to the unit through the remainder of the conflict was invaluable.[20]

The Texans earned a reputation in the Mississippi Delta for being absolutely ruthless in their means and indiscriminate in killing and torturing northern sympathizers as well as Union soldiers. There were several skirmishes and other incidents in the vicinity of Greenville in the summer of 1864. Across Rattlesnake Bayou on the edge of Plum Ridge Plantation ran a dirt road to a river landing which the raiding Federals would use on their frequent forays inland. Often Collier and his comrades would lay in ambush and attack them from the bushes.[21]

Decades later, Mamie Bowen Warfield recounted seeing Captain Perry Evans's Delta Rangers when she was a child, "Several Confederate soldiers were captured in our yard in a circle of cedar trees, when unexpectedly a band of Texas scouts dashed up, surrounded them, and the situation was reversed. A thrilling sight met my childish gaze as the sun flashed upon those glittering bayonets, and brilliant uniforms of the enemy as they dismounted and in turn were made prisoners by our men."[22]

Sam Worthington's recollection of the Texas scouts describes the attitude and manner in which they served, "In 1864, I think it was, Captain Evans appeared with his Confederate scouts. They were sent to Washington County to break up Yankees who were trying to raise cotton near Skipwith's Landing. They were as wild a lot of outlaws as ever followed 'Robin Hood.' I verily believe they would have braided the tail of a cyclone if commanded to do so by Captain Evans. They caught some of the civilians who were trying to raise cotton, frequently, and the first stop they made was at Wayside to get breakfast. They usually 'lost' their prisoners going through the canebrakes from father's Redleaf Plantation to what was the Sims plantation just above Arcola on Deer Creek. Going out there once just after them, I scared the buzzards from three bodies they had 'lost.' They caught Colonel [Louis] Dent, a kinsman [brother-in-law] of General Grant, on one of their raids, but my father saved his life, which fact was afterwards to be of great benefit to our family. Evans' scouts did not 'play any favorites.' One of their number, breaking into a house near Greenville and robbing it, was promptly shot. The Reverend Stevenson Archer was sent for to shrive the man and say a miserere over him. I merely mention this to show what a state of 'admired disorder' this country was in."[23]

Stevenson Archer, like Howell Hinds, was a native of Jefferson County who had settled near Greenville. He was a military chaplain during the war, and for many years thereafter was pastor of the Presbyterian church at Greenville. He had several dealings with Evans's Scouts, and recorded one of the most telling descriptions of the battle seasoned unit.

"General Ross, in command of the Confederate forces in this state, concentrated his forces not far from Yazoo City, leaving Captain Evans in command of a body of scouts to keep an eye on the movements of the Federals, and make reports to him from time to time. Captain Evans was a gallant and efficient officer and did his duty well. He had fifty to sixty scouts under his command, sometimes more and sometimes less. Besides their duties as scouts, these men were expected to protect the people from the marauding enemy, prevent horse stealing and drive out scattering bands of raiders.

"On one occasion, I was called upon to marry a couple at the place known as Winterville, then called the Ireys plantation. I met Captain Evans within a mile of the place. He said, 'Where are you going, sir?'

"I am going to marry Miss Copeland to Lieutenant Johnson.

"He replied, 'It ain't any use, I have just had him shot and flung into the river.

"Why, you are mistaken.

"No, it is a fact.

"What did you do that for?

"He stole Mr. Halsey's mules, and I had orders from General Forrest, who commands the cavalry in this section, to shoot all such marauders, and simply executed my orders.

"I repaired to the house and found that what he told me was literally true.

"On another occasion, he ordered the arrest of two of his command, one of them a man named Fowler, and the other Gallagher. Fowler's arrest was accomplished, but Gallagher escaped. I intervened and begged to go to Refuge where Judge Advocate General [Robert] Lowry was at the time. I laid the case before him and plead for the life of the gallant young soldier. He refused to intervene. I went back to Swiftwater and met Fowler at the gate. He said, 'I know my fate. You failed.' He said that he would like for me to come in and say a prayer for him, during which he wept bitterly and said there was not a crime I could name which he had not committed. He then called for water and washed his face. He said, 'I do not want the boys to see that I am chicken-hearted.' He combed his hair, made his toilet, and walking out, selected two men to fire the fatal shot. They were Texas boys and his best friends.

"Fowler was one of the handsomest men I ever saw, fair skinned, blue eyes, a figure perfectly symmetrical in build. When he stepped out on the ground, he threw off his coat and said to the men selected to shoot:

"Now I have loaded one of the guns and one of them is empty. Neither of you will know which killed me.' Holding his hand over his heart, he said, 'Shoot me just here.' Raising his hand to heaven, he said, 'Oh God, I have lived well on earth, receive my spirit, fire!

"Fowler's grave may still be seen on the Swiftwater Plantation near the scene of his execution.

"Captain Evans was a gallant soldier, gainly and of courtly bearing. The scouts were usually men of genteel manners and attended dances and other social functions. The Evans Scouts sometimes did things everywhere condemned, but they did not think it was any more than right. They thought the people they robbed were in sympathy with the Yankees and that it was right to rob them."[24]

• • •

Dr. Orville M. Blanton, a respected physician in Greenville before the war, was a member of one of the most influential and wealthy families in the area. Evans's Scouts often robbed and threatened him with execution because of his well-known sympathies to the Union. About his treatment he wrote years later that "I was taken back to Indian Bayou by the Confederate Scouts because I turned some mules over to the Union Army and they threatened to hang me on account of my intimacy and supposed friendship for the Union officers and soldiers." Dr. Blanton deeply resented the treatment he received. Speaking of Captain Perry Evans's Scouts, he felt that, "No pronounced Union man's life or property was safe and even a breath of suspicion was enough to bring down upon him the vengeance of the Rebels." He complained that Evans's men came and carried his plantation bell away, killed off some of his stock and burned seven hundred bales of his cotton, all because he was considered an enemy of the Confederate cause.[25]

Once, while Howell Hinds was staying at Plum Ridge Plantation, he and a party of Evans's Scouts were riding about twelve miles north of Greenville near Goodrich Landing when they realized that they had run into an ambush. When they dashed for safety, Hinds's horse stumbled, pitching him off. Holt Collier, far in advance and out of danger, looked back to see Hinds, who signaled him to ride on. Hinds was obviously injured. He was bleeding profusely from the head. Ignoring orders from Evans not to return, and ignoring the certain danger to himself, Collier wheeled his horse around and dashed back to rescue Hinds. Running with his arms raised high, Hinds was jerked up as Collier, riding through the fire, "came abreast of him and without stopping his horse, reached down and jerked Col. Hinds up onto the horse with him." The act very probably saved Hinds' life, because vigilantes, when captured, were summarily executed.[26]

John Crawford Burrus, from neighboring Bolivar County, tendered his service in defense of the Confederate cause in 1864, enlisting as a private with Perry Evans's company of Delta Rangers. In this detached duty, he took part in many spirited skirmishes. Burrus's son Archie Clement served with his father in Evans's Scouts, enlisting when he was only sixteen years old.[27]

J. C. Burrus and his son were friends of Howell Hinds and Thomas Hinds, and often found themselves in the company of Holt Collier. Burrus was ambushed on another occasion while riding with Collier. They were in the thick cover of a canebrake riding toward a slough when they realized that they had been surrounded by the enemy. Burrus decided to surrender but Collier convinced him to make a wild dash through the lines, firing two pistols each and shouting with all their might. Their escape was successfully made without any casualty, and Burrus lived to document the incident.[28]

The surviving accounts provided by Collier's own recollections add little to the details of the actual history of Evans's Scouts. According to Collier, "Evans Company was detailed for scout duty along the Mississippi River and up near Old Greenville. We did a heap of good too; saved our folks property and ran the Unions out. During that time I did a great deal of scout duty. The whole country was a wilderness and if our boys got lost I could always find the way out. I had been raised in this part of the country and had hunted in the woods all my life."[29]

• • •

On September 30, 1864, a company of the Fourth Wisconsin Cavalry along with a band of scouts under the command of Lieutenant I. N. Earl, entered Fayette, Mississippi, on a foraging mission, taking prisoners and confiscating horses. Howell Hinds was in Jefferson County at the time, where he continued to hold the title of provost marshal, although his effectiveness by then would have been limited. Lieutenant Earl was known as "a terror to the Confederate citizens in the vicinity of Natchez." On a local level he was described as one of the most ardent enemies of the South who pursued his rancor with "unprecedented violence." To his enemies, he was known to possess one qualification that always wins respect, whether found in friend or foe, the quality of "indisputable courage."[30]

As Earl's advance column entered Fayette, it was fired upon from a nearby residence. The bluecoats were unable to ascertain whether the shots were fired by soldiers or citizens, and the town was immediately seized. In the limited action at Fayette that day a southern cotton agent who was attempting to escape with the mail was captured. While Earl's men were ransacking the house from which they had been fired upon they seriously wounded Howell Hinds and left him to die. In his brief but official report of the matter Lieutenant I. N. Earl reported, "Killed Lieutenant Hinds, the provost marshal of the place."[31]

According to a newspaper article in the *Fayette Chronicle* thirty years later, Lieutenant Earl met his fate about two months after the assault on Howell Hinds when a Confederate soldier quietly awaited Earl's arrival into Fayette. With his target about forty yards away, the soldier raised his gun with as much nonchalance as if shooting a squirrel and fired one barrel, mortally wounding Earl. The identity of Earl's assassin has never been determined.[32]

Earl's report of Hinds's death was premature. Against great odds, the tough old colonel survived his wounds and outlived the notorious Union officer who had declared him dead. Although he survived, the long and difficult war left Howell Hinds a broken man, both financially and physically. At the surrender, Holt Collier and his unit of Texans went to Vicksburg, where they were mustered out under the command of General Edmund Kirby Smith of Texas.[33]

CHAPTER 9

# OCCUPATION AND COURT-MARTIAL

*"No rude alarms of raging foes
shall here disturb my long repose."*
— Epitaph of Captain James A. King
Wittemberg Cemetery
Newton County, Iowa

When the Civil War began, College Farm was a remote Iowa village near the valley of the north fork of the Skunk River, just a few miles above Newton, the county seat. It was the home of the Wittemberg Manual Labor College, a small educational institution around which the close-knit community was built. The residents were of diverse origins united by the maxims to which the school was devoted: an affordable education for all, freedom of evangelical religion, the use of manual labor to equalize social barriers, and the total abolition of slavery and all forms of societal discrimination.[1]

It was an idyllic communal setting created with the goal of abandoning the spirit of aristocracy through the benefits of regular labor shared by all. According to the articles of incorporation, instructors and students alike were expected to perform manual labor at least two hours a day.[2] The school was situated on a ten acre site with agricultural tracts of forty acres located at the corners. Adjacent to the farms were the residences of the instructors and students. It was surrounded by gently rolling terrain blanketed by the great western prairie.[3]

For almost six years John King had made College Farm his home. He was a farmer who served on the college board of directors and was influential in the area.[4] Raised in Sullivan County, Tennessee, he migrated north through Illinois. King and his first wife, Elizabeth, had six children, three of whom died in infancy. After the death of his wife in 1858, King married Elizabeth Meyer, a widow, who remained his faithful companion until his death. All of the King children were raised as radical abolitionists. The desire to see slavery ended was so strongly held that John King withdrew from his ancestral affiliation with the Presbyterian Church, which he considered pro-slavery, and joined the Free Presbyterian Church, for which the abolition of slavery was its stated mission.[5]

James A. King, John's youngest son, was nineteen years of age when, on June 24, 1861, he volunteered to serve in the U. S. Army. He was a well-educated farm boy with high ideals and had probably not traveled further than Newton since moving from Illinois six years earlier. On July 15, less than a month after his enlistment, he reported for duty at the Mississippi River town of Burlington. There he was mustered into Company B of the Fifth Iowa Infantry. At the conclusion of the war, the Fifth Iowa boasted that they had never surrendered the field of battle to the enemy and had never served in any campaign where the field was lost.[6]

Border ruffians and bushwhackers of Missouri created a demand for the Fifth Iowa Infantry to be rushed into service. In early August the regiment reported to St. Louis and then to Jefferson City. The border states, including Missouri, were vitally important to the northern cause, and their stabilization was of initial importance to the war planners in Washington. From August 1861 through April 1862, while serving in the Fifth Iowa Infantry, James King's principal service was in Missouri.[7]

The early encounters experienced by the Fifth Iowa were generally skirmishes and police actions. It was not until they crossed the river in April 1862 after the carnage of Shiloh that King and his comrades were truly baptized by fire. The first military objective of significance was the railroad crossing at Corinth, Mississippi, where General P. G. T. Beauregard had retreated after Shiloh. The Fifth Iowa joined in the victory when Corinth was occupied, and pursued the Rebels to Booneville and Clear Creek. They bivouacked at Holly Springs in early July 1862. Among the Rebels King and the Fifth Iowa Infantry pursued after the Battle of Corinth were Howell Hinds and Holt Collier.

James King returned to Corinth in mid-July and remained there until September 18, when his regiment advanced on Iuka for their first encounter with an enemy force of considerable strength.[8] Among the Confederate units confronting the Iowans at Iuka were Company I of the Ninth Texas Cavalry and the Mississippi Cavalry Regiment under Colonel Wirt Adams.

• • •

Iuka was a small village on the Memphis and Charleston railway. It was occupied by Confederate forces under General Sterling Price. The value of the town was the rail line the Federals needed to supply reinforcements to and from Kentucky. The control of Iuka was fiercely contested. The Fifth Iowa was subjected to the brunt of the action, and suffered killed and wounded of almost fifty percent, an unprecedented rate of loss.[9]

The commander of the Fifth Iowa, Colonel C. L. Matthies, received high accolades for his unit from Major General Schuyler Hamilton, who referred to "the brilliant conduct of the Fifth Iowa at Iuka....[M]y heart thrilled with pride and satisfaction at the splendid conduct of the regiments composing my old division, especially that of the Fifth Iowa."[10]

Confederate General Earl Van Dorn, with Collier and his Texas comrades in his command, made his ill-fated attack on Corinth a few days later, and the Fifth Iowa was again called into action. To the relief of the Iowans, they were held in reserve and saw no action there until ordered to pursue Van Dorn after his repulse.

James King accompanied the regiment with General Grant on his Central Mississippi expedition which began in Grand Junction, Tennessee, and advanced south through Moscow, Davis Mills, and into Mississippi through Lumpkin's Mills (Holly Springs), Oxford, and Yocona Creek. The Fifth Iowa was among the units pressing Van Dorn and the Confederates south to Grenada, and they were with Grant in Oxford when Van Dorn and the Texans raided Holly Springs in December 1862, bringing about a swift end to the Central Mississippi expedition. After Van Dorn's raid on Holly Springs, King and his regiment withdrew through Lumpkin's Mills, Memphis, and Grand Lake, Arkansas.

King was also with Grant's ill-fated Yazoo Pass expedition in March 1863. The action, which involved the naval forces under

Admiral David Porter was intended to avoid a bloody frontal assault by flanking Vicksburg at Snyder's Bluff, a risky river passage. If the action was to be successful it would be necessary to land a sizable force east of the river and north of Vicksburg by way of the low Delta passage.

The great Delta swamp contained slow draining waterways–the Yazoo, Sunflower, Tallahatchie and Coldwater rivers–that could provide passage for naval transports if a route were found from the Mississippi River. Six miles below Helena was the entrance to the old Yazoo Pass, a meandering bayou which, before the levee was built, had been navigable to light draft boats in high water. It was thought that the old bayou could be made navigable again if the Mississippi River levee was blown.

On February 2 and 3, 1863, when Federal engineers mined the Yazoo Pass levee, the water on the river side was more than eight feet higher than on the Delta side. When the sappers ignited the buried charge, an explosion displaced huge quantities of earth from the levee and softened the surrounding soil to such an extent that the powerful surge of water immediately widened the crater. By late evening the breach in the levee was forty yards wide, and by morning it was seventy-five yards wide. It took several days for the water levels on either side of the levee to equalize.[11]

The gunboats and transports on which James King and the Fifth Iowa journeyed down the inland waterways above Vicksburg were so crowded that each company was assigned to some definite portion of a boat and was there confined until called on for fatigue duty. The experience was unpleasant, as the men were attacked by swarms of mosquitoes and plagued by snakes, heat, and biting insects of all varieties. The rivers were mostly impassable due not to low water, but to overhanging branches, leaning trees or fallen timbers left by the courtesy of patrolling bands of Rebels. The tall smokestacks were constant impediments to free passage. Removing the natural and man-laid obstructions became a regular fatigue duty for the Iowans. The greatest problem was finding and handling tackle heavy enough to lift the enormous trees that measured four feet across and weighed as much as thirty tons. One member of the 33rd Iowa wrote in his diary, "This was now peculiar soldiering. Heavy fatigue-details were made each day, or twice a day. The men had to get at the logs in the channel, cut them in two, or get them apart in some way, and then fasten ropes to them, by which to draw them out."[12]

Fortunately for James King, this duty lasted only a few weeks, as the fleet was repulsed at Fort Pemberton near Greenwood, at the confluence of the Yazoo and Tallahatchie Rivers. The Union force approaching Fort Pemberton consisted of nine gunboats and twenty seven transports, all loaded to the gunwales with troops. Its size, estimated at five thousand infantrymen, prompted the Confederates to take a drastic measure. In their possession was the captured steamer *Star of the West*, the historic ship that had drawn the first shots fired in Charleston harbor on January 9, 1861. With more than two hundred and fifty holes drilled in her hull she was scuttled abreast of the fort and broadside to the current. Passage further downstream was rendered impossible.[13]

On April 5 the transports began their retreat back upstream. When the soldiers saw the wide Mississippi River they became overjoyed to be relieved from the suffocating detail. One soldier wrote in his diary, "When our boat reached the Mississippi river, we fired a 'grand salute' of all the muskets on board, and the one six-pound brass field-piece on the bow—as a kind of greeting to the noble river. Cramped up as we had been for almost six weeks, on the narrow rivers in the swamps, it gave us a great feeling of relief, to come out again on the broad Mississippi, where there was room enough to breathe." Another observation revealed that the expedition was not without its casualties: "In some respects it was the hardest of our soldiering. Even when men have plenty of the roughest exercises, the army ration as usually issued, is not very well calculated to continue health; and when men are confined so closely on boats, and almost totally deprived of exercise, as we necessarily were, ill consequences must be expected. Diarrhea was universal, almost unanimous. Few of us remained in as good health as usual, and many contracted diseases to whose sad end the lonely graveyard on the bare Helena hills, within the next few months bore witness."[14]

Grant's movements carried James King further south down the Mississippi in anticipation of a landing beyond Vicksburg. He passed through Milliken's Bend, Perkin's Landing, and Hard Times, Louisiana, before taking part in the massive naval transport of men and material at Bruinsburg, Mississippi, on May 1, 1863.[15] Once on land King and his unit advanced through Port Gibson, Raymond, Clinton, Jackson, Champion Hill, and Big Black River Bridge and were at the outskirts of Vicksburg on May 19.

When the Fifth Iowa Infantry was shipped out in February 1864 to serve in the east, James King remained behind and accepted a promotion to become second lieutenant of the 11th Louisiana Colored Infantry. This unit was a new company of freed Louisiana slaves, formed during the previous summer. The 11th Louisiana had been tested in a hotly fought battle at Milliken's Bend on June 7, 1863. In that contest the Negro soldiers had proven to their skeptical command that they were worthy of praise and admiration. Up until that time the Negro soldier was considered untested in battle and, as Howell Hinds once put it, thought of by both sides only as a "wall" for the Union soldiers to hide behind.

At Milliken's Bend the Union forces faced an opposing army of fifteen hundred soldiers. Confederate General Henry E. McCulloch stated later that "The white or true Yankee portion ran like whipped curs almost as soon as the charge was ordered," while the colored troops resisted with "considerable obstinacy."

The action at Milliken's Bend was reduced to a vicious hand-to-hand fight and all witnesses agreed that the valor exhibited by the black troops was exemplary. General Grant observed of the action, "the capacity of the negro to defend his liberty, and his susceptibility to appreciate the power of motives in the place of the last, have been put to the test under our observation as to be beyond further doubt." A Union captain in the action stated more plainly, "I never more wish to hear the expression, 'The niggers won't fight.'"[16]

It was to this proven unit that Lieutenant James A. King was transferred by promotion on February 8, 1864. In March the 11th Louisiana Colored Infantry was reorganized as the 49th Regiment, U. S. Infantry. It remained stationed at Vicksburg with post and garrison duty until they were mustered out on March 27, 1866.

• • •

With final surrender at war's end came the realization that the aristocratic lifestyle of the southern planter was lost forever. Holt Collier "returned to Plum Ridge Plantation where the gin was burned, fences down, workstock gone and labor scattered."[17] He found on his return "a vastly different situation. He now had no indulgent master to dress him up in fine clothes, to give him breechloading shotguns and thoroughbred horses."[18] Though the conditions were vastly deteriorated, Howell Hinds, Thomas Hinds, and Holt Collier had no other real choice but to rely on each other to survive.

Postwar Mississippi was a grim place. Much of the country was devastated. Land was stripped of its very identity. With the exception of the occupying force of Union troops, there was no one to feed the homeless refugees. Nor was there anyone to care for the free roaming emancipated slaves who numbered in the thousands. Harvesting crops was absolutely essential to the immediate stability of the region, especially in the area of the Delta lands where so much wealth had been lost and so many freed slaves were without means. Greenville was completely destroyed. What had not been burned by the Union army had fallen victim to the meandering Mississippi River. The labor force necessary to rebuild the southern economy was scattered, but the planters did not want any outside influence mandating how it was to be collected or put to use. The vast wealth of the area was gone. All that was left was the blind pride of a vanquished people who deeply resented being subjected to the yoke of an oppressive occupation.

• • •

A soldier's wartime habits and practices were hard to leave behind in times of a fragile peace. The instinct to respond with deadly force, learned by Holt Collier during hostilities, would control him in several instances afterward.

Following the end of hostilities, Howell Hinds made a train trip to Kentucky to deliver his daughter Alice to school. Collier accompanied them as a manservant, much in the same manner as before the war. Just north of Memphis, Collier entered the sleeping car to assist Howell and the girl. The conductor protested his presence, presumably because of his race. The man grabbed the young former slave and, as Collier described the incident, "dragged me out same if I was a dog." Howell Hinds was not amused. Collier said of his former master that he "warn't goin to stan' nothin' like that. He jes' hauled off an' knocked that conductor down flat." Though Hinds never carried a weapon, Collier carried a pistol. At the time of the altercation, no one was aware that he was armed. According to Collier the conductor "pulled a six-inch bowie knife on the Cunnel. It was kinder fashionable in those days to carry a bowie knife; everybody had 'em 'cept the Cunnel; he never did carry nothin." To protect the unarmed Hinds, Collier did not hesitate to use his pistol. He drew and fired, intentionally striking the conductor in the hip. "I didn't want to kill 'im but I warn't goin' to let him kill the Cunnel. Co'se I would ha' kilt him, but I knew if I shot 'im it would keep him from stabbing the Cunnel. So I jes' shot 'im in the hip where 'twouldn't kill 'im."

Holt Collier was a grown man almost twenty and jaded by the experience of a bloody war, but after shooting the conductor, he was earnestly worried for his life. "I didn't know but what I would be killed the next minute, but I was sho' goin' to keep him from killing Cunnel Hinds." The authorities threatened to press charges, but were dissuaded by several of Hinds' friends on the train. Collier commented on his good fortune: "The white folks got me out of that trouble, 'cause the Cunnel had a world o' friends on that train. Gen'l Cheatham, he was there, and Doctor Newman, and they all took care o' me."[19]

• • •

James King's war experience earned him a promotion to captain by war's end and rendered him familiar with the Mississippi Delta. He remained in the state after his company was disbanded, and was assigned to Greenville, where he served with the Freedmen's Bureau. Bureau officers took custody of abandoned or confiscated lands, and issued rations, clothing, and medicine to destitute refugees and freedmen. They established schools, hospitals, and dispensaries and supervised tenements and camps for the homeless.[20] In this capacity it fell upon James King and others to educate, clothe, feed, and employ the former slaves.

The planters in need of labor were required to use the bureau to obtain farm hands. Contracts for employment were made with the bureau, and all payments were received by it for disbursement to the workers. Captain King and the uniformed northerners were a measure of salvation to the freedmen. However, like the Bureau of Indian Affairs in later years, the agency was fertile ground for corruption and graft. It was distrusted by defeated southern planters, who could not bring themselves to trust Captain James A. King or any of the occupying force.[21] According to Holt Collier, King raided Plum Ridge Plantation on several occasions, insulted the women, and tormented the impoverished Howell Hinds.[22] To Holt Collier, Captain James A. King was nothing less than a petty thief and tyrant who sought to punish the unreconstructed Howell Hinds.

• • •

In the spring of 1866, under a dire need to get his cotton planted and harvested, former slave master Thomas Hinds struck a deal with the abolitionist King for the supply of labor at Plum Ridge. From all indications King got the better part of the arrangement. In exchange for the use of twenty-five Negro laborers for the season, Hinds would deliver to King at harvest time a total of fifty bales of cotton–two bales for every laborer. The workers occupied themselves throughout the season, but some were slackers, and some became sick. As a result the cotton yield was light, and the price at market was much lower than expected.

By late summer it was readily apparent that Thomas Hinds would not be able to maintain his part in the bargain. When Howell Hinds learned that his son had struck a deal with King, and that it was a terribly poor business arrangement, he became livid and threatened to forever disclaim his son and to disinherit him for making such a contract with the much-hated Northerner. Thomas did all he could to redeem himself and cancel the contract, but King was steadfast in his refusal to renegotiate. Thomas went so far as to write the captain challenging him to a duel, but in a fashion typical of the younger Hinds, it was not specific as to time and place, and the challenge could not be answered.

When Howell Hinds confronted the much younger Northerner, King became physically aggressive and assaulted him. Although Hinds had been seriously wounded twice during the war, he was able to deflect the attack, knocking King down in the process. To gain the advantage King overpowered him, pulled a knife, and threatened to kill the unarmed Hinds. Rich Collier, Holt's cousin, intervened and prevented King from doing further damage. Such conduct, especially when the aggressor was so much younger and stronger, was considered an insult by Holt Collier.[23]

By harvest time it appeared that all was forgotten as Captain King ultimately compromised his position at one bale of cotton per laborer. On December 22, 1866, after King returned from a selling trip to Memphis, Holt Collier called upon him at his boarding house and delivered a note to the effect that King was invited to Plum Ridge that evening to collect his money. Soon after Collier departed Captain King saddled his horse and started for Plum Ridge.

The next morning King's riderless but saddled horse was found wandering the streets of Greenville. For some time no one paid any attention, as it was thought that the horse had simply broken loose. Later in the day, King's friend and possibly his stepbrother, Lieutenant John Meyers, rounded up some of his friends and went to Plum Ridge Plantation to investigate. The Hinds family claimed total ignorance of King's whereabouts. A search was conducted and tracks followed to a place where the horse had obviously left the road. From the marks it appeared that a person had fallen, and signs of a scuffle were clearly present.

The civil authorities refused to act on the matter. Meyers kept up the search and after a few days, the submerged body of James A. King was found in the hollow of a canebrake. He had been shot through, and his body was rifled of a watch, pistol, and as much as two hundred dollars. The killing and the disposal of the body was noticeably consistent with methods used by Evans's Scouts during the war.

The day of King's disappearance Thomas Hinds moved his cotton, including that portion contracted to King, to the river landing where it was shipped to New Orleans and sold. Thomas returned home several days later, but Holt Collier did not resurface for some time.[24] It was widely suspected by those investigating King's death that Thomas committed the murder and had disposed of Holt Collier in a similar fashion so as to allow for no witnesses.

King's death was reported in Iowa with obvious resentment. The Des Moines *Daily State Register* reported that a "few days after, Hines [sic] returned home without the negro, and many surmise he sleeps at the bottom of the Mississippi–'dead men tell no tales.' Hines [sic] lives and flourishes unmolested on his father's plantation, in possession of $2,000 of Capt. King's money; a murderer beyond all doubt, and the authorities refuse to interfere in the matter; it is considered no crime in the South to murder a 'Yankee' or a freedman."[25] In February 1867 King's body was removed by his heartbroken father to the bereaved Wittemberg community where it was interred with great ceremony.

With the exception of officers, the soldiers occupying Greenville were black. The death of Captain King was a blow to their morale. He had been a friend from the beginning, having fought mortal combat for the principle of their freedom, led them and trained them in service, and remained with them when he could have easily returned home. To those in the chain of command, the murder of an officer in uniform could not go unpunished.

As would be expected, the incident prompted harsh reaction from the bureau headquarters in Vicksburg. Correspondence began immediately following the discovery of King's body.

*January 18, 1867*
*letter from W. S. Meyers, Sub-Commissioner to Headquarters*

*"Requests that a small detachment of troops be stationed at Greenville. States that once the murder of Jas. A. King (illegible) a general feeling of insecurity exists not only among northern men but among the freemen. Says his life has been threatened and he has been publicly assaulted on the streets and unless he can have protection he will resign his position as Sub Commissioner."*[26]

Senior officers were not moved by Meyers' threatened resignation. Upon receipt of his alarming request he was summarily dismissed.

*January 25, 1867*
*directive from Headquarters*

*to the effect that W. S. Meyers is relieved of duty.*[27]

The Federal command did not ignore the request or the situation that existed in Greenville. King's death brought more undesired attention to Washington County than anyone might have expected. The day after Meyers was relieved, the counties of Washington, Bolivar, Sunflower, and Coahoma became an independent district of the Freedman's Bureau detached from the District of Vicksburg. As a result, the counties were occupied by Federal forces under the direct supervision of Major W. L. Ryan, who was ordered to Greenville immediately.

> *January 26, 1867*
> *Headquarters District of Mississippi*
> *Bureau of Refugees, Freedmen and Abandoned Lands*
> *Office of Assistant Commissioner for Mississippi*
> *Vicksburg, Miss. Jany 26, 1867*
>
> *General Orders*
> *No. 2 — The Counties of Washington, Bolivar, Sunflower and Coahoma in this State are hereby detached from the District of Vicksburg and will hereafter constitute the District of Washington, headquarters at Greenville, Mississippi, Brevet Major W. L. Ryan, sub commissioner in charge.*
>
>          *A. W. Preston, A.A.A.Genl.*[28]

Reaction to the killing of Captain King was not limited to the Mississippi Freedmen's Bureau. An unprecedented order was received from Washington, D. C. to use "terror" in the investigation and pursuit of the parties responsible for the outrage.

> *February 9, 1867*
> *Order from the War Department, Washington*
>
> *Orders that the murder in Mississippi, and assault on Capt. James in W. C. (Washington County) are so followed up as to strike the vile perpetrators of such outrages with terror.*[29]

Occupation and Court-Martial • 115

The directive to use terror in the pursuit of King's murderer did not go unheeded. Because of his military service with the Confederates, Holt Collier was much disliked by the black soldiers occupying Greenville and his capture was much anticipated. When he returned he was immediately arrested and charged with the killing. If convicted he would have certainly been hanged.

Collier's lifelong loyalty to Howell Hinds was reciprocated in the defense Hinds provided at Holt's trial. The impoverished Hinds found the funds to retain attorney William Alexander Percy to plead Collier's case before a military court-martial. Percy was an extremely capable man who, because of his prematurely graying hair and piercing eyes, was widely known as the Gray Eagle of the Delta. When Lincoln was elected, Percy had argued widely against the secession of the southern states. Nevertheless, he did not hesitate when called into Confederate service, organizing the Swamp Rangers, the first company to leave the Delta for active duty. Like Hinds, he became a general staff officer (to General John Bowen). Percy served in Mississippi until Vicksburg fell. He was transferred

*WARREN COUNTY COURTHOUSE, circa 1866.*

to Lee's Army of Northern Virginia where he served until returning to his home state in the war's last year.[30]

The court-martial of Holt Collier was conducted at Vicksburg. In addition to having Howell Hinds and Colonel Will Percy by his side, Collier was accompanied by several other distinguished leaders of Washington County. Also in attendance to help him escape if he were convicted were several of Evans's Texas Scouts. As the trial progressed, it became obvious that there was little or no credible evidence and that the prosecution was motivated by its resentment of Collier's previous service to the Confederacy.[31]

Of the killing of Captain King and the trial following, Harris Dickson wrote, "To the end of his life Holt would never tell the facts of this killing, not even to his best friend Senator Leroy Percy. He gave the details of his various trials, but not a syllable about how the officer got killed." Additionally Dickson wrote that six of Collier's "Texas comrades" were known to have been "loafing around the court to rescue Holt" in the event he had been convicted.[32]

The death of Captain John A. King and the trial that followed were the subject of speculation for generations and no one was ever convicted or brought to justice. Collier spoke in detail of the trial, the circumstances leading up to it, and his subsequent treatment at the hands of the Federal garrison after his acquittal.

"That's how come they tried to hang me after the war—because I was a soldier. They had me in the military court at Vicksburg; but Cunnel Percy and Cunnel Tom Marshall and all my white friends stuck to me and got me out. The whole lawsuit came up about a Yankee captain controlling a lot of colored soldiers over the levee yonder, in the cottonwood bushes. His name was Cap'n King. He put people out on all these plantations in companies, and they had to make crops. He had the bossing of them and the planters could not get labor. Cap'n King had men all over the country on different plantations. He put about twenty of them on this plantation of Mr. Howell Hinds. Cap'n King and the old Cunnel had some trouble about their business and had a fight. Cap'n King was a young man and Cunnel Hinds was about sixty years old; but he was tough, and mighty hard to whip. He never carried a pistol, only during the war. Cunnel Hinds was wrangling, and Cap'n King tripped him and threw him down. Old man Rich Collier, a cousin of mine, separated them. Cap'n King pulled out a knife on the old Cunnel, but finally they got separated.

"This fight happened in the negro quarters, 'bout three or four hundred yards from the big house. I was in the woods huntin' and didn't know nothin' about it until old man Rich Collier told me how 'twas. It sho' did rile me up. I jes' couldn't help saying, 'I'm mighty glad I warn't here— no, I ain't; I wisht I was here.

"Twarn't long after that 'til Cap'n King got killed alongside the road, down on the Ridge. These carpet-baggers 'cused me of killin' 'im. They arrested me by the military laws, but they never could prove anything and they turned me loose. Five different times the provost marshals come and got me. It looked like every little while they would send another provost marshal to investigate, and I would have to go up again.

"The last one that came here, he asked me a few questions and then he said, 'You go ahead. That's all right. If you did do it, you ought to have done it.'"[33]

• • •

Holt Collier did not return to Greenville immediately after his acquittal. His life would have been in great peril, and in all likelihood, he would have suffered retribution for the death of Captain King at the hands of the occupying forces. He certainly would have been a marked man. Hinds, Percy, and his other friends advised him of what confronted him if he returned. For once, Howell Hinds could not assure his safety. Ignorant of how long the occupation would last but confident he would one day return to the service of Howell Hinds, Collier joined his Texas comrades and traveled west to Fort Worth where he became a Texas cowboy.

# PART TWO

*HOLT COLLIER,
THEODORE ROOSEVELT
AND
THE ORIGIN OF
THE TEDDY BEAR*

# CHAPTER 10

# TO TEXAS AND
# A DISTANT FAREWELL

*"Shucks, I couldn't hang around no town."*
— Holt Collier

For Holt Collier the move to Texas in 1867 was a pleasant reunion of his soldier comrades with whom he had ridden and suffered in three years of war. He was especially anxious to see Captain Perry Evans and Colonel Sul Ross, and from Collier's account, they were pleased to see him. Through these connections he obtained employment near Fort Worth with Tom Evans, a brother of his former captain. He served as a ranch hand, breaking horses and herding cattle. While in Texas, Collier visited both Perry Evans and his former commander, Sul Ross, who, according to Collier, "had done got to be a justice o' de peace, or governor or somethin' out in Texas." Lawrence Sullivan Ross became a very important figure in Texas politics. He was elected governor of Texas in 1886 and reelected in 1888. When he retired from office he became president of Texas A&M College.

Collier's description of part of his Texas adventure survives. As Collier told the story, Ross and Evans "was glad to see me, but, shucks, I couldn't hang around no town." He had to get a job, and he wanted to work in the open range. "I met up with one ole soldier what said he could git me a job drivin' cattle, so him an' me went out an' tackled the foreman. It was way out on the open prairie jes' as level as a floor." The open prairie must have been unusual country for the young man, who had spent so much time of his life in the covered swamps and dense growth of the Mississippi wilderness.

When he arrived at the ranch, Collier was greeted by a host of strangers, all seasoned cowboys. Holt remembered that there "was a lot of cowboys standin' aroun' an' they sorter smiled when the foreman axed me, solemn-like, 'Holt, kin you ride a hoss?' I 'lowed I had rid a hoss several times back in Mississippi."

As was certainly the custom, every prospective hand on the place had to go through an initial test, an initiation, to become one of the chosen cowboys. The foreman met Holt and pointed out one particular wild mustang in the corral.

He asked: "There's a pretty good sorrel over yonder. Kin you ride 'im?"

Holt was apprehensive but answered. "Yes, sir, I kin ride 'im."

The new recruit must have been uncomfortable. Around him circled the other cowboys who paid particular attention to the small framed young black man.

"All the cowboys grinned, an' I seed a lot of 'em come ridin' up kinder keerless and whisperin' to each other."

The foreman told Holt: "Well, if you kin ride *dat* hoss I kin give you a job; but if you can't I ain't got no use fer you."

Holt described the horse as "a slim-built sorrel mustang with a left 'hind stockin' foot — an' mo' white in his eye than there is on a bedspread. He kinder stepped high, a-lookin' all ways at once."

Showing no fear, Holt accepted the challenge. Observing the large audience that had gathered Holt knew that to decline this test would be an invitation to leave this select group immediately. "Six or seven cowboys, all at once, brought out the hoss.... It took three men to put a saddle on 'im, and it sholy was a good seventy-five-dollar saddle, stropped down tighter'n Dick's hatband."

When the animal was ready, the foreman turned to Holt: "There he is,... 'them two men'll hole 'im while you gits on."

Holt was smarter and more confident than his appearances indicated. If he was going to ride the beast, he was going to do it his way. He was not about to be used purely for the pleasure of these men.

"Wait a minute, Cap'n,' says I; 'lemme have a pair o' spurs.' When I said that the man what was holdin' the sorrel's head kinder grinned an' dodged behind the hoss so I wouldn't see 'im." The foreman protested that Holt wouldn't "need no spurs with *that* hoss." The unexpected request surprised the foreman and amused the others.

The foreman was trying his best to keep a straight face when he told Collier, "An' when you git on 'im you'll be devilish glad you ain't got none."

Insisting on the spurs, Holt further horrified his tormentors by asking for some loaded pistols.

Holt said, "Cap'n, I want them spurs, anyhow–an', furthermore, I wants a pair o' six-shooters.' I kep' insistin' until I got the spurs an' six-shooters."

It was a new day on the ranch. The men had never seen a rounder arm himself and use spurs to tame a wild animal. They withdrew as a group to a safe distance.

Collier described the scene: "Then the cowboys began to move away, 'cause a skeered nigger on a bucking mustang ain't gwine to be perticular whichaway he shoots."

As Holt approached the animal he instructed the two men holding it, "Now, you two gentl'men what's holdin' o' this hoss, you let *me* have 'im."

Collier took the bridle and put as much tension on it as the horse would allow. "They let go o' the bridle, an' I pulled the hoss' head around jes' as hard as I could an' helt 'im tight."

It wasn't until this point in the tense moment that the group began to sense that this scrappy newcomer had merit. "The cowboys begun to look at each other as ef I mout know somethin' 'bout a hoss, after all."

The ride was made in the classic bronco bustin' style. Collier's own description needs no elaboration. "I got one foot in the stirrup an' made a spring — that is, *we* made a spring together, me an' the hoss, straight up in the air. An' we wouldn't never come down 'ceptin' there warn't nothin' in the sky to hold us up. I wrapped the bridle 'roun' the pummel o' the saddle, an' dug 'im with the spurs; an' every time he hit the groun' I let off a couple o' shots — you know that encourages 'em to go ahead instead o' jumpin' up an' down in one place. An' he sho' *did* go ahead."

The confident rider welcomed the openness of the land. There were no trees to impede his efforts and there was no limit to how long he could ride the horse before it exhausted itself. The pistol was used to maximum effect.

Collier described his ride, "Twarn't nothin' to knock ag'inst, no tree in a milyun, an' I knowed he couldn't git me off. So we lit out, him and me, like hell-a-beatin'-tan'bark, acrost the prairie. An' when he wanted to quit I'd job 'im with the spurs an' let off another shot."

Horse and rider traveled for a long distance before the animal finally wore out and gave up the fight. According to Collier, "After a while I turned 'im 'roun' an' rid back to camp, jes' as nice an' easy as ef I was a lady goin' to church."

The cowboys were thoroughly impressed. Collier became one of them. He was exuberant. "That's how I got a job drivin' cattle."[1]

For more than a year Holt enjoyed the solitude of the saddle and the camaraderie of his cowboy friends, far removed from the discord he had left in Mississippi. Collier claimed to have met the outlaw Frank James while in Texas. Though this claim cannot be confirmed, several soldiers who rode with Frank James and William Clarke Quantrill during the war did settle nearby, including one named Tom Evans. During the war Quantrill had made his headquarters near Sherman, Texas, just north of Fort Worth.[2]

• • •

Back in Mississippi, partisan divisions were deeply felt between close neighbors and were no longer confined to political borders or men in uniform. Occupation by the Federal army brought favoritism toward old allies and "bayonet rule" against those known to have taken up arms against the Union. Blind eyes were turned in many cases, and often the local civil authorities, many appointed by the occupying forces, were reluctant to act.

Extreme poverty knew no racial barriers. It existed among whites and blacks alike. Howell Hinds and Thomas Hinds were not exempt from poverty. Having wagered their all on the success of the Confederacy, their postwar existence was burdened by ever-increasing debt. Desperate efforts were made to save Home Hill in Jefferson County, but Hinds lost it to creditors in 1867 and moved his family to Plum Ridge, never to return. At Plum Ridge Plantation, Howell schemed to avoid his obligations by conveying substantial tracts of land to his son Thomas. This ruse was unsuccessful, as a mortgage on the property had been properly recorded. One creditor sued Hinds for a debt of more than thirty-nine thousand dollars, an impossible sum for him to repay in the depths of such despair. Other civil suits were brought, and it seemed only a matter of time before Plum Ridge Plantation would be lost as well.[3]

Neither were Howell or Thomas free of criminal litigation, and it is unlikely that the authorities filed false charges. Howell was involved in "an indictment for an affray" against Henry Richardson in December 1867. No disposition is recorded.[4]

The problems facing Thomas Hinds were more serious, and much more personal in nature. He had been married to Victoria Sullivan on January 30, 1858, but there is no record of children from the marriage. Nor is there any record of a divorce or of the death of Victoria. What became of her is unknown. In 1867 Thomas was charged with the offense of "fornication," almost certainly having been committed with twenty-five year old Augusta, a former slave and sister to Holt Collier. Along with her daughter, Anna, she had been listed on the deed of gift from Howell Hinds to Thomas Hinds dated July 16, 1861. There is no proof of a conviction on the fornication charge, but the court costs were assessed against Thomas, normally an indication of some degree of culpability.[5]

Other litigation included a civil suit filed by the destitute Howell Hinds against his neighbors, the prominent Harriet B. Theobald and William C. Blanton. Mrs. Harriet Blanton Theobald was considered the "Mother of Greenville." At the conclusion of the war, she had sold a substantial portion of her Blantonia Plantation for the new site on which Greenville would be rebuilt. The Blanton family were early settlers of the county. They were loyal unionists, and unlike so many others, had survived the war financially intact. The court case was initiated by Hinds and involved a property dispute. The merits of the suit are unknown, but the existence of the litigation is a clear indication that real tension existed between these adjoining landowners.

• • •

The Carvelle saloon in Greenville was a popular local tavern frequented by several of the town's gentlemen. On the early summer night of May 13, 1868, Howell Hinds and E. P. Byrne, Thomas Hinds's former artillery commander, were there to drown away their mutual financial woes. Also present were Dr. Thomas G. Polk and Dr. Orville M. Blanton. Blanton was a son of Harriet Theobald and brother of William C. Blanton, defendants in the property dispute with Howell Hinds. Described by his wife at their Belle Air Plantation in 1859 as "having a mania for buying negroes," Dr. O. M. Blanton had nevertheless been a Union sympathizer during the war and, as previously mentioned, claimed to have been victimized and threatened with execution on several occasions by Perry Evans's Scouts, Holt Collier's old outfit with whom Howell Hinds sometimes rode.[6]

It had recently been published that the two physicians had taken an oath of allegiance to the Union and had been successful in having their political disabilities removed by Congress. Dr. Blanton had been appointed justice of the peace the previous January and in that capacity was a likely consort of the occupying forces.[7] The thought of the Unionist doctor in such a position of authority angered both Byrne and Hinds. Calling the two doctors out, Byrne claimed that he "could whip any man born north of Mason and Dixon's line, or any man that would affiliate with them."

Not willing to be abused in public, Blanton and Polk quietly left the Carvelle saloon through the rear door and made their way across the yard to the Courtney House, where they hoped to enjoy more pleasurable company. Edward Byrne followed the men into the yard intending to press the point. Though Byrne was unarmed, Blanton became infuriated, displayed a knife, and stabbed Byrne several times. When it became evident that the assault had turned deadly, Hinds grabbed Blanton from behind so as to limit the bloodshed, but this act only angered the doctor further. With a backward thrust Blanton imbedded the knife deeply into the abdomen of Howell Hinds mortally wounding him. He died painfully several hours later.

Howell Hinds was buried in Greenville's city cemetery. A simple stone bearing his name once marked his grave but was removed when the lot was converted into a playground. Soon after his funeral, the Greenville paper reported a gruesome tale "that ghouls had opened his grave and severed one of his hands–no motive could be ascribed for the perpetration of such a wretched deed."[8]

Dr. Blanton claimed not to remember stabbing Hinds. The verdict of the coroner's inquest fixed the cause of death upon him and no other person. Blanton's friends claimed that he wept bitterly when he learned of Hinds's death, all the while he proclaimed his innocence. His actions revealed a different intent, however, as he immediately fled certain arrest and went into an extended self imposed exile.

Years later Blanton gave testimony on his wartime treatment and on the murder of Howell Hinds before a federal commission considering a war claim of his wife: "I was taken back to Indian Bayou by the Confederate Scouts because I turned some mules over to the Union Army and they threatened to hang me on account of my intimacy and supposed friendship for the Union officers and soldiers. After the war I was frequently accosted and upon one occasion when I was assaulted by Col. Howell Hinds and Major E. P. Byrne, I had to use my knife. I killed Hinds and inflicted several dangerous wounds on Byrne. For this I was hunted with dogs by the same mad disunionists that had their sway during the war, who threatened to hang me if I was captured."[9]

Blanton's exile lasted five years. With an indictment pending, he would have been arrested immediately upon his return. He claimed to have hidden out in a foreign country immediately following his hasty departure, and later he lived with his wealthy mother at her Elizabeth, New Jersey, home.

Blanton's mother, Harriet Theobald, was a woman of means and a tyrant in her personal affairs. During her son's absence she made several unsuccessful attempts to sell the family holdings in Mississippi. She advised her son "never to look back on Sodom." She was in control of the family situation and often refused to deliver Orville's letters to his wife and his "three helpless little girls," whom Dr. Blanton had left without support. Other family members asked among themselves, "Will Mrs. T. never get too old to think of meanness?"[10]

• • •

Although he had every fear that returning to occupied Greenville would present life-threatening difficulties, Holt Collier, upon receiving news of the murder of Howell Hinds, wasted no time in making the journey home. His purpose was unmistakable. He would exact retribution on the man who had committed the dastardly act, regardless of his social position or wealth. Collier's intentions became known by the friends of Howell Hinds who, like him, were outraged.

Holt Collier spoke many years later of the way his beloved friend had died. "It sho' did seem like a pity for my ole master to git kilt right here in dis street, stabbed to death with a knife, and 'twarn't none o' his fight no way. He jes' went in to separate 'em an' cotch de lick."[11]

Collier's return caused an immediate and expected reaction from the Federal authorities who continued to occupy the state. He remained the most likely suspect in the unsolved murder of Captain James A. King and for that crime he was arrested several times. Each time he was released, but the intimidation was clearly to maintain pressure until he confessed or until charges could be brought and proven.

Collier described those experiences often, "After the war there was a whole lot of carpet-baggers come down here and I had a heap of trouble with 'em.... I sho' did have a tough time in them reconstruction days. I had to look out for myself all the time, and didn't sleep much."

To Collier, the reasons for the difficulties were clear. "They all hated me, because I had been a soldier. I reckon I was the only colored man down here that had been a soldier in the Confederate war." The animosity felt against Collier was returned in kind. "I never would have anything to do with the carpet-baggers. They came down here and misled the colored people and sold 'em out, then ran off and went to the Northern countries."

On one occasion when Collier was severely intimidated by the soldiers, he started shooting at them. He did not intend to harm anyone, but the act served to complicate his problems. Whenever he would tie his horse in town and be seen by the "colored soldiers at old Greenville...they'd be jumpin' on 'im and galloping off jes' to make me mad. You know how biggety a nigger is when he gits on a uniform."

Collier said that he "stood it as long as I could; then we had a rookus and I took a crack at some of 'em, but didn't kill none."

The authorities reacted as expected. "Dat brought on a whole lot more talk an' 'sputin' an' jawin' back an' forth 'bout me shootin' at the soldiers."

Thomas Hinds, inadequate in past difficulties, seemed to be effective in mediating some of Holt's problems with the military authorities. Unlike his predecessors, the Federal officer in charge at the time did not press charges. The soldiers had been away from camp without leave. Collier recalled that, "They had a white cap'n, an' me an' Mr. Tom Hinds had to go over there to explain it to him. The cap'n acted mighty nice 'bout it. The soldiers didn't have no right out o' camp, nohow. He put 'em all in the guard-house right away."

The Federal officer supported Collier in the incident, lecturing his men for their insolence. "I told how they were treatin' me an' he went out and read out of a great big book to 'em. He had a whole lot to say. He told 'em they must remember that I had as much right to be in the Southern army as they had to be in the Republican army." The officer went even further making it clear to his men that Holt Collier had "a right to carry my pistol, an' he told me if anybody bothered me, an' I got the best of it, jes' to light out and make it there to him. He'd see that I got a fair chance. He treated me mighty nice. I got out of that trouble an' they let me alone."[12]

• • •

By harvest time in 1868 both Edward P. Byrne and Thomas Hinds, whose families were considered wealthy prior to the war, had lost everything. They filed for bankruptcy that year in the U. S. District Court for the Southern District along with several prominent citizens, including Blanton's friend, Dr. Thomas G. Polk.[13]

Holt Collier returned to Plum Ridge and worked in the field alongside several other former slaves doing what he could to help make it profitable. Harrison and Daphne Collier were aged and Thomas was the only white person on the property. Holt lived with twenty-two-year-old Mary, who was likely his sister or a member of the family who was listed on the July 16, 1861, deed of gift from Howell to Thomas. Others living with Holt in 1870 were twenty-two-year-old Meriam, a male, and Benjamin, aged twelve.[14]

In 1872 Thomas Hinds and the Collier family relocated to the nearby vicinity of Stoneville and abandoned the dwelling house at Plum Ridge, which was finally lost to debt. A small portion of the plantation was allowed to be kept by Howell's widow as exempt homestead property, even though she had lived in St. Louis for years.[15] Mary Ann Hinds relocated out of state soon after Howell's death. Her move was a result of her impoverished status and her desire to protect her four daughters from the social stigma associated with the well-known tryst existing between Thomas Hinds and Augusta Collier.

• • •

In the same year a movement began in the Reconstruction state government, then very much under the control of the Republicans, to allow Dr. Blanton to return to Greenville. An indictment remained pending, and his return would have meant instant arrest and trial for the murder of a southern patriot by a unionist.

Local opinion against Blanton ran high as fliers were circulated and displayed in area homes. The circulars bore a likeness of Hinds and read: "*Colonel Howell Hinds, murdered by Dr. Orville M. Blanton, at Greenville, Mississippi, May 13, 1868, while trying to save his friend Maj. Edward P. Byrne, from assassination by Blanton.*"[16] Continued community interest in prosecuting the case precluded Blanton's supporters from having the charges dismissed at the local level.

Political favors were summoned, and the full weight of Mrs. Theobald's influence was called upon. Beginning in May petitions were received in the office of Governor R. C. Powers, seeking a grant of executive clemency. Governor Powers was a Republican and an 'affluent carpetbag landowner.'[17] The petitions were signed by several prominent citizens described as "southern gentlemen, most of whom served in the Confederate army."

The final petition, received by Governor Powers on November 1, 1872, was from veteran politician William Lewis Sharkey. He wrote a long persuasive appeal for Blanton reciting erroneously that the doctor had been protecting "the character of his wife who had been grossly slandered." William Lewis Sharkey was a noted Mississippi politician of long standing who ironically had political ties to General Thomas Hinds dating back to 1828, when they joined together to support Andrew Jackson for President. Sharkey had been the chief justice of the Mississippi Supreme Court, provisional governor by appointment of President Andrew Johnson in 1865,[18] and a United States senator following the war. Sharkey's plea must have been effective. A full pardon for Dr. Orville M. Blanton was granted by the governor that same day.[19]

Before Dr. Blanton could return home, one final measure had to be taken. Mary Ann Hinds, Howell's widow and the former mistress of Home Hill and Plum Ridge and probably the only person who could have succeeded in the mission, visited Holt Collier at Stoneville. She persuaded him to allow Howell's death to go unpunished. Collier gave her his promise that he would "never carry the matter any further."[20]

• • •

As though destruction from the war were not enough, cotton prices during the early 1870s fell to an average of only seventeen cents per pound. The depression of 1873 brought about an end to stable wages for blacks and arrested the modest progress of the late 1860's and early 1870s toward the growth of a class of independent black farmers. Disastrous floods affected the Delta in 1874, making crops even more difficult to plant and harvest.[21] From these harsh financial realities was born the practice of sharecropping, a process whereby the laborer was no longer paid a wage. He was rented a parcel of land upon which to work and raise a crop, and he paid a percentage as rent when his crop was harvested and sold. The contract made the sharecropper heavily reliant upon the land owner, who advanced seed, tools, and other provisions on credit against the final harvest.

The freedmen were not willing to farm the most productive lands because they were more expensive to rent and more accessible by the land owner. Instead, they preferred to use the unimproved lands along the edge of the Delta wilderness which were cheaper and more remote. "Not only was the rent lower under this arrangement, but direct supervision by the planter was more difficult, and tenants could supplement their rations from the game that the forest harbored."[22]

Other than mules and horses there was little livestock to speak of in the Delta, as all cleared land was in cultivation. Yearly flooding was an ever present risk of owning cattle. Plentiful wild game provided an ample supply of meat, and to the hunter an occasional supplementation of income. It was to this particular endeavor that Holt Collier was drawn. He was an accomplished marksman, had been raised with hunting dogs and horses, knew the swamp wilderness, and, being of independent personality, was an unlikely candidate for sharecropping.

CHAPTER 11

# THE HUNTER

*"Money don't buy nothin' in the cane-brake, nohow;
and a man's dog don't care whether he's rich or po."*
— Holt Collier

•••

Carpetbag rule officially ended in 1875 with an election that ousted the Republicans and brought into power the Democratic Party that would rule Mississippi politics for the next one hundred years. The election in Washington County was a hard-fought political battle, and Holt Collier was involved because of his influence with others of his race. Collier later said of the election of 1875 that it "was against the white people. And when we was having so much trouble in this country with the Republicans and colored people, these carpet-baggers tried to bribe me to turn and go with them. They offered me three thousand dollars to go with them and I wouldn't take it. The party offered me that. They wanted me to go with them and canvass, and go all around the country helping them to get up riots and one thing and another. They had a red wagon with guns in it. But I didn't accept it." Holt's loyalty was clearly with the old guard. "I went with the Southern people to all the voting places. I had this same rifle with me then that I am shooting now."[1]

•••

During the last quarter of the nineteenth century three new industries dramatically altered and expanded the economy of the Mississippi Delta. Timber production became a thriving enterprise as the vast forests were slowly cut back to bring more land into cultivation. The demand for virgin timber from the Delta swamps in turn prompted the expansion of a rail system, and large-scale levee con-

*HOLT COLLIER, erect in the saddle at the age of 61.*

struction was initiated as the planters began an organized effort to protect their cotton fields from the annual flooding that had devastated crops for so many years. With each industry came the employment of laborers and the need of additional resources for an expanding population.

In these prosperous circumstances Holt Collier recognized an opportunity to earn a living without having to pick cotton or work in the fields. An abundance of wild game and Collier's knowledge of the vast wilderness made him well suited for an occupation as a professional hunter. Mississippi white tail deer was a prime source of meat, and it was plentiful and considered an easy kill. Deer meat was not as much in demand as the meat of the black bear. Deer were small and sold for only thirty cents per pound field-dressed. A full-grown bear could earn a hunter sixty dollars or more.[2]

Hunting game in the Delta swamps was a seasonal matter that began after the animals had foraged in the late summer and early fall.

# The Mississippi Delta
(circa 1902)

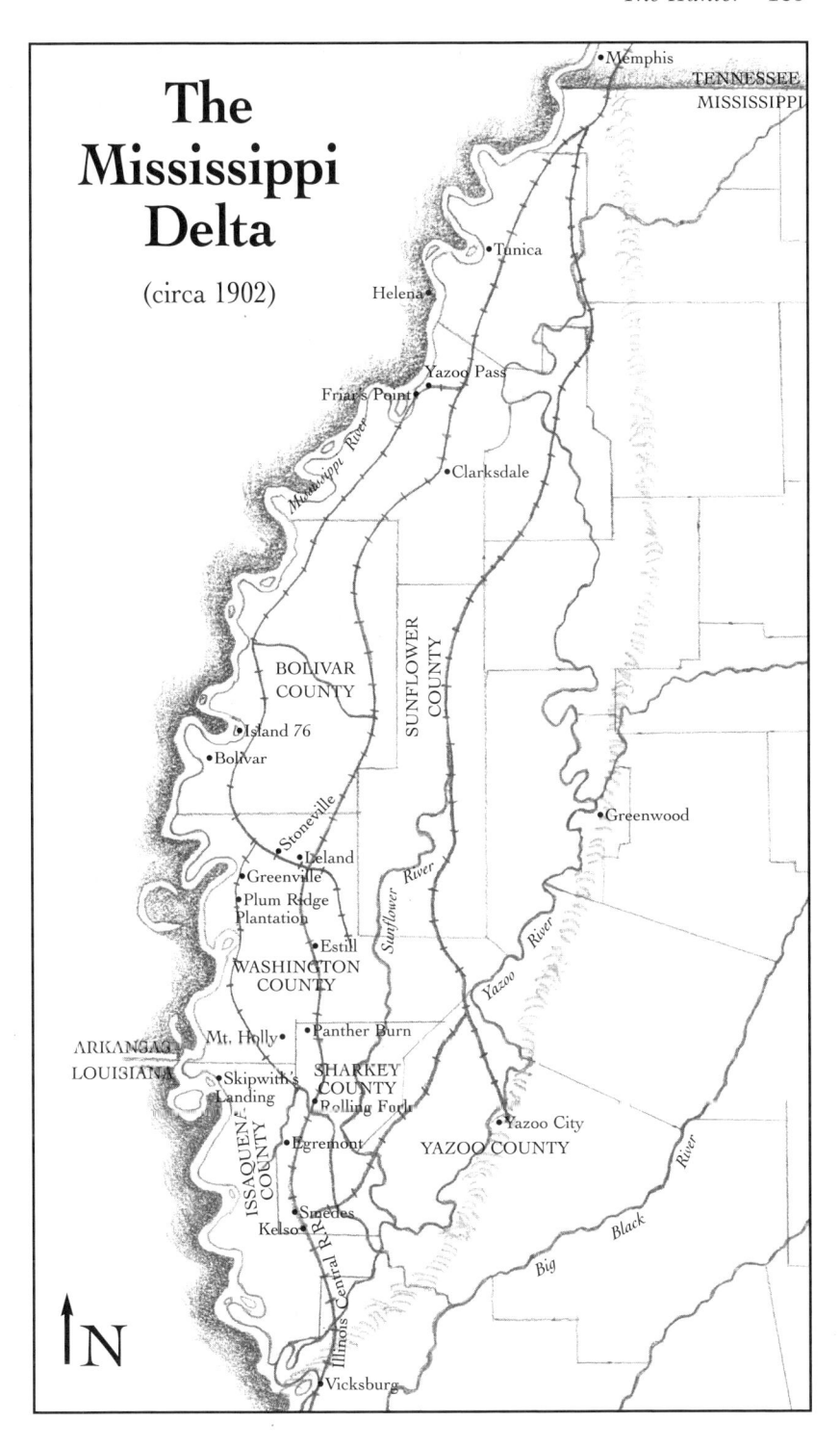

They would gorge themselves to gain weight and supply their bodies with sufficient strength and energy to survive the lean winter. A hunt in the swamps could not begin until the miasmatic organisms, mosquitoes, and other insects had been killed or reduced by the first frost. Terrain in the swamp was always marked by the alluvial deposits from the previous spring's overflow. The annual floods destroyed the undergrowth and left high water marks of mud stained rings on the tall cottonwood trees normally twenty feet high overhead. The high grounds of the swamps were the natural levee ridges running along the banks of the bayous where the stands of cane grew their thickest.[3]

Louisiana black bears *(Ursus americanus luteolus)* were plentiful in the Mississippi Delta but very difficult to track and kill. The bears were not particularly ferocious unless hungry, wounded, protecting their young, or at bay. Hunting them was an extreme physical challenge, and any man successful at the sport was a respected nimrod, regardless of his race or background.

In fact, it was a common test of courage to kill a bear with a Bowie-style knife rather than a gun. This method of achieving the kill was well-accepted by the experienced Delta hunters. The bear would be approached from the side while distracted by the dogs and the knife plunge was always made on the opposite side of the bear from the position of the hunter. James Gordon, author of an 1881 article on the subject, wrote, "The experienced hunter always strikes a bear from the opposite side to which he stands, as the bear is sure to turn to the side from whence he receives the blow; and woe to the unlucky hunter caught in his death-grasp."[4]

Canebrakes were almost impenetrable masses of growth and made the most secure lairs for the panther, wildcat, and bear, all of which Holt Collier hunted. These hunting grounds were difficult to reach, and to make a camp required specialized equipment. A good mule or horse capable of withstanding these harsh conditions was a necessity. It was in and about these vast domains, often covering hundreds of acres, that the majority of Collier's kills took place.

Theodore Roosevelt described these vast domains of cane in 1908 when he wrote that, "The canebrakes stretch along the slight rises of ground, often extending for miles, forming one of the most striking and interesting features of the country. They choke out other growths, the feathery, graceful canes standing in ranks, tall, slender, serried, each but a few inches from his brother, and springing to a height of fifteen or twenty feet. They look like bamboos; they are well-nigh impenetrable to a man on horseback; even on foot they make difficult walking unless free use is made of the heavy bush-knife. It is impossible to see through them for more than fifteen or twenty paces, and often for not half that distance. Bears make their lairs in them, and they are the refuge for hunted things."[5] In addition to the cane, the Delta was thickly crowded with cypress, oaks, gums, and sycamores and cottonwoods of immense size, some measuring ten feet in diameter.

The black bear would usually make its bed by cutting and piling stalks of cane into a comfortable pallet, and it was known never to sleep on a wet bed. Its diet consisted of wild grape, acorn, muscadine, persimmon, pecan, hickory nuts, the farmer's corn or melon crop, a small rodent or piglet, and honey, of which it was excessively fond. Though it was considered unsportsmanlike, some pothunters would place in the bear's path a vessel of a honey and whiskey mix which would easily intoxicate it.[6]

A successful bear hunter relied heavily on his pack of mixed-breed dogs to chase and corner the bruin. It is said that "a bear dog belongs to no particular breed, that he is an accident," and that of a large number of such animals only one might be found that "takes to b'ar." Holt Collier once described Mandy, the most reliable dog he ever owned. She had been badly cut by a bear once. Afterward she would hunt only deer or wildcat, "but when ole Mandy come in and got right between my legs I knowed it was a bear an' no mistake. Mandy never guessed wrong 'bout a bear — not one time."[7]

James Gordon explained that there were dogs of varying sizes in each pack, "A few rough-haired terriers, active and plucky, that can fight close to Bruin's nose and dodge under the cane when pursued; some medium-sized dogs to fight on all sides, and a few large, active curs to pinch his hindquarters when he charges in front or crosses an opening in the woods."[8] Most varieties of dogs would have to be able to fight close to their prey, though not necessarily to hold the bear.

The pack was a social organization whose members would bite and seize hold of the bear only when another from the pack was in the bear's clutches. Once their comrade was released, they in turn would release the bear. The dogs would continue to intimidate and malign the beast until it would take to a tree and there become easy prey for the hunter following not far behind.[9] Collier often spoke of his dogs as if they were old friends. "My dogs would fight a bear three or four days an' nights until they 'most starved to death, waitin' for me to come. I often found 'em the third or fourth day treein' or fightin'. Me an' them both has lived off o' raw meat, an' not cared whether 'twere cooked or not."[10] Collier's pack of dogs was his pride and joy, and were envied by other hunters in the Delta. He was once offered one thousand dollars for the pack, an offer he refused even to consider.

Tracking the bear was an art unto itself. The bruin was a creature of habit that always followed an existing trail. An experienced hunter would be able to examine the tracks of a bear and determine the bear's size and its gender. The fatter the bear, the further his hind toe marks would be from his fore toe marks, indicating an obstruction in its stride. After following the bear for some distance, indications would always be detected if the bear had marked tree bark and how high. If the tree was marked, the animal was a male. The higher the mark, the bigger the bear.[11]

For an avid hunter the chase through the wilderness swamps on the bear hunt was one of the finest thrills known. Harriet Theobald once wrote that, "Hunting was the gentleman's one unalloyed sport. Who can describe to those who never felt it, the thrill of excitement and pleasure 'when the huntsman winds his horn,' and the pack leap out on the scent in full cry. To the isolated settler there was a bond between him and his dogs. They were a joy by day and a guard by night. No modern music ever made my heart leap as the sound of the cry in a spirited chase has done."[12]

• • •

With the passing of years, Holt Collier's reputation as a bear hunter grew until by the turn of the century it had reached heroic proportions, at least on a local level. He averaged about 125 kills a season, and kept a book count of more than 2,100 kills until the book burned in his brother Marshall's house about 1890. Collier earned more than nine hundred dollars in one season and was known to have as much as two thousand dollars in his possession at one time. These

*Holt Collier on the bank of the Little Sunflower.*

were phenomenal amounts of money for a black man in the Mississippi Delta and more than most people earned in a year.

When not on the hunt, Collier led what could easily be described as a cavalier lifestyle. He indulged in the one vice that haunted him his entire life, gambling. It is apparently from several sources that he never drank alcohol. At the annual spring fairs he played poker and faro and wagered heavily on horse races. In the summer he enjoyed playing baseball, and in 1877 he financed a team that received local attention. It was named 'Holt Collier's Club' from Deer Creek.[13]

Following the hunting season every year, Collier traveled in any direction and to any destination that suited him. He sometimes went west to Texas and followed the spring fairs. He went south to the racetracks and fairs of Louisiana. Most years he would return home penniless.[14] His friends urged him to save money, settle down, and buy some property for a house. Collier did not heed their warnings. He preferred to live in the swamp or with friends while storing his meager belongings at the Greenville stable and at the home of his brother Marshall.

The spring immediately following one of his most successful years, Collier was wealthy by Delta standards. With two thousand dollars in his pocket he went north to follow the seasonal races and local fairs, much in the same manner he had done with Howell Hinds in the prosperous years before the war. Collier was confident that he knew horses and could pick the winners. He took the train north but soon discovered that a "free negro with cash had a different appeal to northern philanthropists." He fell victim to the experienced gamblers who stripped him clean, and he had to telegraph home for railroad fare.[15]

This routine was an annual ritual for Collier. "In the spring I'd go away an' foller the races, same as I used to — St. Louis an' Saratoga an' New Orleans, an' way out in Texas takin' in the fairs. Then in the fall I'd come home, git my dogs together and hit the cane-brake again — I jes' nacherly loved a hoss and loved to hunt bears. Didn't do nothin' much 'cept hunt."

The yearly loss of his hard-earned money had little effect on the unregimented sportsman. It was not his desire to be domesticated, and he had little use for money in the swamp. His life revolved around his dogs, the hunt and his "frolicking around."

Collier freely admitted his wasteful habits. "'Now, Holt, you must buy you a home an' settle down; that'll take care o' you for de balance o' your life' — Cap'n he talk mighty sensible — but money sho' do burn a hole in a nigger's pocket. Ev'ry time I put my hand in there an' felt a dollar I cotch the travel itch, until I jes' couldn't keep off'n the train. So I slipped off from the Cap'n and went back to Kentucky to visit some friends near Bardstown. Den I cotch the racin' fever, an' lit out for Brighton Beach. Well, you know how 'twas — got home without a cent, but didn't make no difference to me. Money don't buy nothin' in the cane-brake, nohow; and a man's dog don't care whether he's rich or po'."[16]

In addition to the money he earned hunting, Collier was also a paid deputy sheriff for his old comrade in arms, Major George Helm. Helm lived in Stoneville and had been elected sheriff after the ouster of the Republicans. During Reconstruction the "rough element of the community had a habit of breaking into the jail whenever they wanted to administer quick justice." Helm was elected on a promise that all prisoners would be protected from mob violence. To accomplish his goal, he approached Holt Collier to serve as deputy with specific orders to guard the jail. "So the Major chose Holt Collier, sat him down at the door with a shot gun across his lap and orders to shoot. No mob ever tried to rush him because they knew that Holt would obey orders, would shoot and wouldn't miss."[17]

During the late nineteenth and early twentieth century, Holt Collier maintained a special, if not unique, relationship with many wealthy Delta planters, all men of considerable influence. Attorney William Alexander Percy, namesake of the author of *Lanterns on the Levee*, remained a life-long good friend, and it fell to Collier to train Percy's son Leroy, a future U. S. senator, the finer points of quail hunting. Wade Hampton III, one of the wealthiest men in America and an accomplished bear hunter in his own right, was one of the many prominent friends of Holt Collier. Hampton was a Confederate general, governor of South Carolina from 1876 to 1878, and U. S. senator from 1878 to 1890. He owned the Delta plantation Walnut Ridge and hunted there frequently. Hampton was once thrown from his mule and injured his leg so badly that part of it was amputated, but according to Collier, "that never stopped him from hunting."[18]

• • •

Over the years Holt Collier's hunting exploits became well known and were given wide currency throughout the region. On one particularly difficult chase Holt followed his dogs to a huge fallen tree that was hollowed by years of internal decay. He could hear the bear that had sought refuge in the log. The beast had been in a desperate fight with several of Holt's dogs, one of which was trapped inside the log with the bear. To allow a dog to be mangled or killed was unacceptable to any hunter of honor. The animals were highly regarded, and the death of one could spoil the others against the hunt. Collier's pack was "famous throughout the lower Mississippi Valley.... This was more than his pack; it was his life."[19]

When he saw what had happened, Collier did not hesitate. With his knife clutched in hand and at the ready he crawled into the open end of the log. One of his companions tried to stop him by grabbing his ankle as he made his way into the fallen tree, but he was only successful in pulling off a boot. The hollow of the tree was a tight fit for man, dog, and bear. Holt had to crawl on hands and knees to get to his dog and also to maintain a defensive posture with which to encounter the enraged bear. He entered the dark lair with no regard for stench, heat, or danger. His only purpose was to save his dog. The bear was cornered and frightened as the light from its only exit was obscured as Collier crawled into the log. As the animal lunged past him in a desperate effort to escape the hunter stabbed the bear several times. From its wounds the bear collapsed and died in the narrow opening trapping Holt inside. Had it not been for his companion who tied a rope to the carcass and pulled it free before it became turgid, Holt Collier would likely have perished that day.

The story of Collier's narrow escape became a legend among the hunters of the Mississippi Delta and was told and retold for years around the campfires of his guided hunts. In later years Collier described the incident in vivid detail, "The closest I ever got was one time in a big hollow log. The bear was plum tired out, and it run into the log. I had a fool young dog that run in right behind him. He was such a fine dog that I hated for the bear to kill him. I heard him whine once or twice. Then I crawled in with a knife in my hand, caught the dog by his legs and pulled him past the bear. I stuck the bear three or four times with the knife, and he cum squeezing out by me; but he didn't make no 'tempt to do nothin' 'cept to git away. The log was pretty big on the inside, but it got kinder nerrer up toward the mouth, and by me stabbin' 'im so swif' the bear got twisted up and died right there. Ef I had been by myself, like I mostin generally was, there wouldn't been no way on earth for me to git out o' that log. I mout've pulled the bear out, but I could never shove him out from behind. The nigger what was with me had done run away, but when he found the bear was dead for keeps, he cum back and pulled him out. That was the closest I ever got to a bear, and the closest I ever wants to git."[20]

Holt did consider that he could dismember the bear and throw it behind him, piece by piece, but this strategy was unnecessary when the carcass of the bear was pulled free The incident was considered by Collier as his most perilous hunting experience.[21]

• • •

According to the census of 1880, Holt Collier was thirty-four years old and lived with twenty-nine-year-old Rose Collier, who was identified in the census records as his wife. There is no record of a civil ceremony between them, though common law marriages were recognized at the time. With them lived three children, daughters Effy, age twelve, Maggie, age two, and son Coley, age seven.[22] What became of Rose and the children is not known.

By 1880 most of Collier's family and old friends had left the old Plum Ridge Plantation and relocated a few miles east near Stoneville, close to the home and plantation of George Helm. Most of the former bondsmen were sharecroppers. Harrison, Holt's father, was dead, and his mother Daphne was very elderly. Several Colliers lived nearby, including his brothers Marshall, Topp, J. B., Marimon, and Allen.

Thomas Hinds was forty nine years old in 1880 and also lived nearby with his ever-growing family. In the census that year he was identified as a farmer and the head of a household. He continued to live openly with Collier's sister, Augusta, who in this census record was identified as a Hinds. Augusta's child Anna was nineteen years old and living with them and, like Augusta, was identified as a Negro and a Hinds in that census. Other children living with Augusta and Thomas were also identified with the surname of Hinds—Ernest, age sixteen, Robb, age fourteen, Evie, age twelve, Floyd, age seven, Alice, age six, and Tulley, age two. All of these children were identified as mulatto. The enduring union between Thomas and Augusta created a blood bond between the Hinds and Collier families that would last forever. The issue of Thomas Hinds and Augusta Collier are the only known Mississippi descendants of the once famous General Thomas Hinds.[23]

• • •

Floyd, Louisiana, an inland community located downstream and across the Mississippi River from Greenville, in West Carroll Parish, was a wild town where liquor was readily available and people were quick to draw their weapons to settle disputes. Bill "Wild Cat" Bradley was sheriff of the parish. One of his recently-hired deputies was Travis Sage, spoken of by his defenders as a quiet, inoffensive, timid young man, although his subsequent actions would belie that description. On May 24, 1881, a local political disagreement that had been festering for months finally resulted in bloodshed.

The incident was believed to have been the result of a well-laid plan to take the life of either or both of the Lott brothers. Richard and Jessie Lott were described as "noble, pure, generous and brave." The young men, both recently married, were sons of Colonel Hiram

R. Lott, a veteran of the Mexican War and a prominent businessman in the area. Richard Lott managed the family plantation just outside of town, and Jesse managed the general store in town. Their brother-in-law had some unpleasant business of a "private nature" with Sheriff Bradley on the morning of May 24, and had drunk to excess at the saloon that evening. When Richard Lott collected his brother-in-law to take him home, he was accosted by Deputy Sage.

Travis Elmore Sage was a newcomer to the community. He was a stranger to the Lott family and to many of the citizens. Exactly why he was chosen by Bradley to be his deputy is unknown because he spent large portions of his time in the saloon stationed around the card table, and "the plane on which he operated was altogether different from that" on which the Lott family moved.

Sage made his appearance in front of the saloon that evening, armed with a pistol, "the largest sized Smith & Wesson improved, very violently and boisterously abusing" Lott and his family. Sage told Richard Lott that if he got down off the mule he would be killed. The sheriff and another deputy were there but did nothing to stop the fracas that was now drawing a crowd. Sage had his pistol drawn and cocked. Richard Lott pulled out a small caliber pocket pistol and twice attempted to fire but was thrown off balance by a bystander. Sage, a fine shot, fired his weapon, and killed Richard Lott instantly.

Jesse Lott had just closed the store nearby when he heard the commotion and came to investigate. The sheriff and his other deputy made no effort to arrest Sage before Jesse reached the place where his brother lay dead. Angered by what had happened, Jesse picked up his brother's pistol and began to fire at Sage, who was retreating to his horse. The gun misfired three times after which Sage turned, drew a bead, and fired deliberately, hitting Jesse and wounding him mortally. Jesse Lott lived about twenty-nine hours and was conscious until his death. Soon after the double homicide Sage disappeared.

The Lott brothers were "two intelligent, high toned and worthy young men." Though Sage was a deputy sheriff and could have easily argued self-defense, his guilt in the affair was evident by his flight. It was reported that "Mr. Sage, immediately after the killing, mounted his horse and left for parts unknown."[24]

Six weeks after the murder of the Lott brothers, on July 6, 1881, Holt Collier was making a summer trek into the Mississippi swamp to scout for game when he encountered a local constable. The officer told him about the double murder across the river and that a man fitting the description of the assailant had been seen en route to the vicinity. Collier was asked to proceed to Washburn's Ferry and arrest the fugitive before he could cross the Bogue Phalia River to hide in the swamps beyond. Collier rode to Washburn's Ferry, where he found a man fitting the description as given. It was not unusual for Collier to assume the role as an *ex officio* officer of the law considering his service to Sheriff Helm after the election of 1875.

The man at Washburn's Ferry was the fugitive Sage, but he was known on the east bank of the Mississippi as "Stacks." He was sitting on his horse in front of the store with a Winchester rifle in his hand. Holt approached, dismounted, and spoke to the outlaw, who knew the hunter by reputation. As they entered into conversation Collier began to admire the Winchester and asked to examine the weapon. Not suspecting an intent to disarm him, Sage freely passed the rifle to Holt, who placed it against the gallery. Keeping himself between the rifle and Sage, Collier announced that he had a warrant and that Sage was under arrest. It probably never occurred to Holt that Sage would take offense at being arrested by a Negro, but he was fully prepared for resistance.

A third man on the gallery attempted to intervene on behalf of the fugitive. He pled to Collier that the Louisiana deputy was a poor man and that he had killed a rich man for trying to "bulldoze" him. It was an obvious attempt to distract. Sage protested that he would not be arrested and lunged his horse forward, pinching Holt against the gallery. Sage called out for the other man to pass him the gun, which he did, passing it over Collier's head. Sage quickly brought the rifle to his shoulder and attempted to shoot Collier, but in the excitement, he brought the gun down onto the horse's head, causing the animal to bolt ever so slightly. The distraction gave Collier the necessary time to defend himself. He quickly drew his revolver, aimed, and fired, killing Sage instantly. The murderous deputy fell to the ground motionless with the cocked rifle in his hands.

Holt Collier immediately surrendered himself to the authorities. Although what became known locally as "the gunfight at Washburn's

Ferry" received considerable attention from the press because of the killing of a white man by a Negro, Holt Collier was discharged, and no action was ever taken against him. The inquest by Justice O'Bannon found that Collier had acted in self-defense.

Sage was buried in Greenville. He was remembered as a man of "very bad reputation." Personal effects taken from the body included a Bowie knife, about sixty dollars, some of which was Confederate money, and a pocketbook inscribed "A. M. Key," believed to have been stolen.[25]

• • •

By 1890, Holt Collier had apparently tired of Rose, with whom he was living in 1880, and on December 18 he obtained a license to marry Maggie Phillips.[26] No certification was filed however, and no other information on Maggie Phillips is known.

In time Holt Collier would no longer hunt to market the pelts and meat of the wild game he killed. The railroad companies, which he had supplied with meat to feed the land-clearing workers, had slowly stolen away the bears' habitat. The expanding cotton acreage and urban sprawl also did much to deplete the old wilderness and swampland. The receding hunting grounds made bear hunting an expensive enterprise. Because finances and substantial commitments of time were required the bear hunt became a sport of the wealthy elite.

In the early 1890s Holt Collier, who killed his first bear at the age of ten and had been hunting ever since, began hiring himself out as an outfitter and guide, earning a respectable livelihood in the process. He provided the dogs, a wagon, guides, camping gear, a cook, and other supplies, depending on the size of the party and the needs of the customer. Because the bear population had been significantly reduced in Washington County, Holt often took his clients south into the largely unsettled swamps of Sharkey and Issaquena Counties, or north into Sunflower County.

Two of the local planters who relied heavily on Collier to track and locate bears for them were Clive and Harley Metcalfe, the owners of Glenbar and Newstead plantations. Their family at one time owned over eight thousand acres of fine cotton land comprising Glenbar, Newstead, Brighton, Courtland and Cold Springs plantations. Their

The Hunter • 147

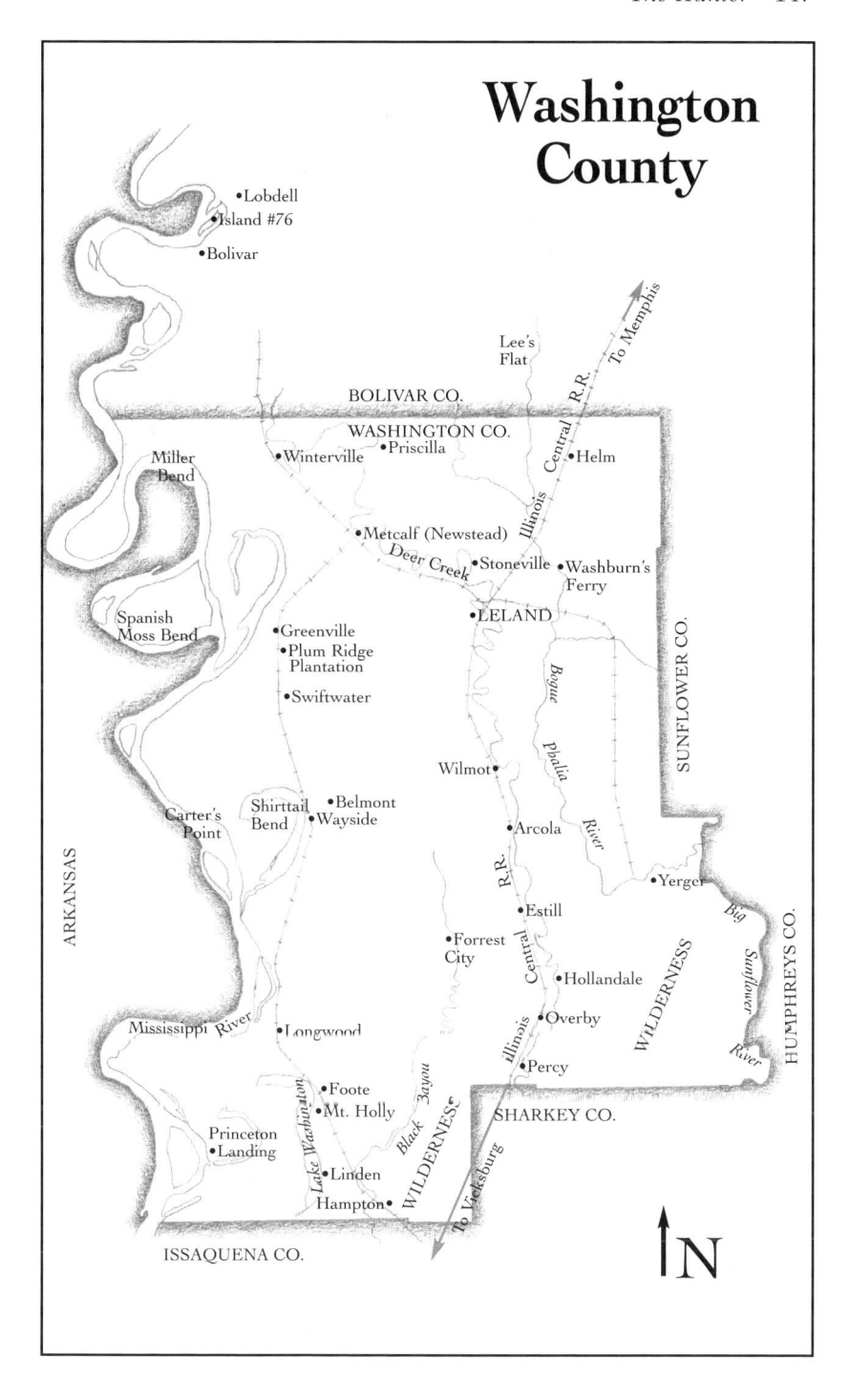

mother, Martha Priscilla Miller, like Howell Hinds, had migrated north from Jefferson County before the war. Their father, Frederick Augustus Metcalfe, was a captain in the Washington County Home Guard during the war and was a good friend of both George Helm and wartime Governor Charles Clark.

Clive and Harley Metcalfe were contemporaries and friends of Holt's good friend, LeRoy Percy. Like the Percy family, the Metcalfes wielded considerable influence in the Mississippi Delta, and Holt taught them to hunt, just as he had taught Percy. With the Metcalfes, however, Holt Collier enjoyed an even closer relationship and a bond that was broken only by the encroachments of age. Harley and Clive Metcalfe ran successful plantations and also maintained positions with the Commercial National Bank of Greenville, Hotel Greenville, the Greenville Compress Company, and the Delta Compress Company. They both dedicated themselves to the hunt at any time their businesses operations would allow. Both were Episcopalian and strongly devoted to St. James's, their local church.

The Metcalfe brothers frequently hunted together and always included Holt Collier. In fact, they depended on him. A few plantation ledger entries from the waning days of the great bear-hunting era are the only surviving records that provide an indication of the frequency of the hunts and the comradery among the hunters. Clive's entries show that he devoted as much time to hunting as he did to his farming operation. The ledgers can be divided into two main sections. The first covers the farm operations during planting and harvest, and the second details the hunts in the fall, winter, and early spring. A few excerpts of the hunting entries follow:

> *Sunday, Nov. 24, 1889*
> *Been to the lake and had found all the boys in the woods on a camp hunt. So off I get and just came back this morning. Did not have the best luck in the world. I killed a very fine panther and Holt killed a bear, the only one that was killed on the hunt.*
>
> *Thursday, Nov. 28, 1889*
> *Holt came out to go into camp.*

*Friday, Nov. 29, 1889*
*Sent my wagon in the woods with corn and provisions for Holt Collier.*

*Sat. Nov. 30, 1889*
*Sent for Mr. Harrison this evening to stay on the place while I was in the woods next week. Laid off my hands too.*

*Sun. Dec. 1, 1889*
*Cold and frosty this morning. Got up at five oclock went out to the camp to hunt bear— Jumped two. The dogs split and we got none.*

*Sat. May 20, 1893*
*Holt and Harley came up this evening and will go out for a drive in the morning.*

*Sun. Oct. 1, 1893*
*Harley came and we went out hunting did not start a single thing. The bear have all disappeared from this part of the country.*

*Thurs. Oct. 12, 1893*
*Went hunting again today. Killed two little deer— No bear again.*

*Sat. Oct. 14, 1893*
*Holt came out from Greenville this evening and we will go hunting in the morning.*

*Sun. Oct. 15, 1893*
*Killed nothing.*

*Tues. Oct. 17, 1893*
*Holt went out hunting this morning and brought no meat back as usual.*

*Fri. Oct. 20, 1893*
*Sent Holt out with the dogs to hunt.*

*Sat. Oct. 21, 1893*
*Holt sent me a piece of poor bear meat today. It was so poor that I gave it to the dog.*

*Tues. Oct. 31, 1893*
*Off on a camp hunt in Sunflower (with Harley)*

*Nov. 1 to Nov. 8, 1893*
*Off hunting*

*Thurs. Nov. 9, 1893*
*Came home from hunting, Having had a good deal of sport. Killed four fine bear.*

Clive also recorded that from November 29 to December 5, 1893, he left home for a hunt, not mentioning his success, but clearly indicating that there were few bear to be found near Glenbar Plantation.[27] By the end of the century a successful bear hunt inside Washington County would be a newsworthy item. On November 24, 1898, the Weekly Democrat reported that Holt Collier, "the great bear hunter," killed a very large black bear at Swiftwater Plantation south of Greenville. Apparently the animal had been seen in the vicinity and when word of it reached Collier, he wasted no time dispatching the beast.[28]

• • •

On June 15, 1895 Mary Ann Hinds, Howell's widow, died in St. Louis.[29] What became of Alice, Mary Ann's daughter by Howell Hinds, is not known. After the Civil War, perhaps to escape the shame of their half-brother living openly with Augusta Collier, John Hinds and Howell Hinds Jr. moved into the New Mexico territory. Howell Jr. was living in Sonora, Mexico, in 1895. John died in Arizona in January 1897.[30]

# CHAPTER 12

# THE GREAT WHITE HUNTER

> *"At 4 the train arrived and the anxious hunter stepped onto the platform dressed in his fringed buckskin hunting suit with a blue flannel shirt and a brown slouch hat. A cartridge belt was buckled around his waist and his favorite ivory-handled knife at his side. He carried his favorite Winchester rifle..."*
> — Gregory C. Wilson, Curator
> Roosevelt Collection, Harvard University[1]

Frontiersman Daniel Boone achieved considerable fame in the last half of the eighteenth century with his skills as a marksman and his talent for tracking bears. The most popular such figure in the first half of the nineteenth century was Davy Crockett, whose fame as a hunter endures along with his gallant stand at the Alamo in 1836.

In the later half of the nineteenth century, many men–including John 'Grizzly' Adams, Wilburn Waters, Wade Hampton III, William Pickett, Robert Eager Bobo, William Wright, and Ben Lilly–vied for the reputation as the greatest hunter of his era. Until 1902 Holt Collier was a stranger to this list except on a local level, largely unnoticed because of his race and because he hunted out of necessity rather than mere sport. First on this distinguished list of bear hunters was President Theodore Roosevelt, not so much for his level of success, but because of his love of the hunt and his popularity as a public figure.[2]

By the turn of the twentieth century the once vast Mississippi Delta wilderness had been reduced and the bear population had declined significantly, but there were still large habitats where the bruins could be found. The aging Holt Collier, who kept his pack of dogs and his mules ready continued to guide wealthy planters and urban dwellers willing to pay his price for the chance to kill bears before the species became extinct as had already happened to other species in the region. Collier's reputation and that of his hounds was unchallenged.

Theodore Roosevelt had become president of the United States upon the death of William McKinley on September 14, 1901. There is no public figure in modern American history whose star rose so high so rapidly. He had held several public offices including New York assemblyman, civil service commissioner, New York police commissioner, president of the New York City Police Board, assistant srcetary of the Navy, governor of New York and vice president of the United States.

After the sinking of the *Maine* in the Havana harbor on February 15, 1898, Roosevelt resigned his position with the Navy and accepted a lieutenant colonelcy with the First U. S. Volunteer Cavalry, better known as the "Rough Riders." His success and daring in Cuba during the Spanish-American War made him a household name. The "Rough Riders" were a mix of Ivy League friends and Texans recruited in San Antonio in May 1898. In combat with them was elderly "Fighting" Joe Wheeler, a former Confederate general with whom Holt Collier had briefly ridden thirty five years earlier during Earl Van Dorn's and Nathan Bedford Forrest's raids into Central Tennessee.[3]

When Roosevelt returned to New York later that year, the state Republican Party drafted him as their candidate for governor, a position he easily won. The death of Vice President Hobart in November 1899 left the Republican slot for the second position open at the National Convention in June 1900. President McKinley threw the nomination to the floor, refusing to choose Roosevelt or any other to join him on the ticket. Though he stated publicly that he would refuse the honor, Roosevelt was nominated overwhelmingly and accepted the post. He was inaugurated vice president of the United States on March 4, 1901. McKinley's assassination only six months later propelled Roosevelt to the presidency, the youngest person ever to hold the office.[4]

• • •

The Civil War held intense interest for President Roosevelt. His father was a Lincoln Republican and his mother was a native Georgian who, in his own words, was "entirely unreconstructed until the day of her death." His two uncles fought for the Confederacy and had been self-exiled rather than be captured or take the oath of allegiance. As a boy Roosevelt had grown up with his mother's stories of the idyllic life on her plantation and of Sherman's destruction of it. At times during the war when Roosevelt's father was away young 'Teedie,' as his mother called him, would assist her in packing boxes of food and clothing to send south on the blockade runners.[5]

After the death of both his mother and his wife on Valentine's Day, 1884, Roosevelt retreated from his life in the city to a sprawling cattle ranch in the unchartered and desolate wilderness of the Dakota Territory. There he began his quest to make a name for himself as a big game hunter. By the time of the Spanish-American War he had established himself as a noted conservationist and hunter by founding the Boone and Crockett Club. He hunted almost all types of American game including the grizzly bear, the buffalo, and the pronghorn sheep.[6] Over the years he read and was often told of the thrill of hunting black bears through the wilderness swamps on horseback with hounds. Bear hunting had been highly recommended by Wade Hampton, and it was becoming increasingly evident that with the diminution of the bear population such an experience would not be possible much longer.

• • •

In the early twentieth century Mississippi political races often turned on racial issues. The Democratic Party was firmly in control, but different factions held widely differing views on the subject. James K. Vardaman, the "White Chief," was known for his anti-Negro views and had received significant public support in his failed 1899 gubernatorial campaign. He was defeated by fellow Democrat Andrew H. Longino, a racial moderate. Vardaman and his ideology were expected to be in the forefront of the upcoming 1903 campaign.[7]

When Governor Longino invited President Roosevelt to join a Mississippi bear hunt with several other distinguished politicians from Louisiana, Mississippi, and Tennessee, Roosevelt could not bring himself to accept. He compared the prospect of such a large contingent to "leading a charge of cavalry on a herd of cattle." However, the invitation prompted him to read again several of Wade

154 • *Holt Collier*

*Theodore Roosevelt* (THEODORE ROOSEVELT COLLECTION, HARVARD COLLEGE LIBRARY.)

Hampton's articles on the Mississippi black bear chase. Roosevelt wanted to go, but not with such a large party. He desired a serious hunt with limited distractions.[8]

Stuyvesant Fish, president of the Illinois Central Railroad, agreed to arrange such a hunt. Fish knew the land from Chicago to New Orleans through which his railroad passed, and he was especially familiar with bear country. He invited the president to join a small private hunt.

Fish wrote to his friend John M. Parker, a man with many hunting connections in the Mississippi Delta. Parker was a native Mississippian who became a power in Louisiana politics. He was an avid hunter, planter, and cotton factor, president of the New Orleans Cotton Exchange and the New Orleans Board of Trade, and a member of the board of directors of the Illinois Central Railroad. He was later elected governor of Louisiana and was a candidate for vice president on the National Progressive (Bull Moose) Party ticket in 1916.

John Parker wrote to E. C. Mangum of Sharkey County, an owner and manager of vast cotton lands comprising four plantations, asking for his help in arranging a bear hunt for President Roosevelt. Mangum wrote to George Helm, Huger Foote, and LeRoy Percy to solicit their assistance. Because public knowledge of the plans might spoil their efforts, secrecy was a priority.

Major George M. Helm had served in the Confederacy as an engineer with Thomas Hinds in Byrne's Artillery and had also served as a staff officer to generals Hardee, Polk, and Breckenridge. After the war he became chief engineer on the Delta Levee Project and served as sheriff of Washington County in the years following Reconstruction. Helm owned over seven thousand acres near Stoneville.[9] Holt Collier was his former deputy and had guided Helm when he killed his first bear.

Huger Lee Foote was considered by many to be the finest shot in the state. He was a state senator, president of the board of supervisors, levee board member, a former two-term sheriff, and a prominent planter who owned Mount Holly on Lake Washington and Egremont Plantation in Sharkey County. Known to have a "sunny and genial disposition," he was the grandfather of noted novelist and Civil War historian Shelby Foote.[10]

LeRoy Percy was the son of William A. Percy, Holt Collier's defender at the court-martial in 1866 and a former hunting apprentice of Collier's. A respected Greenville attorney, Percy would later become a governor of the Federal Reserve Bank, a trustee of the Carnegie and Rockefeller Foundations, and U. S. senator.

Stuyvesant Fish also invited Jacob Dickinson to accompany the party. Dickinson, another native Mississippian, had volunteered and served in the Confederate army at age fourteen, had been a Tennessee Supreme Court justice, a former assistant U. S. attorney general, and at the time served as general counsel for the Illinois Central Railroad. He would later become the U. S. secretary of war. LeRoy Percy once described Dickinson as an "intense southerner."

Fish's invitation of Dickinson was apparently of some concern to Roosevelt. The president had no objection to Dickinson but was concerned at having too large a hunting party. He wrote privately to Fish that "I have never before been accustomed to ask favors, but I find that for reasons it is hardly necessary to explain I have to. I want to kill one bear myself without fail. Under ordinary circumstances of course each man would take his chance, but I am going on this hunt to kill a bear, not to see anyone else kill it; and unfortunately the people at large are sure to misunderstand what happens in case I don't kill it and some one else does. Now I hope you won't regard this as churlish. It is not. As a rule, when I go hunting I do not like to take more than one friend with me, because when I hunt, I hunt. I don't go for companionship — I go to get the game and I want to get it;

and all I have felt unfavorable about this trip is that we should have too many men with us. Mr. Cortelyou and Dr. Lung will not hunt. John McIlhenny's desire is that I should get a bear, and I think that is Mr. Parker's. I hope Mr. Dickinson won't object to the hunt being arranged with a view to my getting the bear. Of course after I have killed one bear, then I am only too delighted that we should all of us take our chances. But, as I say, my only hesitancy about going on a trip was lest we should have so many men as to make it unlikely that I would get a bear." Roosevelt entered his own handwritten post script, "In short, my experience is that to try to combine a hunt and a picnic, generally means a poor picnic, and always means a spoiled hunt. Every additional man on a hunt tends to hurt it. Of course I am only going because I want to <u>hunt</u> — and do see that I get the first bear without fail."[11]

Roosevelt sent a private letter to John Parker the same day expressing his glee that Parker would accompany him. He added, "I am sure you will not misunderstand me when I say that I trust every effort will be made to have me personally get the chance to kill a bear....Now when I hunt I go out purely and simply to get game and to enjoy the wilderness while doing so; and the only hesitancy I had about going on this trip was lest we might have too many men, and it might result in my not getting a bear. I am willing to hunt every day and all day in foul weather and fair, and after I have gotten my bear then let us all take our chances; but for reasons I gave you when you were up here I do most earnestly wish to get a chance at a bear personally, without fail."[12]

Roosevelt also requested that John McIlhenny be allowed to join the hunt. McIlhenny had served as a lieutenant in the Rough Riders. He was from New Orleans and served as a member of the U. S. Civil Service Commission. His family business continues today to produce and market worldwide the condiment Tabasco sauce.

Roosevelt would be accompanied by George Cortelyou and Dr. George Lung. George B. Cortelyou was the private secretary to presidents McKinley and Roosevelt. He would serve in later years as secretary of commerce and labor, chairman of the Republican National Committee, postmaster general, and secretary of the treasury. Lieutenant George Augustus Lung, U.S.N. Medical Corps, had

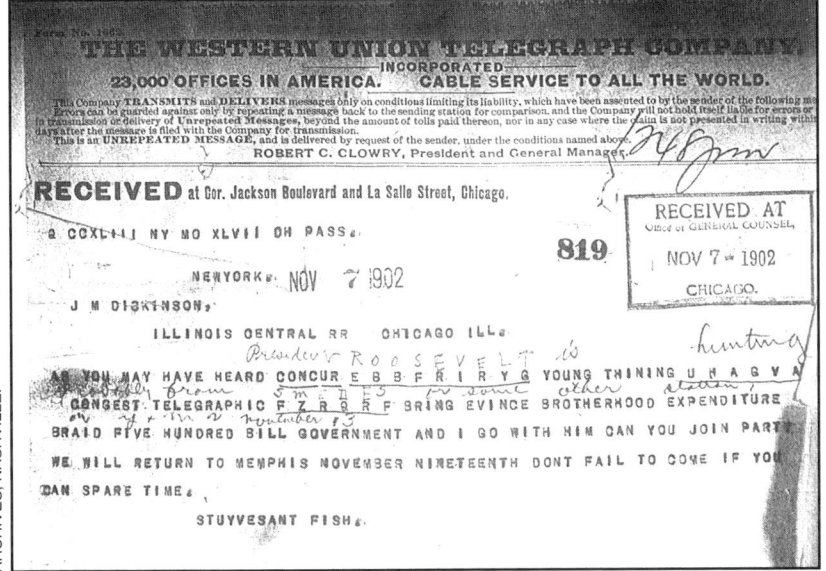

CODED TELEGRAM FROM STUYVESANT FISH TO JACOB DICKINSON,
Translation reads: "As you may have heard President Roosevelt is hunting probably from Smedes or some other station, on Y & M on November 13. I go with him can you join party? We will return to Memphis November nineteenth. Don't fail to come if you can spare time."

been assigned by the Navy to the president as his staff physician. It was expected that there would be the regular contingent of the president's personal guards and several members of the press.[13]

Despite all good intentions to keep the expedition to a manageable size, it was obvious that this would be no small endeavor.[14] Secrecy was involved in all communications. Telegrams informing others of arrival times and points of arrival had to be sent in code.[15]

George Helm was given the task of locating his old hunting guide and giving him instructions of what would be expected. Major Helm visited Collier and explained that "[i]f you can get things ready in a month and not let anybody know what you're doing, President Roosevelt will go hunting with us."[16] Though Roosevelt and his company had immeasurable finances and manpower, almost every aspect of the presidential hunt, including its success or failure, was the responsibility of the uneducated fifty-six year old former slave, Holt Collier.

GUIDES ON THE 1902 ROOSEVELT HUNT, *Holt Collier's guides on the hunt were Frank Dorsey, Calvin Dorsey, Bill Ennolds and Thomas McDougall. Swint Pope served as cook. Ben Johnson and Freeman Wallace served as guards.*

    His first task was to assemble a crew of guides and locate the bear. Once done, wide paths had to be cut through the thick cane and underbrush, and a camp site had to be cleared. Soon before the arrival of his guests, the camp would have to be provisioned and set up. It was a time-consuming, difficult job. Holt chose Swint Pope, a local justice of the peace who would serve as the cook; Bill Enolds; brothers Frank and Calvin Dorsey; Ben Johnson; Freeman Wallace;[17] and Thomas McDougall to accompany him on the hunt.[18]

    Collier did all in his power to find the perfect camp site where there were ample bears to insure the possibility of a kill by the president. Holt explained in a later interview: "Of co'se, him bein' a stranger, we wanted to make sho' he kilt a bear; 'twouldn't never do to have a gentl'man come that fur an' not git a bear. So they sent me to pick out a huntin'-ground."

The best place Holt could find for the hunt was about forty-five miles south of Greenville, in Sharkey County. As Holt explained years later, "Down 'bout Smede's Station there is a lot of overflow land, right between the Big Sunflower an' the Little Sunflower — kinder wild in there, 'cause didn't nobody live there."

Holt used his tried-and-true methods to find the best area to set up camp. As he once explained his process, "[w]hen I go into the woods to locate bears I only carries one dog, an' I don't let 'im run none. It's jes' to find out where they is an' where they feeds. After that it's easy enough to come in with a pack o' dogs an' kill 'em. Of co'se, a man has got to know how."

The location on the banks of the Little Sunflower River was ideal. Holt and his men started the rigorous tasks of clearing the camp site and cutting cane immediately. "This was a pretty good place fer bears. I located plenty of 'em in there, an' then I set to work to cut the trails....[A] bear has always got his own particular path through a cane-brake, an' ef you have got a good eye it's easy enough to foller 'em. But you can't shoot in a bear path, 'cause it's so crooked and all tangled up. 'Sides that, you'd be might apt to shoot somebody else instead o' the bear. That's why we cut trails jes' as straight as strings. You can ride through 'em on a horse an' see from one end to the other. Yes, sir, it is a heap o' work — but when a gentleman comes all the way from Washington City to kill a bear we wants to show 'im a good time."[19]

The site Collier selected was about fifteen miles west of the Smedes and Kelso plantations near the Little Sunflower River. The closest access was Smede's Station, a small railroad platform which served to transport cotton from the field to gin. Located near the station was a commissary, E. C. Mangum's large six chimney house, and several sharecroppers' cabins.[20] It was from this remote station that Holt Collier's crew "would load up all sorts of camp plunder" to make the camp.

Food and tents were the only responsibility of the local hosts. Holt Collier and his men had prepared the camp days in advance,

# Sharkey County (circa 1902)

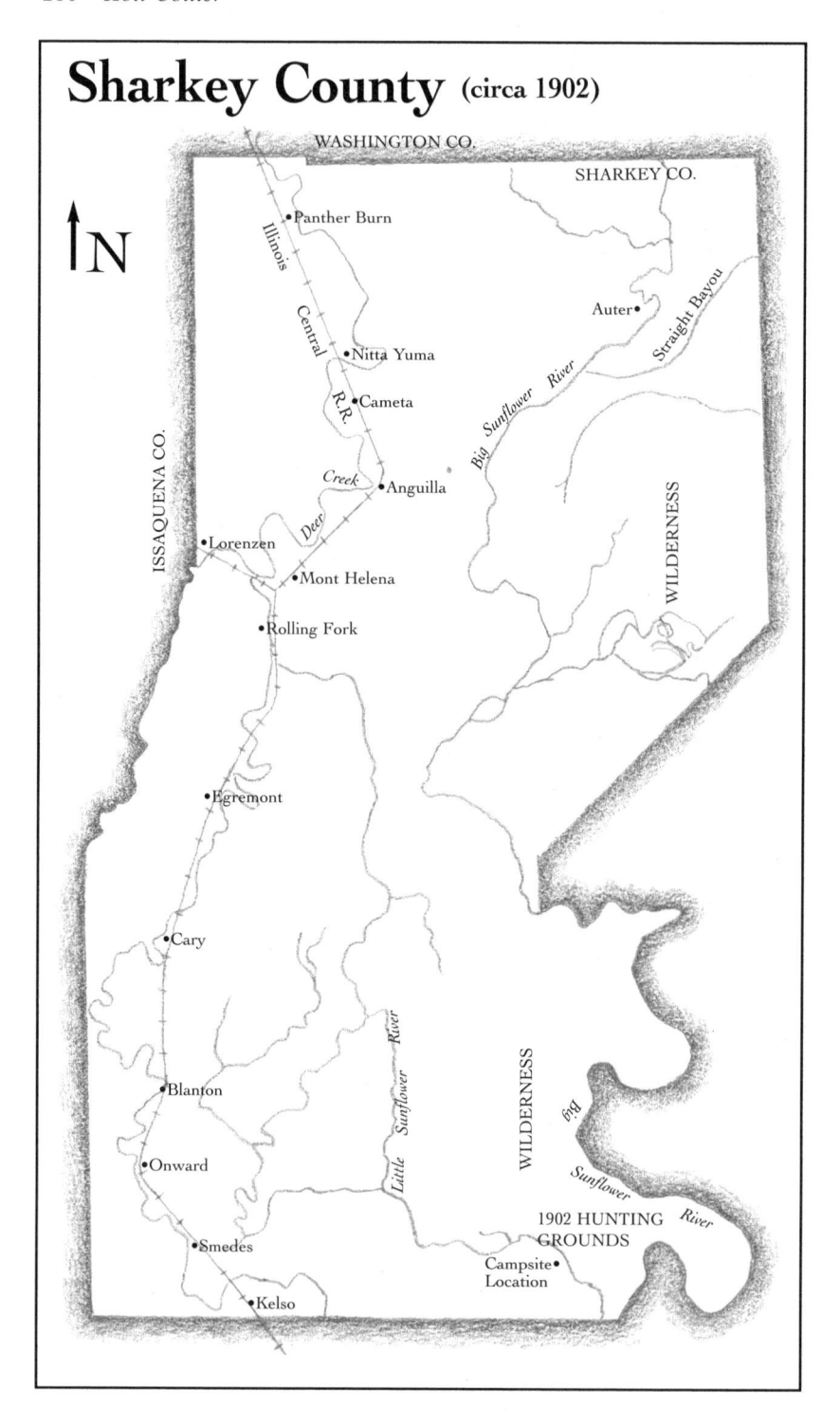

and they all waited "in feverish impatience with little to do but feed their dogs and polish their guns" until they got the signal—at which time it was Collier's responsibility to "drive out to the railroad for the President."[21]

• • •

Roosevelt's train traveled through Columbus, Cincinnati, Louisville and deep into Kentucky on November 12, 1902. Reports were sent out by the press at stops along the way. Huge crowds met the train at every station. The anticipation of the Mississippi bear hunt and the president's travels were widely reported and followed by the newspapers across the country. Headlines through the week read "President Speeds Toward Bruin Land," "President Hunts Bear," "In the Mississippi Canebrake," "President Ready to Meet a Bear."[22]

At Memphis on the morning of November 13 Fish, McIlhenny, Dickinson, Parker, Helm, Mangum and Foote joined Roosevelt for the remainder of the trip to Smede's Station. They donned their hunting attire while in transit so as not to be delayed upon their arrival. Through the flat Mississippi Delta stops of Tunica, Dundee, Lula, Clarksdale, Bobo, Alligator, Hushpuckena, Mound Bayou, Cleveland, Leland, Estill, Panther Burn, Nitta Yuma, Anguilla, and Rolling Fork the engineer pushed to make the maximum speed of seventy miles per hour, in consideration of the president's wishes.[23]

When Theodore Roosevelt stepped from the train at the remote Smedes Station into the chill moist air on the afternoon of November 13, 1902, he was ready for the hunt and in typical fashion was anxious to move directly to the camp site. The several hundred African Americans who greeted him, all children and grandchildren of slaves, were in awe of his presence. He was "clad in hunting costume, khaki riding trousers, leather leggings, blue flannel shirt, corduroy coat, and a brown slouch hat. About his waist was a cartridge belt from which hung a very handsome ivory-handled hunting knife."[24] According to the newspaper accounts, Roosevelt also carried his famous fringed buckskin coat and his favorite Winchester 40-90 that bore the scars of an encounter with a Colorado mountain lion.

Holt Collier was immediately impressed by the man and his manner. Roosevelt was not a big man, only five feet, eight inches tall, but "seemed palpably massive" especially about the chest, being a full two hundred pounds of muscle. It has been said that: "Were it not for his high brow, and the distracting brilliance of his smile, Theodore Roosevelt would unquestionably be an ugly man." He had small ears, heavy jowls, large wide-spaced eyes of pale blue, and he wore rimless pince-nez glasses. His most celebrated feature were his dazzling large white teeth.[25] The President introduced himself by walking straight to him with his hand extended and according to Collier said "So dis is Holt, de guide. I hyar you's er great bear hunter."[26]

Guns, blankets, baggage, and other personal effects were placed on a four-mule wagon for the ride to camp. The hunting party, except for Fish and Dickinson, rode off on small, wiry, tough, little horses and were last seen dashing away along a field road east toward the woods at a "breakneck canter." Fish and Dickinson followed in a buckboard drawn by two mules. The president's black horse did not appear to be spirited; he was described, however, as "just the sort of animal needed to force a way through the dense undergrowth."[27]

As usual, the president was accompanied by an entourage of support personnel, a stenographer, a security detail, reporters, and others. Most of this entourage, including the bodyguards, were ordered to remain at or near the isolated rail platform where they would await the president's return four days later. The number of reporters, who usually traveled in a gaggle, was limited to three, and they were required to present a press pass for admission into camp. Like the other members of the president's retinue, the reporters established their headquarters at the small isolated train platform at Smede's Station, Mississippi, which for the next five days was the telegraphic source of all news relating to the president of the United States of America.

To insure that no stragglers or sightseers interfered with the hunt, the road between Smedes Plantation and the Little Sunflower camp was guarded by Ben Johnson and Freeman Wallace, two trusted farm hands armed with repeating rifles. Several people attempted to penetrate the cordon but were turned back. To the local whites, this was considered highly objectionable as it "was a new thing in Sharkey County for a negro to presume to raise so much as his little finger against a white man."[28]

• • •

The field road ran eastward from the railroad track for four miles through the Smedes and Kelso Plantations. Wide stretches of seemingly flat cultivated land were bright with cotton from a second eruption of the bolls ready for scraping. The vast forest of gaunt, deadened timber at the edge of the fields was a clear line of demarcation between the new land being brought under cultivation and the receding frontier beyond. The sharecroppers' white-washed cabins, not much improved since the days of slavery, were spread along the field road, in the fields, and back in the "deadenings," and every so often a black-faced woman would appear at a cabin door. All of the men were at the station, and not evident at the cabins or in the fields.

Just beyond the plantations, Roosevelt, Holt Collier, and the other riders entered a stretch of forest several miles long carpeted with knee-high briar tangle. The towering forest of oak, ash, and cypress was majestic except for the mud dark color of the lowest fifteen feet, a reminder of the annual flooding from the backwater of the Yazoo and Sunflower Rivers. Then came the long stretch of Coon Bayou, a mud gully where floodwater lay stagnant through the summer and fall, attracting all types of wild game. On the other side of Coon Bayou, the hunters entered the primeval Delta swamp with briars and thickets thirty feet high and knit so thickly that it would have been difficult to leave the trail. The passage itself had been cut out of the jungle as though to create a corridor through which they might pass.[29]

The presidential camp was pitched on high ground on the west bank of the Little Sunflower River, then a fast-flowing, mud-banked stream of clear water full of moccasins and small mouth bass, locally known as "trout." Collier had prepared a neat row of four large A–shaped tents for the white hunters and hosts, a cooking tent, and a large shelter tent for Holt's crew at the back edge of the clearing. Mules and horses were tethered in a wide semicircle between the

*1902 campsite*

tents next to large piles of fodder and bedding. In the center of an open space was a great cypress log, against which the campfire would be built. There was a bench laden with water pails and washbasins, and at the end of the row of "white men's tents," next to the cook tent, was an uncovered dining table. It was described as "too high for a man to eat from in comfort if sitting, and just too low for one who would eat standing."

Dogs were everywhere, followed "about by negroes armed with blacksnake whips, and shouting protests about the uttermost impossibility of teaching any four-footed creature the deference due to the President of the United States." Someone had brought a large armchair of rustic construction which the campers dubbed "The Throne." The president was an imposing figure as he sat in the armchair deep in the Delta wilderness, but he scorned it for the purpose intended. Among his comrades around the campfire that night Roosevelt announced that on the hunt he was not to be referred to as President, and that from that time on he was to be addressed only as "Colonel."[30]

# CHAPTER 13

# THE "PICNIC"

*"C" is for Collier, old Holt*
*Who stopped that Bear's run with a jolt.*
*He caught him with a sling*
*And tied him with a string,*
*Just like he had been a mule colt.*

*"T" is for Teddy on the scoot,*
*He tore up the canes by the root.*
*When he got to Holt's side*
*And found the bear tied,*
*He swore he never could shoot.*
— Author Unknown[1]

On the eve of the first day's hunt Roosevelt could barely control his excitement. He made it clear to his hosts and especially to Holt Collier that he fully expected to see a bear on his first day out. As Collier remembered it years later, "Me an' the President was talkin' that first night — it was on a Thursday — an' he says to me, 'Look here, Holt, I'm bound to see a bear the first day.'" Collier tried to explain that it was not going to be that simple even for the President of the United States.

"I said to him: 'Lissen to me, Cunnel, real good, suppose I get away from everybody — which I most ingen'rally do — off with the hounds, an' I don't know how to get you to me. How are we goin' to fix it?' The Cunnel he jes' shook his head kinder stubborn."

Roosevelt persisted. " I can't help that, Holt. I'm *bound* to see a bear the first day." All Collier could do was assure the president that he would do his best to "put one up a tree" and "I will blow my horn, and I'll stay there all day and all night for you to come and kill it."[2]

The president's good natured but high expectations caused Holt to make an unusually difficult promise that a bear would be had on the first day if he had to lasso one with his "Texas" rope. The President and Huger Foote laughed off this idle boast as something no man could do. LeRoy Percy and George Helm, who had hunted often with Holt, knew that it was no idle boast.

Roosevelt said "All right; I am *bound* to see a bear the first day." Collier "thought about that a while, an' he 'peared to have his heart sot on it, so I couldn't help but laugh."

Holt responded with confidence that, "I don't know any way to be sure of that without I put my lariat on it." When this prediction was made the men in the camp began to tease Holt insisting that such a feat could not be done. "There was a whole lot of gentl'men in the camp, and they buzzed me consid'able. None of 'em ever heard of such a thing." Collier, not one to be chided, "said no more, but I jes' made up my mind I'd show 'em."

According to Collier, he "heard the President asking Mr. Percy 'bout it. Mr. Percy said he didn't know. He had never heard me say I would do anything but when the time came to do it I didn't do it. He told him I had hunted with him all my life, and I learned him how to hunt when he was a boy — that was Mr. Percy. Mr. Foote made fun of me. The President looked doubtful, but Mr. Percy and Major Helm said I could do it."[3]

Although Roosevelt wanted to ride and participate in the chase, his demands for a shot on the first day and the timidity of his hosts condemned him to a stationary blind overlooking one of the well-used bear trails Holt had explored the previous month. Mangum, the President's intended partner for the day, became ill with "indisposition" from the evening before and was replaced by Foote. The idea was to place Roosevelt so that he would have a clear shot when the bear, driven by Holt's pack of about forty dogs, watered at a clearing.

Holt Collier described the first day of the hunt: "The next day we went out to the lake where I knew the bear was waterin'. I found that out when I was cuttin' the traces. We struck a track, an' I went with 'em. But first I put the President on a stand at that lake with Mr. Foote. I knew I could drive that bear right by him — same as anybody would drive a cow — an' he'd get a shot ef he jes' waited.

The "Picnic" • 167

*PRESIDENT THEODORE ROOSEVELT mounted and ready for the 1902 bear hunt guided by Holt Collier on the Little Sunflower River, Sharkey County, Mississippi.*

That was 'bout eight o'clock in the morning. I told 'em to stay there 'til I got back."[4]

Once the hunters had been placed, Collier started out with his dogs across the river into the thick jungle which extended several miles further to the Big Sunflower River. The pack was made up of clean limbed, gaunt beasts, some resembling no particular breed, but all consistent with the "conglomerate and unlimited variety that hangs about every negro cabin." Old Remus, the oldest and most experienced, had a "foxhound's body and a bloodhound's head." Jacko, Collier's fice dog was a "valiant little scoundrel." It would be this fice dog that would "harry the bear and bite his flanks, and run away to bite again as soon as the bear has turned his head."[5]

Collier followed the dogs on horseback accompanied by John Parker, Bill Ennolds, Frank Dorsey and Calvin Dorsey. They found the trail of a bear early on, but the animal led the dogs on a long chase that took them several miles, crossing the river two or three times. It was a warm day and Collier was exhausted when the bear finally turned onto the trail that led to Roosevelt's stand.

Roosevelt and Foote waited on the stand all morning listening to the baying of the dogs and the trilling of the hunters' horns. Through the forest the sounds would fade in and out as the pursuit ranged great distances along the wooded rises and into the canebrakes.[6] About mid-afternoon the baying of the pack died out of hearing. Occasionally they heard it again, but it never sounded as if the game was coming in their direction. Foote told the president that "Holt has either gone across Big Sunflower or the Yazoo River, following his dogs" and suggested to the president that Holt was far too distant to return and that he might kill a bear and bring it back camp. Roosevelt asked, "Do you reckon Holt crossed the river?" Foote told him, "Yes, he will go anywhere the dogs go." At Foote's suggestion they abandoned the stand and broke for camp and a late lunch.[7]

• • •

The impatience of the hunters cost the president his trophy but gave the world a children's toy that would become an international icon beloved by generations. Holt Collier told the story hundreds of times in the years that followed. His disappointment at not having his instructions followed plagued him long after the hunt. "That was eight o'clock in the mornin' when I hit the woods an' roused my bear where I knowed I'd fin him. Den me an' dat bear had a time, fightin' an' chargin' an' tryin' to make him take a tree. Big ole bear but he wouldn't climb nary tree. I could have killed him a thousand times but Mr. John Parker warned ev'ybody not to shoot, to save ev'y chance for de Cunnel. I sweated myself to death in that canebrake. So did the bear. By keeping between the bear and the river I knew he'd sholy make for that water hole where I left the Cunnel. After a while the bear started that way and popped out of the gap where I said he'd go. But I didn't hear a shot, and that pestered me....It sholy pervoked me because I'd promised the President to bring him a bear to that log, and there he was."[8]

The camp was about "two miles from this waterin' place, and 'bout the time they got to camp I got that bear." The bear "bayed up against the very log where I had left the Cunnel sittin.'"

When the bear turned it came into immediate conflict with the dogs in hot pursuit. This presented a dilemma to Holt Collier that he could not have anticipated. He had been given specific orders to save the bear for Roosevelt to kill and was now angered that the president had disregarded his very specific instructions. The president was not where he was supposed to be and Holt had to protect his dogs from the raging beast they had brought to bay. If not muzzled or somehow allowed to escape, the bear would certainly kill many of his treasured hounds.

Holt was struggling. He shouted at the dog, "Catch him, Jocko, Catch him." In obedience to his master, Jocko jumped on the bear from behind.[9]

Lindsay Denison, one of the correspondents on the expedition described the scene, "There was a flashing confusion of black, hairy fore feet beating them off — of white teeth snapping here and there at the squirming mass: squeals of wrath and pain from the dogs were lifted in a deafening chorus. Then the bear rose straight up on his hind legs and stood waist deep in the water. In the grasp of his mighty fore legs he had a curly yellow cur that was Holt Collier's especial pet.

"'Leggo mah dog, bear!' howled Holt, leaping from his saddle, rifle in hand. Bear and dog fell back into the muddy pool. Collier could not shoot without the risk of killing two or more of the pack, as well as the bear. He clubbed the rifle and leaped into the battle.

"'Leggo mah dog!' he shouted again, and swung the stock of his gun through an arc that landed at the base of the bear's skull. The bear let go of the dog; but it was too late, the dog was dead."[10]

According to Collier, "I whooped and hollered and the bear went over the log right down into the lake of water. The dogs were all fightin' him pretty brash. But the Cunnel warn't there. I didn't want to kill the bear, but I jes' *couldn't* let him git away. I rode out into the clear of the lake through the bushes and got my horse."[11]

"I hollered to Frank [Dorsey], a colored man, to fetch the lariat off my saddle. But Frank wouldn't bring it to me. Neither would his brother. Had to get the lariat myself and waded into the lake where Jocko, my little Scotch terrier, was fighting the bear from behind and watching me for orders. Had my rifle in my left hand, the lariat in my right."

As Collier prepared to hobble the bear, Calvin Dorsey "rushed hotfoot to camp for the Cunnel."

At that point, Collier desperately positioned himself beside the raging animal. As he told the story many times, "I put my foot right between the bear's legs, and when he raised his head out o' the water I dropped the lariat over his neck and went out o' the water and tied the other end to the willow tree. He caught another dog in there and I ran in to save the dog and hit the bear with both hands across the head with my rifle. That knocked him down and broke his skull. When he reared up he looked higher than I was. He *was* higher than me. I bent the breech of my rifle so I could not shoot it."[12]

A short time later Roosevelt, Foote, and several others arrived "as hard as they could ride." According to Collier after Roosevelt dismounted he ran into the water, and Collier humbly suggested to him "[d]on't shoot him while he's tied." Others called for the president to shoot the bear but like any hunter of honor, Theodore Roosevelt would not shoot an animal under restraint. Collier objected to the calls to shoot the bear. "Some of the other gentlemen wanted to shoot the bear, but I knew the dogs would rush in and get killed before the bear died, so I told 'em if they gave me fifteen hundred dollars for the dogs they could have the bear. They didn't want him after that."[13]

The president raised his hand haltingly and declared "Gentlemen, no magazine bears for me, or something like that, and everybody laughed." Though he refused to shoot the bear, Roosevelt was nevertheless in awe of the feat he was witness to. "Then they all laughed. The Cunnel looked at it a long time an' asked how it was I did it, then he said: 'That's wonderful, wonderful — I never saw anything like that before.'"[14]

In life the bear towered over Holt Collier. It was described as weighing over three hundred pounds, but according to Collier was "poor as a snake; if he'd been fat he'd a-weighed over five hundred."[15] A memorandum on White House letterhead with details of the hunt noted: "Old male bear. Weight 235 pounds. Measured from tip of nose to tip of outstretched hind foot, 6 feet 7 inches."[16]

John Parker, who had ridden with Collier the entire day, wanted to claim the bear after Roosevelt refused to shoot him. Parker, who Collier said was "one of my best friends," asked Collier how to put the bear out of its misery with a knife, in the true bear-hunter fashion. Collier teased the bear out on its tether and told Parker where to plant the blade. "I told Mr. Parker to take the knife out of my belt

*Theodore Roosevelt, John McIlhenny, and Holt Collier crossing the Little Sunflower River.*

and stick the bear. I put my finger over his heart, where I wanted him to stab him. Parker's attempt missed the mark, and in Collier's words, when "the knife went in, the bear jumped. Mr. Parker nearly pushed me on top of the bear, trying to get out of the lake, and left me to pull the knife out of the bear he had stabbed."[17]

After returning to camp that night Theodore Roosevelt told Holt Collier that he "was the best guide and hunter he'd ever seen."[18]

• • •

In the early mornings of that Delta autumn the temperature was low enough to form sheets of thin ice along the shore of the Little Sunflower River. Roosevelt amazed the other campers by taking a plunge into the river for a bath every morning. In the evenings there was much fun as the white hunters and the black guides gathered around the campfire trading stories and telling tall tales.

Even in the company of such dignified and powerful men, Holt Collier was the center of attention. His background and experience excited the president's imagination as he told stories of his years as a slave, his service as a Confederate scout, and his many years hunting bears. Holt Collier was described by some contemporaries as having had good diction and speaking "correctly," and one interviewer wrote that he had a "rich, colorful Mississippi dialect."[19]

Judge Jacob Dickinson wrote of those evening sessions around the campfire. "Every night we sat up late around the fire, black and white, a large company of us, and were regaled with hunting and fishing stories and reminiscences, illustrative of the days before, during and after the civil war. With the exception of the famous bear hunter, [Robert Eager] Bobo, Collier had killed more bear than any man in that country. He was a good raconteur in a quaint, homely, sportsmanlike way, and by his vivid and intense descriptions aroused and sustained unflagging interest."[20]

Lindsay Denison, one of the assigned correspondents on the hunt wrote that there would be "long talks around the camp-fire at night, when Collier, sitting apart, as he felt that a dependent should, but speaking simply and fearlessly, as became one who knew, despite his color, he was no less of a man than any of the officials or planters or lawyers or brokers about him, told the wonder-

*1902 HUNT IN SHARKEY COUNTY, MISSISSIPPI, Mr. Mangum, Huger Foote, John Parker, Dr. Lung, Swint Pope, Holt Collier, Jacob Dickinson, John McIlhenny, Dr. Richardson (note the empty seat for Theodore Roosevelt).*

ful story of his life...[how] he had killed white men and had gone unscathed, how he had met Union soldiers in hand-to-hand conflict; how he fought off a band of vigilantes that had planned to take his life without just cause."

"There was the instructive picture of Holt Collier and of some of the white men, too, dipping their horns into the water hole where the first bear had died, and drinking their full of a purée of bear and dog and mud, all held in solution in water that had been standing for at least eight months."[21]

As always around a campfire there were humorous moments. Swint Pope, the "cook and justice of the peace," was a "homely figure." He prepared the game meat and served it with "sweet potatoes fairly candied with their own sweetness, and pork gravies and turkey hashes, whose odors, floating through the wilderness, were a more certain recall signal to the hunters than all the horns." One evening Pope asked "Mr. Fish to excuse him for a moment while he went to the outpost and signed some papers which had been brought out to him from civilization." The men were curious as to what could be so important and Pope explained to Fish that, "They's some appeal bonds in some cases I decided against yo' railroad, suh."[22]

Collier was proud to be "the boss of the hunt." He later said that Roosevelt had brought with him "a car-load of guards, but he left all but one of 'em in the car. Anyway he was safer with me than with all the policemen in Washington." Roosevelt and Collier became very friendly towards each other and entered into many lively conversations. "The President was a pleasant man; when he was talking he'd stop every little while to ask other people's opinion. Sometimes he asked my opinion about something, and he talked to me about as much as he did to anybody else; he had a thousand questions to ask. We sat on a log to talk and in ten minutes, thirty-five people were sitting on the log."

Roosevelt asked Collier in private one day about his domestic life. It was a humorous account that Roosevelt repeated to Harris Dickson years later. While sitting on a log in the woods, the President asked Collier if he were married.

"Yassuh. I got a wife." answered Holt.

"Any children?" asked the President.

"Yassuh a few."

"How many?"

Holt leaned back with eyes half closed and counted on his fingers, then replied, "Nigh as I kin come at it, I got fo'teen chillun."

Roosevelt reacted astonished.

"No suh. No suh. All of 'em aint my wife's. She had two, an' de balance I got jest frolickin' around."[23]

The president was a "master leader in evoking and directing conversation." Collier was reluctant to tell all, but Roosevelt eventually "drew him out." Collier described "with vivid details" how he had run off with his master to join the army.

As might be expected with several of his old friends at camp including George Helm, a fellow Confederate veteran, and LeRoy Percy, the son of his able defender, Collier's difficulties during Reconstruction were discussed. Roosevelt was told about the death of the Captain James A. King, but Collier steadfastly refused to answer his questions. Only after being pressed by the president did Collier reluctantly explain how he had killed Captain James A. King in the canebrakes in what he described as a pistol duel on horseback. The details of King's death that he had kept secret for thirty-six years were revealed by Collier on those nights around the campfire in the Delta swamp to a sitting President of the United States of America.[24]

According to all who knew him and those who interviewed him, Holt Collier, with the exception of this one occasion, never admitted any involvement in the death of Captain James A. King.

At the conclusion of the hunt, President Roosevelt declared that "before he is three years older, he will go back to the Little Sunflower, and, with Holt Collier as his only guide, will chase bears until he comes up with one and kills it, running free before the dogs."[25]

• • •

Although the bear hunt had not been a success for Roosevelt, it was of enormous public interest. The reporters naturally resented being prohibited from covering the event firsthand and having to wait out the results of the hunt until they could briefly visit the camp. They were also frustrated by the additional insult of being held at bay by armed Negro plantation workers with orders to shoot anyone trying to sneak into camp.

On that first day, after the bear had been put out of its misery, Collier tied the carcass onto the back of his horse and returned to camp, while Roosevelt, Foote, Parker, and the other guides followed the dogs in hopes they might start another chase. When Holt arrived back at the camp with the dead bear, he found Lindsay Denison and some other correspondents looking for something to report. They inquired if the president had killed a bear and Holt replied naively that "[i]f the Colonel had stayed whar' I put him he would done got this yere one."[26]

Denison and the other reporters had a field day with the story. Although factual, the headlines, reports and editorial cartoons depicted the usually confident president as having lost his opportunity for a successful hunt by satisfying his appetite for an early lunch. One headline read: "President Lost a Shot by Not Obeying Instructions."[27] A story about Roosevelt being out-smarted by a lowly guide invited ridicule. The account of Holt Collier's heroic and seemingly super-human efforts actually received much more detailed coverage.

The hunt lasted five days. Overall there were three bears killed, but none by Roosevelt. Parker provided Roosevelt with an inventory of the hunt trophies. It was sent on his letterhead, "John

*BLACK BEAR BROUGHT TO CAMP–1902 HUNT, John Parker, Mr. Mangum, and an unidentified guide. This is one of three bear killed on the 1902 hunt with Theodore Roosevelt and Holt Collier.*

M. Parker & Co., Cotton Factors, New Orleans, La.," and dated November 26, 1902.

*Memoranda —*

*Large Bear Skull,—*
  *Old Male. — Very poor. — Weight 235#. Struck on head by Holt Collier with his rifle. — Little Sunflower River — Sharkey Co., Miss., Novr. 14/1902.*
*Small Bear Skull. —*
  *Three year old female. — Very fat, weight 220#, caught by dogs. — Then shot in head. — Same location as above and same date.*
*Old She Bear. — Poor condition. — Weight 235#. — Killed after long chase by Thos. McDougall, Novr. 17th, Kelso, Miss.*
*Deer is young swamp doe. — Not weighed. — Killed by Maj. Geo. M. Helm. — Sunflower River, Novr. 17/1902.*[28]

Other than refusing to kill the hobbled and tethered bear, the president never had an opportunity to raise his gun. Under normal circumstances the fact that a particular hunter had not personally contributed to the success of the hunt would have been worthy of little comment. Bear hunting was considered a communal matter and not an individual sport. Therefore, by the standards of southern hospitality, the hunt with three bears taken should have been considered a success.

The president, who took great pride as a marksman and huntsman, now had to face critical headlines and reports, some even comical. From all indications, he considered the press coverage of the Mississippi hunt to be unfavorable. On November 24, 1902, President Roosevelt wrote confidentially to Philip Bathell Stewart:

> *Now about our hunt: I have just had a most unsatisfactory experience in a bear hunt in Mississippi. There were plenty of bears, and if I had gone alone or with one companion I would have gotten one or two. But my kind*

> hosts, with the best of intentions, insisted upon turning the affair into a cross between a hunt and a picnic, which always results in a failure for the hunt and usually in a failure for the picnic. On this occasion, as a picnic it was pleasant enough, but as a hunt simply exasperating, and I never got a shot. Naturally the comic press jumped at the failure and have done a good deal of laughing over it.
>
> [I] had to compromise on taking three thoroughly reputable newspapermen to the station from which I got off and letting them occasionally come out to visit the camp; and even under these circumstances it was literally only by the use of guards armed with shotguns that I prevented the yellow journal men from coming along too. These same papers, having in vain tried to get into the camp and accompany us with kodaks, etc., turned around and have been industriously insisting that I had been trying to advertise the hunt and was ostentatiously endeavoring to attract public attention.[29]

To his prominent and well-meaning hosts, Roosevelt's disappointment was "something of a blow to the sense of southern hospitality to find that the president had a vigorous desire to kill a bear himself," and "even more of a blow to find, after this prejudice of the distinguished guest had been discovered, and a bear had been captured at least half-alive to await his pleasure, that he refused, with something very like scorn, to put the finishing bullet into it."[30]

• • •

Clifford Kennedy Berryman, who was then a cartoonist for the *Washington Post* and a 1944 recipient of a Pulitzer Prize, could not allow the occasion of Roosevelt's Mississippi bear hunt to go unnoticed. On November 16, 1902, the Washington Post ran a grouping of five Berryman editorial cartoons under the title "The Passing Show" on the front page. One cartoon depicted Roosevelt in his hunting attire with a rifle at his side, posturing that he would not shoot the tethered bear being held at a distance. The cartoon was titled "Drawing the Line in Mississippi," It remains the subject of

*The "Picnic"* • 179

CLIFFORD BERRYMAN CARTOON "DRAWING THE LINE IN MISSISSIPPI,"
The Washington Post, *November 16, 1902.*

debate what underlying purpose the title was to convey. Was it a statement about a civil rights issue of that day? Perhaps it was a reference to a boundary dispute between Louisiana and Mississippi. Whatever else it might imply, the cartoon was an accurate depiction of the events on the hunt when Roosevelt refused to shoot an animal that was bound to a tree.[31]

The scene depicted by Berryman, however, was incorrect on two major points. The inaccuracies were clearly a result of artist's license, but were nonetheless significant. First, the bear appeared to be very young and small, a cub with an anguished look on his face, not the 235-pound bear described in press reports and confirmed in Parker's inventory. Second, the guide holding the roped bear was clearly depicted as a white man. The reason for this discrepancy is not known. It could be that Berryman simply did not have all the facts when he drew his subject. It is possible that depicting an African American in such proximity to the president and as being the person whom he had disobeyed was not "politically correct" for the day.

180 • Holt Collier

**AFTER A TWENTIETH CENTURY BEAR HUNT.**

CLIFFORD BERRYMAN CARTOON
'AFTER A TWENTIETY CENTURY BEAR HUNT',
The Washington Post, *November 19, 1902.*
Note the bear on the hill '"Can you bear to leave me?".

After the 1902 Mississippi bear hunt Berryman employed the bear cub as an agent of comic relief in his work when portraying Roosevelt, and he continued to use it throughout his long and distinguished career. Although he is credited with much of its enduring popularity, he was not the only artist to incorporate the cub bear in political cartoons. Following Berryman's lead, other political cartoonists began using the cute little creatures, which were immediately and fondly dubbed "Teddy bears."

*A HAPPY DAY IN BEARVILLE, MISSISSIPPI*,
The Fort Wayne News, *November 19, 1902.*

*NO HIT, HE WHO LAUGHS LAST LAUGHS BEST*,
The Chicago Tribune, *November 21, 1902.*

182 • *Holt Collier*

*MISSISSIPPI, cartoon by W. L. Evans from an unidentified publication.*

*'THE EFFECT OF A REPUTATION',* The Pittsburgh Gazette, *November 20, 1902, Note the small bears hiding under the map. The racoon was the most recognizable Roosevelt mascot prior to the 1902 hunt in Mississippi.*

Coincidentally, toy stuffed bears had recently become popular in America at the turn of the century. The first were manufactured in Giengen, Germany by Margarete Stieff's toy factory. That winter large orders were received in the United States. They were known as Steiff bears but with the popularity of the Teddy bear phenomena their product in time became known as the Steiff "Teddy bear."

Others sought to profit from the popularity of the little bear, the most successful of whom was Morris Michtom, a Russian Jewish immigrant living in Brooklyn. He saw the Berryman cartoon and was inspired to design a toy bear which he called "Teddy's bear." He displayed the stuffed toys in the window of his candy store, and they became an overnight success and were in much demand by his customers. Michtom supposedly wrote Roosevelt asking permission to use his name. Roosevelt reportedly responded and gave permission, but downplayed any significance his name might have on the popularity of a cuddly toy.

Michtom soon began mass production of the Teddy bear. His success selling Teddy bears for a dollar and fifty cents resulted in formation of the Ideal Novelty Company in 1903. When Michtom died in July 1938 the Ideal Toy Corporation was a multimillion dollar industry producing and selling more than one hundred thousand Teddy bears every year.[32]

# CHAPTER 14

# IN THE LOUISIANA CANEBRAKES

*"He taught the boy the woods, to hunt, when to shoot and when not to shoot, when to kill and when not to kill, and better, what to do with it afterward. Then he would talk to the boy,...And as he talked about those old times...those old times would cease to be old times and would become a part of the boy's present..."*
— William Faulkner[1]

Holt Collier's notoriety from the newspaper coverage and a national magazine article after the 1902 hunt added to his local fame, but the measure of national attention was of short duration as the public interest moved on to other matters.[2] Roosevelt had been serious when he had pledged to hunt again with Collier within three years. Much to the disappointment of both men, the president was unable to fulfill that promise on schedule.

While waiting for the opportunity to guide the president, Collier continued to carve new trails through the dwindling wilderness. He was often on the hunt, frequently with the Metcalfe brothers. He trained dogs and taught his skills to the children of prominent planters in a tradition spanning generations, from Harrison Collier to Howell Hinds and from Howell Hinds to Holt Collier. He was an "ancient" as in Native American lore, one of the wise elders who passed his knowledge to the young men of the tribe with little payment in return other than the respect of the community.

• • •

On April 24, 1904, at the age of fifty eight, Holt Collier made one final effort at domestic life. He married Frances Parker, a twenty-six-year-old woman of unusual beauty. She brought into the union a child they called Toots.[3] Like all other legal documents signed in his later years, the 1904 marriage application is signed using a simple "x" known to be Collier's mark. Holt Collier had never learned to read or write. Throughout his entire life, he never learned how to sign his own name.

When Collier applied for a Confederate servant's pension on April 6, 1906, he answered affirmatively that he was "indigent and unable to earn a support by [his] own labor."[4] He claimed in a form completed by someone else that during the entire war he had served "Lieut. Tom Hinds," in "Maj. Burns Artillery in which Lieut. Tom Hinds served." He also claimed to have been wounded in the ankle at Shiloh. It is probable that Collier's application was engineered by some of his white friends to help him get financial support, and with "evidence furnished by J. C. Burrus, very shortly before his death, Holt was allowed the pension."[5]

The misstatements contained in the application were either the result of simple error, or the name of Thomas Hinds was used, since, although an outcast, he was certainly better known than Howell Hinds, who had been dead almost forty years. Further, the claim of a wound was probably made to increase the chances that a pension would be granted. If that were not enough, the application was accompanied by an unusual testimonial from the highly-regarded United Confederate Veterans, who stood united in their support of Collier. They wrote on their official letterhead:

*Greenville, Miss.*
*April 5th, 1906*

*To the Board of Supervisors of Washington County:-*

*I, with Everman, Major Robb, Capt Hunt, and I expect the entire W. A. Percy Camp of U. C. V., are anxious to have Holt Collier put upon the State pension list, and receive a pension. He is getting old, is in bad health—and is the only negro ever enrolled in our army.*

*He went out with Colonel Hinds, and at Bowling Green, Ky., joined Captain Evans' Texas Scouts, and remained with him until the end of the struggle.*

> *Colonel Hinds was off on a retreat after a charge, Holt missed him, called for volunteers, re-charged, and brought "Mars Howell" out.*
>
> *I know him to be as brave as any living man, not only loyal to the cause, but to the whites ever since, and during our most trying ordeal, "Reconstruction."*
>
> *Our implicit confidence in him was evidenced by our selecting him as body-guard for President Roosevelt on his hunting trip to this section.*
>
> *Yours truly,*
> *G. M. Helm, Brig.Gen.*

By W. W. Everman, Lt. Col. and A. A. Genl.

> *We indorse the above.*
> *J. H. Crouch, Sheriff of Washington County*
> *LeRoy Percy*
> *D. F. Hunt*
> *Clive Metcalfe*
> *J. H. Robb*[6]

The application was acted upon favorably on September 29, 1906. Although he was approved only for actions rendered as a servant, it was the first official recognition by any agency or office of the State of Mississippi of Collier's prior service to the Confederacy.

• • •

Theodore Roosevelt's continued popularity during the early 1900s was unparalleled by any other politician on the national scene. He was an early advocate for conserving America's natural resources and the preservation of the nation's natural habitat. In 1903 the first federal wildlife refuge was established at Pelican Island in Florida. The next year he established by executive order fifty-one national bird reserves in seventeen states and established the Breton Wildlife Refuge of 7,512 acres in Louisiana. He established the Game Preserve in the Wichita Mountains of Oklahoma in 1905, and in 1906 wildlife preserves or similar institutions were established in Nebraska, Oregon, Florida, and Alaska.

To some extent Roosevelt's aura and popularity was enhanced through his identification with the Teddy bear which had become so popular by the time of the presidential election of 1904 that editors and cartoonists used it almost daily in flattering portrayals of the president. When Seymour Eaton published the universally popular *The Roosevelt Bears, Their Travels and Adventures* in 1906, the Teddy bear was a popular icon of American culture.[7]

Theodore Roosevelt won the presidential election of 1904 and began his first elected term of office with the overwhelming support of the American people, except in the South. Mississippi was controlled and dominated by the Democratic Party, which was committed to the tenets of white supremacy. James K. Vardaman was a Greenwood newspaper editor who had been highly critical of Roosevelt prior to his 1902 visit. He was a relentless white supremacist who frequently targeted President Roosevelt for his racial views.

"Negro baiting" in Vardaman's 1903 race for governor "became so venomous that some predicted his election would result in four years of radicalism and riot; four years of whitecappism and lynching; four years of ignoring the law and of trampling the Constitution underfoot." Because Roosevelt had dined at the White House with Booker T. Washington and had clearly made it known that he was progressive on the race question, he became a magnet for a "smoldering race prejudice" in Mississippi. Vardaman frequently called Roosevelt a "coon-flavored miscegenationist" in his speeches. He referred to the president as "that wild, untamed, self asserted, bronco busting negro dining man who sits in the chair of Washington, Jefferson, and Wm. McKinley." These extreme racial views were not limited to Mississippi, nor were they even limited to the southern states.[8]

Although Booker T. Washington had dined with Roosevelt in October, 1901, the southern politicians and newspapers kept the issue alive for several years. The Memphis *Scimitar*, which had a wide circulation in the Mississippi Delta, wrote of Roosevelt's meal with Booker T. Washington. "The most damnable outrage which has ever been perpetrated by any citizen of the United States was committed yesterday by the President when he invited a nigger to dine with him at the White House....he went out of his way and extended a special invitation to a nigger to sit down at table with him — a nigger whose only claim to distinction is that, by comparison with the balance of his race, he has been considered somewhat superior."[9]

It was into this race-baited political atmosphere created by the likes of Vardaman that Roosevelt returned to the South in 1907, for another hunt with Holt Collier. This time, he came at the invitation of John M. Parker and John A. McIlhenny. Roosevelt was to stay for two weeks near Stamboul, Louisiana, and participate in a hunt of significantly longer duration than the one in 1902.[10] They would hunt in Louisiana, on about seven thousand acres owned by Parker, and Roosevelt would participate in festivities in Vicksburg and travel through Mississippi immediately afterward.

• • •

Several weeks before the hunt was to begin, sixty-one-year-old Holt Collier joined Alex Enolds at the Rescue Plantation in Louisiana to scout the area for bears. Enolds insisted that there were large numbers of bears in the woods along the Tensas River. Collier strongly doubted this, having found very little evidence to support Enolds's claims. With "misgivings", Parker and McIlhenny decided to follow Enolds's recommendation, disregarding those of the older but trusted Collier. For two weeks the men and their crews set out on the difficult task of cutting trails and clearing a camp site out of the canebrake in anticipation of another presidential visit.

On Saturday, October 5, 1907, Roosevelt arrived at the railroad siding in Stamboul, Louisiana, and proceeded on horseback immediately to the camp site. He was greeted by a driving rain that lasted several days. In the presidential party were Dr. Presley M. Rixey, surgeon general of the Navy; Major Amacker; Dr. Hugh Miller; Dr. Alexander Lambert, a regular hunting partner of the president's; John M. Parker; and John McIlhenny. Alex Enolds led the party to the camp, keenly aware of his position as the lead guide of the hunt. Holt Collier was not there when Roosevelt arrived. He had returned to Greenville to collect his pack of dogs.

To avoid the "picnic" atmosphere of the 1902 hunt, Roosevelt had given strict orders that the hunting party not be interrupted. Harris Dickson wrote of the secrecy involved, "Twenty miles away secret ser-

BEN LILLY

vice men rode on every train and observed every traveler. It would have been impossible for a stranger to set foot in the country without being stopped and asked his business. Not a negro on any of the plantations could have been hired to guide a visitor to the President's camp. The planters had seen to that. No man could have threaded those swamps without a guide."[11]

Parker and McIlhenny had invited the notoriously famous bear hunter Ben Lilly to help manage the hunt. Ben Lilly was raised in Mississippi and moved to Louisiana as a young man, where he had worked as a blacksmith. He was a fifty-three-year-old eccentric pothunter who had a reputation as a master tracker and crack shot, but he was an indiscriminate killer. He had piercing blue eyes and an unkempt beard and was small but muscular, weighing about 180 pounds. Lilly has been described as "a bit addled," "a goofy old coot," and one "whose oddness went far beyond anything that could safely be called eccentricity." Roosevelt later wrote confidentially that Lilly was a "religious fanatic." When Roosevelt met him, Lilly had abandoned "house living" and had taken up living in the wild, much like the animals he hunted.[12] Roosevelt had never met any other man so indifferent to fatigue and hardship. The president compared him to "Cooper's Deerslayer in woodcraft, in hardihood, in simplicity — and also in loquacity."[13]

On the morning following Roosevelt's arrival at camp his party was joined by Lilly, who must have looked pitiful as he wandered onto the camp scene. Roosevelt wrote, "The morning he joined us in camp, he had come on foot through the thick woods, followed by his two dogs, and had neither eaten nor drunk for twenty four hours; for he did not like to drink the swamp water. It had rained hard throughout the night and he had no shelter, no rubber coat, nothing but the clothes he was wearing, and the ground was too wet for him to lie on; so he perched in a crooked tree in the beating rain, much as if he had been a wild turkey."[14]

Other than the impression he made on his arrival, Ben Lilly's presence was of little note during the hunt. The first day it continued to rain, and only one old she-bear with a yearling was jumped. Roosevelt had again been placed on a stand, this time by Lilly and Enolds, but they were unable to herd any game to him. Afterward, Roosevelt and his hosts took it upon themselves to search the area for signs of bears and found very few. When the hunters complained, Enolds insisted that the cutting of the trails through the canebrake had frightened them off.

That afternoon, Monday, October 7, Holt Collier arrived with Clive and Harley Metcalfe and their pack of twenty-two dogs, including two veteran canines named Rowdy and Queen. This addition swelled the size of the pack to thirty-four. Immediately Harley Metcalfe took issue with the progress of the hunt and challenged the way it was being conducted. He based his challenge on the negative reports he received from Holt Collier.

According to Roosevelt, "The Metcalfs were young men—swampers, planters, Mississippians, gentlemen in the old English conception of the term — and bear hunters from the heart." The president had little knowledge of the preparations for this hunt or of the individual conflicts of personality that had resulted in the selection of the site.

"Look here, Colonel,' said Harley Metcalf, 'you have plenty of good bear hunters, and lots of dogs, but you've got seventy-five miles of country and no bear in it."

"How do you know that?"

"I sent Holt Collier over here to investigate it."

"Don't you know,' urged the Colonel, 'there are reported to be fifteen or twenty bear in here?"

"Yes, that may be reported, but there are only five bears in the whole seventy-five miles of country. Holt knows what he is talking about."[15]

Roosevelt later provided an account of the arrival of Holt Collier and the Metcalfes, giving them the ultimate credit for the success of the hunt. "Late in the evening of the same day we were joined by two gentlemen, to whom we owed the success of our hunt. They were Messrs. Clive and Harley Metcalf, planters from Mississippi, men in the prime of life, thorough woodsmen and hunters, skilled marksmen, and utterly fearless horsemen. For a quarter of a century they had hunted bear and deer with horse and hound, and were masters of the art. They brought with them their pack of bear hounds, only one, however, being a thoroughly staunch and seasoned veteran. The pack was under the immediate control of a negro hunter, Holt Collier, in his own way as remarkable a character as Ben Lilley. He was a man of sixty and could neither read nor write, but he had all the dignity of an African chief, and for half a century he had been a bear hunter, having killed or assisted in killing over three thousand bears. He had been born a slave on the Hinds plantation, his father, an old man when he was born, having been the body-servant and cook of "old General Hinds," as he called him, when the latter fought under Jackson at New Orleans. When ten years old Holt had been taken on the horse behind his young master, the Hinds of that day, on a bear hunt, when he killed his first bear. In the Civil War he had not only followed his master to battle as his body-servant, but had acted under him as sharpshooter against the Union soldiers. After the war he continued to stay with his master until the latter died, and had then been adopted by the Metcalfs; and he felt that he had brought them up, and treated them with that mixture of affection and grumbling respect which an old nurse shows toward the lad who has ceased being a child. The two Metcalfs and Holt understood one another thoroughly, and understood their hounds and the game their hounds followed almost as thoroughly."[16]

Ben Lilly took a hand in the discussion of the bear population and informed the others that he had seen several signs of bears near Bear Lake, about fourteen miles away. As a result of his recommendation the Tensas camp was abandoned and the party moved. The move was an unprecedented change in plans, considering the camp had been cleared and the trails cut for weeks beforehand.

Bear Lake was created from an old riverbed a few hundred yards wide and several miles long. Situated in the deepest of swamps, the

*IN THE LOUISIANA CANEBRAKES, 1907, Dr. Rixey, John Parker, John McIlhenney, Harley Metcalfe, President Theodore Roosevelt, Clive Metcalfe, Tom Osborne and Icabod Osborne.*

cane grew thick and the matted vines reached out from the shore to rest upon the waters. On a bit of high ground someone had built a shack, a poor man's hunting lodge, in which the presidential party set up camp.

Again, Roosevelt was required to still-hunt from a stand. The difficulties attendant to this procedure were self-evident. In order to be successful a bear would have to be herded in his direction. By the time the guides could get a bear to him the animal would have made himself a target several times, and the danger to the dogs was considerable. On the first morning, Holt and his hounds jumped a bear, but it got away during the pursuit. A second bear was killed, but not by the president.

The camp was similar to the arrangement in 1902. There were two fires started every night, one for the white hunters and one for the guides. Inevitably "the negroes clustered about the other," and often "the Colonel left his own fire and went down to talk with the negroes, finding keen enjoyment in their novel point of view. Most frequently it happened, as the stories began to pass around, that the negroes gradually deserted their own fire and circled round the gentlemen. Every man had his chance, and whosoever knew aught of interest was at liberty to tell it. The discussion frequently turned upon the dangers of the hunt."[17]

• • •

One morning near Joe's Bayou the dogs jumped a wild boar and chased it a few hundred yards until it turned on them. By the time Collier arrived at the scene three of the most aggressive hounds were killed, torn through by the animal's sharp tusks. Holt quickly dismounted, raced in, and grabbed the boar by the hind leg. Tom Osborn, a Louisiana planter's son who had joined the hunt the night before, quickly joined in the fray and stabbed the boar to death.

It was a revealing incident among these hardened men when Holt Collier returned to camp from Joe's Bayou that night. He was wet, shivering and suffering from the elements. Without hesitation, both the Metcalfe brothers placed him by the fire, rubbed his body dry, and warmed him with their own towels before dressing him in their own dry clothes. Clive Metcalfe was kneeling before his old mentor, tending to his every need, when he noticed Roosevelt studiously observing. When he finished dressing Holt, he rose and said as though embarrassed, "Holt, don't you ever let me do that again!"[18]

For ten long days the hunt continued without success. The activity had been intense and persevering, yet the president had not gotten a bear. Parker and McIlhenny were distressed. The Metcalfes suggested that Holt Collier take over as manager of the hunt. On Thursday evening with time rapidly approaching for his return to Washington, Roosevelt called the elder nimrod over to the fire.

"Holt, I haven't got but one or two more days. What am I going to do? I haven't killed a bear."

The old guide answered promptly, "Cunnel, ef you let me manage the hunt you'll sho' kill one to-morrow. One of 'em got away to-day that you ought to have killed."

"Whatever you say goes, Holt."

"'All right, Cunnel."

Collier called Clive Metcalfe and instructed him to "take the Cunnel and bum around with him in the woods like you an' me always does, and don't put him on no more stand. He ain't no baby.

He kin go anywhere you kin go; jes' keep him as near to the dogs as you kin. Mr. Harley and me'll follow the hounds; when we strike a trail you and the Cunnel come a-runnin."[19]

The next morning Holt went with Alex, Tom Osborn, Ichabod Osborn (Tom's father), and Harley Metcalfe to follow the dogs. Roosevelt held back with Clive Metcalfe to await the sound of the hounds and bear at bay. About six miles into the cane the dogs jumped a bear, which proceeded to run in the wrong direction. They pursued knowing that "when the cane got thin, the bear would turn around and come back again — for a bear will not break cover if he can avoid it." This bear never did stop, never treed, and never went to bay. "When the cane grew thin he doubled on his tracks and started toward the President."[20]

Clive Metcalfe and Roosevelt separated from the others at the place where tracks had been found the day before. They waited between two canebrakes for about two hours when they heard "the notes of one of the loudest-mouthed hounds, and instantly rode toward it." They rode hard to the point determined by Metcalfe to be the "probable line of a bear's flight" based on the direction of the "babel of the pack."

Roosevelt appreciated the chase and wrote that the horses "kept their feet like cats as they leaped logs, plunged through bushes, and dodged in and out among the tree trunks; and we had all we could do to prevent the vines from lifting us out of the saddle, while the thorns tore our hands and faces." They traversed the swamp several times always attempting to anticipate the direction of the chase. After a few hours without result, they heard the "cheering of Harley Metcalfe and Tom Osborn and one or two of the negro hunters...trying to keep the dogs up to their work" in the thick canebrake.

When they heard the lead dog at bay in the thickest of the cover, they galloped as close to the place as possible and dismounted. Making their way into the dense stand of cane, it was impossible to keep totally quiet. As they approached, they could tell by the sounds that the bear was again on the move, making what is called a "walking bay." The hunters quietly made their way through the thick cane until Clive suggested they wait. Roosevelt wrote later that he "crouched down...with my rifle at the ready" until he "made out the dim outline of the bear coming straight toward" them. The president quietly cocked and half-raised his rifle and waited for a clear shot. The bear sensed danger, "turned almost broadside" to Roosevelt, and walked "forward very stiff-legged, almost as if on tiptoe, now and then looking back at the nearest dogs." Roosevelt took aim and fired through the dense cane.

The shot was fatal, penetrating both lungs of the animal. When the bear fell, the dogs came forward in typical reckless fashion. Believing the bear to still be a danger to the dogs, Roosevelt ran forward and fired a final round into the back of the neck, severing the spine. The president later wrote that the bear went down "stark dead, slain in the canebrake in true hunter fashion."[21]

*ROOSEVELT, By Alexander Lambert, 1907 Louisiana hunt.*

The great white hunter was overwhelmed. He threw down his gun, joyously pulled Harley Metcalfe from his horse and proclaimed the hunt a great success. The bear was mounted on the back of Collier's horse and taken back to camp. Roosevelt claimed the bear weighed two hundred and two pounds. The press reported that it weighed three hundred and seventy-five pounds. At the end of the day Dr. Alexander Lambert photographed Holt Collier and Theodore Roosevelt standing among the dogs, but the photograph has never been found.

The final count of the 1907 Louisiana hunt was three bears, six deer, one wild turkey, twelve squirrels, one duck, one possum, and one wildcat. All of the game animals were eaten by the hunters with the exception of the wildcat.

*WARREN COUNTY COURTHOUSE, 1907, on the occasion of the visit of President Theodore Roosevelt.*

On October 20 President Roosevelt arrived at the residence of Leo Shields to stay the night. He enjoyed his final meal with his hunting companions and enjoyed his last visit with some of the guides, including Holt Collier, Alex Enolds, Brutus Jackson, and numerous cooks, teamsters, and messengers.

The following day Roosevelt departed for Vicksburg for a grand reception and parade through the city and a newly dedicated monument at the National Military Park. He was met there by LeRoy Percy and many other friends. Governor Vardaman did not attend. On the steps of the Warren County Courthouse where Holt Collier had been tried and acquitted for the murder of Captain James A. King forty years earlier Roosevelt gave a stirring speech honoring Jefferson Davis and thereby neutralizing much of the criticism earlier made by Governor Vardaman. That evening his train carried him to Leland, just a few miles from the Metcalfes' Newstead and Glenbar plantations, where he again addressed a large crowd. A little after 8:00 p.m. his train left Leland and traveled through the Mississippi darkness to Memphis. He would never again visit Mississippi. Upon his return to Washington, Roosevelt ordered three guns to be delivered to his friends in Greenville. The 45-70 caliber model 1886 Winchester lever action rifles President Roosevelt presented to Harley and Clive Metcalfe and to Holt Collier were treasured keepsakes that all three displayed with great pride.[22]

• • •

In December 1908 Roosevelt invited several of his hunting friends to a dinner at the White House. Dubbed the "Teddy Bear" dinner, it was held in the State Dining Room and included as guests Clive and Harley Metcalfe, John Osborn, Tom Osborn, John M. Parker, J. M. Dickinson, Fitzhugh Lee, and others. Ben Lilly had been invited, but did not attend, the explanation given that he was too bashful.

Roosevelt described the dinner as one of his most memorable meals in the White House. "[T]here was one feast at the White House which stands above all others in my memory....This was the bear-hunters dinner. I had been treated so kindly by my friends on these hunts, and they were such fine fellows, men whom I was so proud to think of as Americans, that I set my heart on having them at a hunters' dinner at the White House. One December I succeeded; there were twenty or thirty of them, all told, as good hunters, as daring riders, as first-class citizens as could be found anywhere; no finer set of guests ever sat at meat in the White House; and among other game on the table was a black bear, itself contributed by one of these same guests."[23]

Holt Collier was invited to Washington by Roosevelt, but the uneducated Collier declined the president's invitation. "The President wanted me to go to Washington with him, and lots o' negroes aroun' here thought I was a mighty big fool for not goin'. But I didn't have any friends in Washington, an' I couldn't hunt up there. So I thought the best thing for me to do would be to stay right here among my own people."[24]

# CHAPTER 15

# PENSIONER

*At first they had come in wagons: the guns, the bedding, the dogs, the food....
But that time was gone now. Now they went in cars, driving faster and faster
each year because the roads were better and they had farther and
farther to drive, the territory in which game still existed drawing yearly inward
as his life was drawing inward....*
— William Faulkner[1]

Holt Collier continued to hunt bears after 1907. He guided others and on one hunt about 1910 he captured a cub which was kept at Newstead Plantation. The cub was named Lucy and was a pet of the Metcalfe children until it grew too large. Rather than kill it, the bear was donated to the Memphis Zoo where it was displayed until it died at an old age.[2]

For many years Collier held out hope that he would manage another large hunt for his friend, Colonel Theodore Roosevelt. After the 1907 hunt the Winchester 45-70 model 1886 that the president gave him was a most treasured item among his many weapons. He heard from Roosevelt through the Metcalfe brothers and claimed to have received several personal letters from him through the years.

The last documented bear kill involving Holt Collier was on November 16, 1912, when the old hunter was sixty-six. He took Albert Gallatin Metcalfe, Clive's ten-year-old son, into the Bolivar County canebrakes along the Bogue Phalia River. The young Metcalfe, who was probably the "youngest bear hunter in the United States," killed a very large three hundred pound black bear. The hunt, which also included Clive, started on horseback early that morning with Holt's pack of dogs. After leaving the horses to travel on foot, the dogs led the hunters more than three miles into the swamp before they started a bear. As the bear ran through the cane,

NEWSTEAD PLANTATION, circa 1908, Fredrick Augustus Metcalfe, Clive Metcalfe, Holt Collier, Harley Metcalfe, George 'Jug' Metcalfe, Albert Gallatin Metcalfe. Note the pet bear 'Lucy' among the dogs.

"young Albert Metcalfe planted nine buckshot behind her shoulder."[3] It was a memory the boy carried for a lifetime.

The world Holt Collier had lived in and the lifestyle he had mastered had almost disappeared when he settled into town life, quietly enjoying his local celebrity. Greenville was a town that was "plumb social." It was not considered a "beauty in those days....The brick stores, most of them still in situ...managed to look stark without looking simple. Curbs, gutters, and open ditches, while satisfactory to such stalwart conservatives as crawfish and mosquitoes, still abided.... Sidewalks were often the two-board sort that grow splinters for barefoot boys, and the roads, summer or winter, were hazards. There were lovely trees and crape myrtles but where they grew was their business. There were flowers, but no gardens. Just a usual Southern town of that period...."[4] Delta jazz great W. C. Handy frequently played at local functions just around the corner from Collier's house. Handy lived nearby and played the river boats between New Orleans to St. Louis.

200 • *Holt Collier*

*NEWSTEAD PLANTATION, 1912, Clive Metcalfe and Albert Gallatin Metcalfe with 300 pound bear from a Holt Collier hunt.*

As Holt Collier settled into town life, the Mississippi Delta began a slow change. LeRoy Percy, who had won a seat in the U. S. Senate, was put out of office in 1911 by white supremacist James K. Vardaman. An unsettling wind of political change had swept over the state. Greenville was a community of about ten thousand people by 1913. The town's growth had been gradual as an increasing number of sharecroppers and white laborers moved into town. William Alexander Percy described the newcomers, "Strangers had drifted in since the war — from the hills, from the North, from all sorts of odd places where they hadn't succeeded or hadn't been wanted....The town was changing, but so insidiously that the old-timers could feel but could not analyze the change. The new-comers weren't foreigners or Jews, they were an alien breed of Anglo-Saxon."[5]

Collier's retirement from a lifetime of hunting was made official on January 6, 1919, when several friends approached the seventy-three-year-old man and told him that Theodore Roosevelt had died. Though Collier was certainly too old to have endured another excursion, he had always hoped that he might take Roosevelt on one last hunt. Over the years he had spoken about one more hunt to several of his friends, men he could depend on to get the word to Roosevelt, and the old guide kept his hunting gear at the ready. The notice of the former president's death "put an end to my huntin' wid Roosevelt," said a sorrowful Collier, who added that "I still got de gun he done give me!"[6]

• • •

In the 1920s several reporters journeyed to Greenville to interview the aging Holt Collier. One of them was Harris Dickson of Vicksburg, a novelist and well-known freelance writer who published several articles about Collier, his experiences in the Delta wilderness, and especially about his hunts with President Roosevelt.

Dickson visited Greenville often and became very fond of the old man. He had calendars and matchbooks made with the old hunter's likeness emblazoned on them, and they were widely distributed around Washington County.[7] Often Dickson had Collier visit at his home in Vicksburg. On one occasion the author wrote that he "kept the old man here in my yard for weeks and talked with him every day, getting a far more coherent narrative than I was able to piece together from fragments" from other sources. Though he tried Dickson could not get Holt to admit that he had killed Captain James A. King. Dickson wrote erroneously that to "the end of his life Holt would never tell the facts of this killing, not even to his best friend Senator Leroy Percy. He gave me the details of his various trials, but not a syllable about how the officer got killed."[8]

Harris Dickson once took Collier to Jeff Snyder's "bungalow on the Tensas River" in Louisiana, where he entertained several friends from New York. "It was too dry for a hunt, but the picturesque old fellow gave atmosphere to the camp and pumped those yankees full of bear stories." Holt's friend, U. S. Senator LeRoy Percy had been expected on that trip, but he was detained in "Washington City."

When Holt returned to Greenville, Senator Percy asked him, "Holt, what kind of a party was it that Mr. Dickson had on the Tensas?"

Collier replied, "Lawd Gawd, Senator, dat was de finest bunch o' yankee white gentlemen what ever hit dis swamp. Never done nothin all day long an' all night long 'cept set up dere on de front gallery an' play poker, drink toddies an' shoot craps. Shoot craps drink toddies and play poker all day long an all night long. Finest bunch o' gentlemen you ever camped wid."

Dickson took meticulous notes and began a nonfiction account on the life of Holt Collier, which for unexplained reasons was never completed. Although Dickson avoided Civil War topics, Holt Collier was his one exception. Dickson wrote that he had "never done much work that touched the civil war, because as a boy I got pretty much fed up on it, especially with the mawkish stuff we had to read. But this seems so real, so human, that I'd be keen to do it. And with such a wealth of material I should make a good job."[9]

• • •

By 1909 there had been articles in five national publications about Holt Collier, his life and the Roosevelt bear hunts. They included several photographs and were all well-circulated. Harris Dickson had written three of those articles for the *Saturday Evening Post*, which included "When the President Hunts" August 8, 1908, "The Bearslayer" March 13, 1909, and "Bear Stories" April 10, 1909. An earlier article was written by Lindsay Denison, who accompanied Roosevelt on the 1902 Mississippi hunt. Denison's account, "President Roosevelt's Mississippi Bear Hunt," was published in *Outing* magazine in February, 1903. The most notable article on Holt Collier, "In The Louisiana Canebrakes," was written by President Theodore Roosevelt and appeared in *Scribner's* magazine in January, 1908. In each of these publications Holt Collier was described in glowing terms as a man of unique talents and unparalleled ability.

*Clive Metcalfe and Holt Collier, circa 1916.*

The same month Roosevelt published his article telling the world about Holt Collier and his hunting experience in the Louisiana canebrake, Frances and Holt Collier purchased from Fay S. Boddie a parcel of property on Broadway Street in Greenville, where they began to build their home.[10] This house on Broadway was Collier's home for the next twenty eight years. His days as a rounder had come to an end.

• • •

By the mid-1920s Collier had achieved legendary status and was a familiar sight on the streets of Greenville. At eighty years of age he kept a horse and buckboard and frequently drove to Newstead Plantation to visit the Metcalfe family, where he was always welcomed and often fed. He dressed neatly and looked sharp in his hunting vest and Confederate hat. "For many years Holt's erect and sturdy figure was a familiar sight on Greenville streets. A stranger would have noticed his bearing, his dark face with iron gray mustache and Vandyke beard and the broad-brimmed felt hat he always wore." The wide hat, similar to those worn by soldiers in the Confederate army, shaded his failing eyes as he sat on the small porch of his home watching the passing scene.[11]

Children black and white followed him as he strolled the streets. They often sat on his porch at night listening to his life history. Two of those young boys, Pete Johnson and Nathan Wilson, jockeyed for position on the steps of Collier's front porch to better hear the tall tales of his long career. They heard firsthand of his life as a young slave and how he had served as an armed combatant in the white army of the Confederacy. He told them of his years hunting wild bear and how in the old days he had confronted his prey with nothing more than a knife. Inevitably, the children always asked to hear how he had captured for the president of the United States the very bear that was the inspiration for the popular children's toy.

Every night he played a game with the children. Before he would share his stories, he required them to pool their pennies to buy him an orange-flavored Nehi soda and a plug of tobacco. Pete and Nathan and others would run to the store next door and return quickly with the offering. For hours on those warm Mississippi nights Holt Collier would enchant the neighborhood children with his idyllic descriptions of a day gone by and of a wilderness lost forever. In those waning years he "took life easy" and enjoyed his time as a positive influence on the children. Three of the surviving children, Pete Johnson, Nathan Wilson, and Luella Anderson, knew Holt both as children and as young adults. In separate interviews six decades after Collier's death, taken hundreds of miles apart, they all recalled that Holt Collier never drank alcohol, never smoked, and never attended church.[12]

Pete Johnson, who visited Collier from the early twenties until 1933 when he "hopped a train and left Greenville," described the old hunter as illiterate, "but he spoke such good English that you'd never know he couldn't read or write." Johnson said Collier would "walk the streets with his cavalry hat, the pipe in his mouth and his Confederate pistol. He had a long-handled mustache and a goatee and folks were a little scared of him. But he was good with us kids. We would worry him to death asking him to tell us stories. I'd go there every day like I was going to the picture show. Imagine, he'd tell us all these stories and I found out that they were true."[13]

• • •

In 1922, Collier was approached by Willa Johnson, a local photographer, and asked to sit for a series of portraits. Johnson was known to everyone in Greenville as an eccentric. She was described as a girl with a "charming child face developed into what is charitably remembered as a plain looking woman."

Willa was the daughter of an early settler of the county who lost his family's substantial land holdings on horses and poker. She rolled her own cigarettes at parties at a time when it was frowned upon for a woman to smoke in public. She was an excellent guitarist and folk singer and was best known in her profession for her photographs of William Faulkner. She was also known for the "severely tailored suits and close cropped coiffure" that she had acquired after a visit to New York, but she was most respected in the Mississippi Delta as "an expert shot with either pistol or rifle."[14]

Willa Johnson's efforts resulted in some unforgettable portraits of Collier, which were the images Harris Dickson used on his calendars and matchbooks. She printed five-by-seven and eight-by-eleven inch black and white photographs that were widely distributed to Holt's friends and to those who knew him only by reputation. The photographs, matchbooks, and calendars were displayed for several years in the homes of both white and black families across Washington County. Holt was, after all, a local celebrity. "The president, millionaires of England and America, and scores of friends have pictures of Holt. They won't let him keep a supply of them. And he does make a fine picture, whether with hat off and irongray hair brushed

*HOLT COLLIER, with the 1886 45-70 Winchester,
a gift from President Theodore Roosevelt, circa 1922.*

back, or with it on, his white beard and steely mustache trimmed to perfection, and in his hands, the rifle Roosevelt gave him."[15]

Holt Collier became a Mississippi Delta icon in the twenties and thirties, a proud and independent man respected by every element of the community. He transcended the barrier of race during a time and in a place where race was a barrier in all things. His color was never an issue with the whites, and his association with whites was never an issue with his black friends. He was respected and beloved by everyone regardless of race, gender, or generation.[16]

• • •

In April, 1927 the serenity of Holt's retirement was shattered by the "Great Flood." The breach in the Mississippi River levee occurred at Mounds Landing north of Greenville on April 21, 1927. A torrent of water thirty feet high and over one hundred feet wide went crashing into the flat lands of the Delta. The volume of water was so great that it "came in as rolling surf...five-foot breakers." In Greenville, the eight foot protection levee was ripped apart "as smoothly as if unzipping it." Hundreds of people were killed, and countless livestock were washed away. Seven thousand square miles that was the lower Mississippi Delta became a whitecapped sea averaging eight to ten feet in depth. The only dry land was found on a few old Indian mounds and the crests of levees. A month after the break, the crevasse in the levee was estimated to be three-quarters of a mile in width.[17]

At Greenville almost eight thousand farm workers and the surviving livestock were encamped along seven miles of levee. When the water poured over the town's own protection levee, the residents knew the last haven of refuge was lost [18] Almost all of the citizens of Greenville had to retreat to the main levee. The flood that took thirty-six hours to devastate the Delta would take over four months to recede into the banks of the Mississippi and its tributaries.

Holt Collier, familiar with the habits of the unpredictable river, had the foresight to build one of the few two-story houses in his section of town. On the cramped second floor he resided with Frances for four long months, relying heavily on friends for food and comfort, of which there was very little.

After the waters receded, Holt and Frances made every effort to adjust to their desperate situation. The flood that devastated the entire region had been no kinder to Holt Collier than it had to anyone else. His home was severely damaged and went without necessary repairs for more than eighteen months. His floor was destroyed, and repairs were desperately needed. He had to wait his turn, as every structure in the city required renovation or demolition. To make matters worse, a storm that year caused serious damage to his roof.

In 1928, largely because of the flood and the economic disruption it caused, many African Americans began leaving Washington County for better opportunities in the North. Collier saw many of his people leave the area. From the effects of the flood, the storm, and the loss of his friends, Collier fell into a state of despair from which he never completely recovered.[19] His wife Frances earned a meager income as a housekeeper, but Holt was too feeble to provide any income other than his pension of two hundred dollars annually. He had for years collected corn shucks from the area plantations which he sold to a stable. He also collected dried bones which he sold as fertilizer, and on occasion he would train and sell a hunting dog. One dog he sold to John and Nathan Adams for thirty dollars would not hunt. When the boys returned the dog, Holt explained that "his ears had to be twisted with pliers and he would have taken to the briars."[20] Collier also made a little money during prohibition by supplying Arkansas corn whiskey to his white friends who did not want to deal with bootleggers across the river.[21]

Holt Collier's Confederate servant's pension was successfully renewed in 1916, and in 1928 Collier was approved for a pension from the State of Mississippi not as a servant, but as a Confederate soldier. No longer was the award based on Holt's service to his former master. He was recognized as a combatant for his service in the Ninth Texas Cavalry.[22] He is the only known African American classified as a combatant by any of the former Confederate states.

• • •

In October 1929 Camille Percy, the wife of LeRoy Percy, passed away. After her death LeRoy's health faded rapidly, and he died on Christmas Eve. LeRoy Percy, the son of the "Gray Eagle" who had saved Collier from the hangman's noose so many years earlier, was one of Collier's last human connections to the parade of valiant and proud men who had passed before him.

After the funeral of LeRoy Percy, Collier visited young William Alexander Percy in the senator's Greenville law office. The young

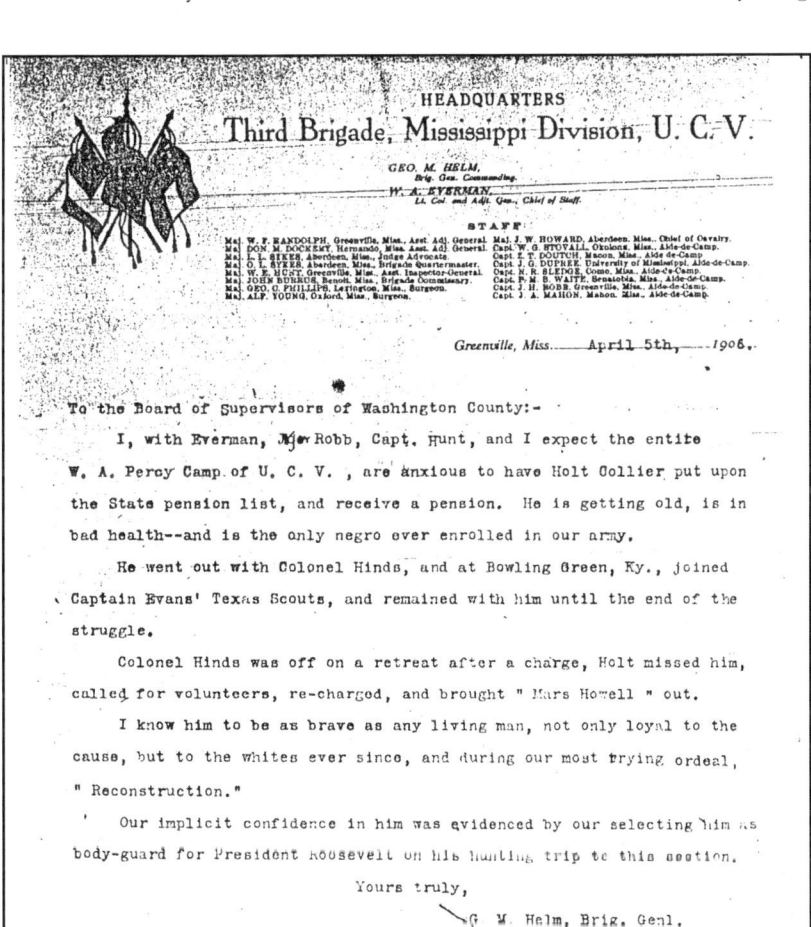

> **HEADQUARTERS**
> **Third Brigade, Mississippi Division, U. C. V.**
>
> GEO. M. HELM,
> Brig. Gen. Commanding.
>
> W. A. EVERMAN,
> Lt. Col. and Adjt. Gen., Chief of Staff
>
> **STAFF**
>
> Maj. W. F. RANDOLPH, Greenville, Miss., Asst. Adj. General.  Maj. J. W. HOWARD, Aberdeen, Miss., Chief of Cavalry.
> Maj. DON M. DOCKERY, Hernando, Miss., Asst. Adj. General.   Capt. W. G. STOVALL, Okolona, Miss., Aide-de-Camp.
> Maj. L. L. SIKES, Aberdeen, Miss., Judge Advocate.           Capt. E. T. DOUTCH, Macon, Miss., Aide-de-Camp.
> Maj. O. L. SYKES, Aberdeen, Miss., Brigade Quartermaster.    Capt. J. G. DUPREE, University of Mississippi, Aide-de-Camp.
> Maj. W. E. HUNT, Greenville, Miss., Asst. Inspector-General. Capt. N. R. SLEDGE, Como, Miss., Aide-de-Camp.
> Maj. JOHN BURRUS, Benoit, Miss., Brigade Commissary.         Capt. P. M. B. WAITE, Senatobia, Miss., Aide-de-Camp.
> Maj. GEO. O. PHILLIPS, Lexington, Miss., Surgeon.            Capt. J. H. ROBB, Greenville, Miss., Aide-de-Camp.
> Maj. ALF. YOUNG, Oxford, Miss., Surgeon.                     Capt. J. A. MAHON, Mahon, Miss., Aide-de-Camp.
>
> Greenville, Miss. April 5th, 1906.
>
> To the Board of Supervisors of Washington County:-
>
> I, with Everman, Maj. Robb, Capt. Hunt, and I expect the entire W. A. Percy Camp of U. C. V., are anxious to have Holt Collier put upon the State pension list, and receive a pension. He is getting old, is in bad health--and is the only negro ever enrolled in our army.
>
> He went out with Colonel Hinds, and at Bowling Green, Ky., joined Captain Evans' Texas Scouts, and remained with him until the end of the struggle.
>
> Colonel Hinds was off on a retreat after a charge, Holt missed him, called for volunteers, re-charged, and brought " Mars Howell " out.
>
> I know him to be as brave as any living man, not only loyal to the cause, but to the whites ever since, and during our most trying ordeal, " Reconstruction."
>
> Our implicit confidence in him was evidenced by our selecting him as body-guard for President Roosevelt on his hunting trip to this section.
>
> Yours truly,
>
> G. M. Helm, Brig. Genl.,
>
> By W. W. Everman, Lt. Col. and A. A. Genl.
>
> We indorse the above.
>
> J. H. Crouch, Sheriff of Washington County.
>
> LeRoy Percy.

*MISSISSIPPI DEPARTMENT OF ARCHIVES AND HISTORY.*

**ORIGINAL UNITED CONFEDERATE VETERAN LETTER REFERRING HOLT COLLIER FOR A PENSION**, *citing that he "is the only negro ever enrolled in our army."*

Percy wrote fondly of that visit, "Holt, a hunting partner of Father's and an ex-slave, came up to the office to express his grief. I met him in the hall, but he motioned me to Father's desk, saying: 'Set there where he sot. That's where you b'long.' He took the chair across the desk from me, filling it and resting his strong hands on the heavy cane he always carried and needed. He was a magnificent old man with massive shoulders and a noble head. For some minutes he struggled silently, sitting there in what had been Father's office, then he let the tears gush unhindered from his eyes and the words from his heart: 'The roof is gone from over my head and the floor from under my feet. I am out in the dark and the cold alone. I want to go where he is.' He rose and hobbled out. Many of us felt that way."[23]

• • •

After the 1929 crops were planted, Collier's economic circumstances were discussed by some of his friends. Arrangements were made for him and Frances to take a loan at the Washington County Building and Loan Association to repair their house. On November 16, 1929, Collier and his wife borrowed six hundred and fifty dollars to remodel their home.[24] When Harley Metcalfe Jr. learned of the old man's plight, he and E. B. LaFoe Sr. visited Collier at his house on the pretense of purchasing some corn whiskey. Metcalfe saw that Collier had a large bundle of split shingles remaining from the remodeling job, and bought them by writing a draft to him on the face of a shingle in the amount of the full cost of the repairs. Collier took this unusual devise to the Commercial Bank of Greenville. It was honored and the money was used to pay the loan. This gift of a new roof by Harley Metcalfe Jr. and the manner of its tender was the source of much local lore for years.[25]

Except for this act of generosity by young Harley Metcalfe Jr. old age was not kind to Holt Collier. In addition to all of the other problems confronting him, Holt Collier was losing the one thing that had never failed him–his eyesight. He was going blind.

## CHAPTER 16

## END OF THE HUNT

*Then he and the doctor and McCaslin and Major de Spain went to Sam's hut.
This time Sam didn't open his eyes and his breathing was so quiet,
so peaceful that they could hardly see that he breathed.
The doctor didn't even take out his stethoscope nor even touch him.
"He's all right," the doctor said. "He didn't even catch cold. He just quit."
"Quit?" McCaslin said. "Yes. Old people do that sometimes."*
— William Faulkner[1]

On October 9, 1931, while rising from an afternoon bath in her kitchen, Frances Collier fell victim to a stroke and died from a cerebral hemorrhage. She was fifty-four years old and had been Holt's wife for almost thirty years. After her death Holt Collier was alone with the exception of Frances's son Toots, whom Holt had never liked, the neighborhood children, a few old friends, and the reporters who occasionally visited.[2]

Clive Metcalfe died in 1924, and Harley was himself too old to be of much help. Holt's brother Marshall was long since dead and Collier's namesake, Marshall's youngest son, died at the age of sixty-five in April 1935. Collier was too feeble to claim the body, which was given a pauper's burial.

* * *

Several of the new faster breed of young hunters sought out the old nimrod of the Mississippi Delta. They would collect him at his home and take him to see their dogs or just visit to swap tall tales of the hunt. Several of the men who claimed to be hunters in the noble old style came from small towns outside Washington County. They worked in Greenville, often had large packs of hounds, and enjoyed a good hunt, but the only quarry a dog would have run by that time were deer, raccoons, and possum, as very few bears could be found.

Holt Collier's treasured collection of artifacts included the Winchester rifle Roosevelt had given him and the letters the president had written him. Some of the men who prided themselves as being among the best of the new local hunters eventually came into possession of Collier's guns and hunting tack. Collier complained in 1932 that "de gen'lemen come an borrow de letters an' de bear skins an' forgit ter bring 'em back! Dat's why' — he caresses the rifle fondly — 'I keep de Pres'dent gun locked up!"[3] In time even the presidential gift would be taken from him. Facing the difficult period of life naturally brought upon him by the plague of old age, it was the ultimate humiliation that he would be taken advantage of by those men he had trusted.

From his front porch Collier reminisced with anyone who stopped by to visit. His temperament was often depressed and reflective. Harris Dickson continued to visit regularly and took meticulous notes of his conversations with the old man. More than sixty years after the passing of Howell Hinds, the feeble Holt Collier often mentioned his old master in devoted terms. Collier was crying openly when he said, "I am black, but my associations with my old Colonel gave me many advantages. I was freer then than I have ever been since and I loved him better than anybody else in the world. I would have given my life for him."[4]

In those final years Collier was often "overcome with emotion, especially when talking of his old Colonel and some very lovely white lady who lived at Bardstown, Ky. in whose charge he was placed when as a boy he was sent there to go to school."[5] The woman he so fondly remembered was Alice Crozier, a cousin of Howell Hinds.[6]

● ● ●

William Von Dresser, a well-known artist from Chicago, frequently traveled south during the Depression, receiving commissions for oil portraits of prominent citizens. While contracted to deliver portraits for several prominent families in Greenville, he was commissioned by one of his subjects to draw a pen and ink sketch of an

End of the Hunt • 213

HOLT COLLIER, *pen and ink portrait by William von Dresser.*

elderly Holt Collier. Collier's nobility at the age of eighty-nine is clearly evident in the surviving sketch.

Collier became so feeble by mid-summer 1936 that he required constant care. He was moved up the street to the home of Sarah Williams, who ran a nursing home caring for the elderly and infirm. There he was visited and cared for regularly by Mrs. T. A. Holcombe, a Greenville lady who volunteered to "minister to his comfort and happiness."[7]

• • •

On Wednesday, August 1, 1936, Holt Collier "just quit" and gave up the hunt. He was ninety years of age. He died at 10:10 a.m. while under the care and attention of Dr. Otis H. Beck, who was at his bedside. The occupation listed on his death certificate was "pensioner" of the "Confederate Army."[8]

The funeral was conducted at the Mt. Horeb Church at the corner of Broadway and Nelson. The church is only a short block from where Collier had lived the previous thirty-two years, but there is no indication that he ever attended it.[9]

The grief of the community for the passing of its most famous citizen transcended all classes, as well as socioeconomic and racial lines. Many "white and colored friends of Collier attended" the services, an unusual display of affection in those days.[10]

Holt Collier was laid to rest on August 3, 1936, at the Live Oak Cemetery in Greenville, near the site of his first bear kill and on the very land that in an earlier day had been Howell Hinds's Plum Ridge Plantation. Though the location of his final resting place was once well-known, like his long dead former master, Holt Collier lies today in an unmarked grave.

# EPILOGUE

The *Daily Democrat Times* ran an obituary of Holt Collier on Monday, August 3, 1936. The fourteen-inch, two-column article was exceptional coverage for an African American in Mississippi. An editorial by R. B. Wells one week later paid tribute to the man. "It was good to talk to Holt Collier, it left one with a feeling that he had gained something, that he had talked to one that was sincere, honest, plain, and unaffected, one that was natural and as God intended him to be. His experiences were many and varied and he could relate them all in an intelligent, interesting and coherent manner. He wasted no words on idle speculations: there was nothing superfluous or unnatural about him, his actions or speech."[1]

Since his death Holt Collier has been the subject of numerous articles in local, regional, and national journals. The details in many of those articles are inaccurate or incomplete, exaggerated or emboldened, but the legend of Holt Collier has endured.

A street in Greenville bears his name, an honor bestowed long before the civil rights movement. Two historical markers now proclaim his achievements or recount his exploits. One is located at Onward in Sharkey County and identifies the location of the 1902 Roosevelt camp site. The other, dedicated in 1996, is at the Live Oak cemetery where Holt Collier lies in his unmarked grave. The Teddy bear is now officially the state toy of Mississippi.[2]

• • •

While the discussion concerning the role of the slave as an armed combatant in the Confederate army continues unabated, there is no doubt that Holt Collier served in a military capacity. In 1970 The Mississippi Department of Archives and History authenticated his role in the Confederate armed forces, "The only Negro for whom we have evidence of service in the Confederate States Army is Holt Collier....Although we do not have an official record of his service, there seems to be no doubt of it."[3]

• • •

After the war Holt Collier's commanding officer, Captain Perry Evans returned to Texas and led a life remarkably similar to that of Holt Collier in many respects. Evans returned home and "trained hounds for the chase, built traps and caught fish, raised hogs and spent his time in hunting. He was expert with a gun and his greatest joy seemed in the training of his neighbor's boys how to shoot a deer...and his dogs were the best. He was liberal in his gifts to all institutions, the church...he supported liberally with his means, but never with his presence. His...was the home of the sport in the chase, on the hunt...he was the life and leader."[4]

• • •

Though the mysterious circumstances surrounding the death of Captain James A. King have never been resolved and are almost forgotten in Newton County, Iowa, there are those who continue to study the facts and try to unravel the mystery. The paradox of a young white abolitionist being killed by an ex-slave he had helped to free is the truest form of irony and an example of what Walker Percy called the "terrible complexities of race" in America. James A. King and Holt Collier "were extraordinary men, who defy the stereotype of a 'carpetbagger' or an 'Uncle Tom.' Such labels do not explain why a young white Iowa abolitionist and former captain of a black regiment was killed while attempting to profit from the work of the very people he sought to free. Nor do they explain why a young black slave became a confederate soldier and a guerilla warrior in the battle against the occupation of Mississippi."[5]

Captain James A. King was memorialized in death, and his final resting place is prominently marked at the Wittemberg Cemetery with a large stone obelisk standing more than six feet tall. Engraved on one side is the following:

*James A. King*
*Assassinated near*
*Greenville, Miss.*
*Dec. 22, 1866*
*Aged*
*24 years, 4 months, 8 days*

The marker is located close to the road on a high point of the cemetery grounds, almost a hundred and fifty yards from the other stones from that same time period. One must wonder why it was placed in such a conspicuous location. Local historian Randal Caldwell posed the question, "Was this a message of anti-southern sentiment to passers by, or a cry for justice by the family and friends of James King? The outrage of the Wittemberg Community over the death of James King is still evident today by the solitary placement of this stone."[6]

• • •

As Harris Dickson was writing the story of Holt Collier, he found the subject of young Thomas Hinds's interracial family perplexing and refused to consider it in his draft. He wrote, "For this chapter I have overflowing material. But would not be willing to write it except upon a full and detailed conference with Senator Leroy Percy of Greenville. Senator Percy is a gentleman of the soundest sense and discretion. His father defended Holt in these various trials. Senator Percy will advise me as to what may be tactful to print so as to avoid offending the relatives of men long dead."[7]

The living descendants of Thomas Hinds and Augusta Collier continue to reside in Mississippi. Their grandmother, Geraldine Hinds, is described as having "very light skin." Geraldine is the same child listed in the 1880 Census as five-year-old Adeline. The census taker also referred to Augusta Collier as Gusta Collier.[8]

• • •

Nothing remains of the Home Hill or Plum Ridge plantation houses nor of any of the improvements that were in use before the war. Although Plum Ridge survived the conflict and was the home of Thomas Hinds until 1874, urban sprawl ultimately took over what once were the plantation's spacious cotton fields and the surrounding swamp. The "path south of the town along the bank of a deep slough called Boggy Bayou" that would in earlier times have led a visitor to Plum Ridge, is now Main Street running north and south through the heart of Greenville. All that is left of Plum Ridge today is a short dead-end road off Main Street named Plum Ridge Street, which probably was the main drive up to the plantation house.

• • •

Long before his term of office was over, Theodore Roosevelt began making plans for an African safari. The African hunt would be his "last chance at something in the nature of a great adventure." In addition to his personal team, he was accompanied by a retinue of naturalists, taxidermists, a group from the Smithsonian Institution, fifteen native soldiers and 260 porters. Roosevelt's most famous hunt lasted for one full year plus travel time to and from Africa. During the expedition Roosevelt penetrated the deepest regions of the continent.[9]

If Holt Collier had known the hunt would last only one year plus travel time, he would have accepted the president's invitation to join the expedition. An interviewer asked Holt:

"Did the president invite you to make the African trip with him, Holt?"

"Yes, he did. But he said he'd be gone three years; I couldn't be away that long. Two years, maybe, and he came back in two years. I sure was disappointed." The interviewer noted that "Holt still feels that he was unintentionally gypped."[10]

• • •

Holt Collier was born in the age of Jackson when James K. Polk was president; America was at war with Mexico; Lincoln had not yet been elected to Congress; the great American West was unexplored;

*"TO GO OR NOT TO GO,"* Berryman cartoon, March 2, 1909.
*This was a comment on Roosevelt's departure from office and his African safari.*

gold had not yet been discovered in California; slavery was the law of the land; and the most advanced weapon of war was a field cannon with limited range. When Holt Collier died, Franklin D. Roosevelt was president; the world was in the seventh year of the Great Depression; Hitler, as Chancellor of Germany, had begun depriving Jews of citizenship with the Nuremberg Laws; Italy was at war with Ethiopia; global war was but a few years hence; and the nuclear age was less than a decade away.

Holt Collier is entitled to a place in the history and heritage of the United States alongside the many courageous pioneers and hunters of fame and legend. His service to the Confederacy will no doubt be debated by those of both races who prefer not to believe it. His contribution as a pioneer to the opening of the Mississippi Delta wilderness cannot be ignored. He is a central figure in the story of the Teddy bear. His courage, tenacity, honesty, integrity, and independence should be an inspiration to all Americans.

• • •

The elderly Holt Collier, possessing an undying loyalty to his friends, was much like Faulkner's old bear hunter Sam Fathers. Both of these proud men had the knowledge that for a while part of their blood had been the blood of slaves. Perhaps Collier's early life as a slave set him apart in his dealings with whites. Perhaps he too had the "mark of bondage," that he felt an affinity with those who had earlier held him in servitude. Faulkner wrote of Sam Fathers, "Like an old lion or a bear in a cage...he was born in the cage and has been in it all his life; he knows nothing else."[11]

Pete Johnson, one of the neighborhood children who knew Collier for many years, and who often drove him when the old man was too feeble to walk, described Holt's complexion as dark olive, similar to that of a native American Indian, and similarly, Harris Dickson referred to Collier as a "yellow man." Johnson strongly believed that Holt Collier had Native American blood and that his lineage would be obvious to a careful observer. The reader can draw his or her own conclusions by studying the von Dresser portrait rendered in 1935. Collier's bloodline of course, cannot be confirmed, and it seems of little consequence in the research of Collier's life until a reference is found in the regimental history of the Ninth Texas Cavalry of an "Indian boy" riding with Captain Perry Evans's Company I who raced horses in the company's popular equestrian contests.

Faulkner's *Go Down Moses*, published in 1940, contains analogous accounts of Sam Fathers, an old former slave, part Indian bear hunter in the Mississippi Delta "who bore himself...toward all white men, with gravity and dignity and without servility...."[12] If Johnson was correct, the similarities would be too great to ignore. Is it possible that the character of Sam Fathers is based on Holt Collier? We may never know.

# CHAPTER NOTES AND SOURCES

## PROLOGUE

1) Edward L. Ayers and John C. Willis, *The Edge of the South, Life in Nineteenth-Century Virginia* (Charlottesville: University Press of Virginia, 1991), 47.

2) Ibid., 49.

3) John Hope Franklin, *From Slavery to Freedom: A History of Negro Americans*, 3rd ed. (New York: Random House, 1967), 288.

4) Ibid., 288. From the beginning of the conflict, many had wanted to arm Negroes and some local authorities had actually permitted free Negroes to enroll for military service. The Tennessee legislature in 1861 authorized the governor to enlist all free Negroes between fifteen and fifty years of age in the state militia. Memphis opened a recruiting office for them. Public opinion was against arming Negroes due to the fear that they would turn on their masters. A company of sixty free Negroes presented themselves for service at Richmond in 1861, but they were turned away. In New Orleans a company of free Negroes was allowed to parade, but not to go into battle.

5) Clarence Gohdes, *Hunting in the Old South: Original Narratives of the Hunters* (Baton Rouge: Louisiana State University Press, 1967), xii.

6) Ibid.

7) Ibid., xiii.

## CHAPTER ONE: A Southern Aristocracy

1) William E. Cox, "The Greens of Jefferson County, Mississippi," *Journal of Mississippi History*, 36, no. 1 (February 1974): 89, 92.

2) Ibid., 81.

3) It has been widely argued and disputed that on this site in 1791 Andrew Jackson was married to Rachel Robards in a ceremony officiated by Col. Thomas Green.

4) "History of the Hinds-Green Family," (Harriette Person Memorial Library, Port Gibson, Miss.), vol. 1: 12, 13; vol. 3: 34. This history consists of records compiled from many sources.

5) Ibid, vol. 3: 15.

6) "Hinds-Green History," vol. 2, 266, citing Corbitt and Corbitt, "Papers from the Spanish Archives," ETHSP, vol. 26 [1954], 60; T-WPA, Davidson County, Ky., Court of Pleas and Quarter Sessions Minute Book B, 240.

7) The earliest property acquired in Mississippi by Hinds was in April of 1793, when he purchased several patents and deeds from Anthony Hart and Edmond Gamble.

8) "Hinds-Green History," vol. 3: 54, 56.

9) Ibid, vol. 3: 57.

10) Ibid., vol.3: 51, 56; May Wilson McBee, *The Natchez Court Records*, 1767-1805, vol. 2, (Ann Arbor: Edwards Brothers, 1953), 510.

11) "Hinds-Green History," vol.3: 14, citing the Virginia Family Registry Index entry for Gen. T. Hinds, 15,432.
12) Fifth Census of the United States, 1830. Jefferson County, Mississippi Marriage Records, Mississippi Department of Archives & History (MDAH).
13) U. S. Department of Interior: National Register of Historic Places, nomination form for Springfield Mansion.
14) "Hinds-Green History," vol. 1: 8.
15) Ibid.
16) Ibid., vol. 2: 249.
17) Eron Opha Moore Rowland, *Mississippi Territory in the War of 1812*, (Jackson: Mississippi Historical Society, 1921), 17. Washington was the capital of the Territory, located just a few miles east of Natchez, and just down the trace from old Greenville.
18) Clarence Edwin Carter, "The Territory of Mississippi, 1809-1817," in *The Territorial Papers of the United States*, vol. 6 (Washington: U. S. Government Printing Office, 1938), 195.
19) Robert V. Haynes, "The Formation of the Territory," in Richard Aubrey McLemore, ed., *A History of Mississippi*, vol. 1 (Hattiesburg: University and College Press of Mississippi, 1973), 208-210.
20) Eron Rowland, *Mississippi Territory*, 97.
21) J. F. H. Claiborne, *Mississippi as a Province, Territory and State with Biographical Notices of Eminent Citizens*, (1880; reprint, Baton Rouge: Louisiana State University Press, 1964), 327, 328, 337.
22) Ibid.; Dunbar Rowland, *Mississippi: Comprising Sketches of Counties, Towns, Events, Institutions, and Persons, Arranged in Cyclopedic Form*, vol. 1 (Atlanta: Southeastern Historical, 1907), 871.
23) Robert V. Remini, *The Battle of New Orleans* (New York: Viking, 1999), 154.
24) Claiborne, *Mississippi as Province*, vol. 1: 342, 344; Dunbar Rowland, *History of Mississippi: The Heart of the South*, vol. 1 (1925; Spartanburg, S. C.: Reprint Co., 1978): 226; McLemore, *History of Mississippi*, vol 1: 234.
25) Eron Rowland, *Mississippi Territory*, vol. 4: 151; Carter, "Territory of Mississippi," vol. 4: 526.
26) Hudson Strode, *Jefferson Davis: American Patriot*, (New York: Harcourt, Brace & World, 1955), 3.
27) Ibid., 12.
28) Ibid., 13.
29) Ibid., 13.
30) Theodore Roosevelt, "In the Louisiana Canebrakes," *Scribner's*, January 1908, 47-60; Harris Dickson, "The Bearslayer", *Saturday Evening Post*, 13 March 1909, 14.
31) Howell Hinds Subject File, MDAH.
32) Claiborne, *Mississippi as Province*, vol. 1: 383; Richard Aubrey McLemore, *History of Mississippi*, (Jackson: University & College Press of Mississippi, 1973), vol. 1: 253.

33) William D. McCain, *The Story of Jackson: A History of the Capital of Mississippi*, 1821-1951, vol. 1, (Jackson: J. F. Hyer, 1953), 1,2. From this acquisition was carved the counties of Copiah, Simpson, Hinds, Rankin, Yazoo, Sharkey, Issaquena, Washington, and portions of the counties of Smith, Scott, Madison, Attala, Holmes, Humphreys, Sunflower, Bolivar, and Warren.

34) Ibid., 128, 130.

35) Ibid., 4, 8; Porter L. Fortune, Jr., "The Formative Period," in McLemore, *History of Mississippi*, vol.1: 262. Peter A. Van Dorn was a successful lawyer from the town of Port Gibson, just north of "Old" Greenville. His son would be educated at West Point and later acquire fame as a Confederate general in the Civil War.

36) Fortune, "Formative Period," in McLemore, *History of Mississippi*, vol. 1: 276; Dunbar Rowland, *Official and Statistical Register of the State of Mississippi*, Centennial Edition, (Madison, Wis.: Democrat Printing, 1917), 238.

37) "Hinds-Green History,"vol.1: 99; Eron Rowland, *Mississippi Territory*, 155.

38) Claiborne, *Mississippi as Province*, vol. 1: 410. Dr. William McKendree Gwin had a remarkable life. His father had been a "fighting parson" with the army of Gen. Andrew Jackson. President Van Buren named Dr. Gwin a U. S. marshal for Mississippi. He served as a liason between President Jackson and Sam Houston during negotiations for the annexation of Texas. He was elected to the U. S. Congress in 1841, and in 1849 he traveled to California to be elected one of that state's first U. S. Senators. During the Civil War he sent his family to France. He was imprisoned twice because of his suspected southern sympathies, once paroled by President Lincoln and again by President Johnson. "Corral Dust, Potomac Corral of the Westerners," Washington, DC., September, 1958, vol. 3, no. 3, 17, 18. Willaim M. Gwin Subject File, MDAH.

39) Thomas Hinds obituary and James S. Fall, "Gen. Thomas Hinds," *The Mississippian*, (September 1840): 2, 4; Eron Rowland, *Mississippi Territory*, 155, 156.

## CHAPTER TWO: Cameron Howell Hinds

1) "Records of the First Regiment of the Second Division, Mississippi Militia." Record of Military Commissions, MDAH. Cameron Howell Hinds was known by his middle name and is referred to as Howell Hinds throughout this work.

2) Dunbar Rowland, *Official Statistical Register*, 238.

3) "They took pride in having a master of wealth and high rank in society–a pride that was partly generous and partly selfish, for the house servant considered himself far above the 'corn field nigger,' as is indicated in a brief conversation between a smartly dressed coachman and a footman." Charles S. Sydnor, *Slavery In Mississippi*, (1933, Baton Rouge: Louisiana State University Press, 1966), 4.

4) Howell Hinds Subject File, MDAH. Coleman Hinds did not survive childhood. He died at the age of nine in 1850.

5) Seventh Census of the United States, 1850; "Hinds-Green History," vol. 1: 56. White servants at Home Hill Plantation at the time of Coleman's death were Julia Devours, aged thirty-two, of Ireland, almost certainly a governess, and M. Hinton, aged thirty-five, of Virginia, most probably an overseer. The last known whereabouts of Mary Ann Lape's daughters was indicated in the obituary of Mary Ann Hinds on June 15, 1895. Listed as surviving were: Mrs. C. M. Currell, Greenville, Mississippi, Mrs. Ben Von Phul, St. Louis, Missouri, Mrs. Godfrey M. Fogg, Nashville, Tennessee, and Mrs. Kate Coleman Buck, St. Louis, Missouri. "Death Notices," *Greenville Times,* 1878-1906, MDAH.

6) What became of this Alice Hinds is not known. After the Civil War John Hinds and Howell Hinds, Jr., moved into the New Mexico Territory. John died in Arizona in January 1897. *Greenville Times,* 30 January 1897. Howell Hinds Jr. ultimately settled in Cleveland, Ohio, married and named his daughter Alice. Estate of Alice Hinds Fallon, Norfolk County Probate Court, Commonwealth of Massachusetts, File Number 175,148 (1967); Death Certificate of Alice Hinds Fallon (daughter of Howell Hinds Jr.), Massachusetts State Department of Health, Boston.

7) Howell Hinds Subject File, MDAH.

8) Ninth Census of the United States, 1870.

9) *Wyatt Epps v. Howell Hinds,* Mississippi High Court of Error and Appeals (October Term, 1854), 5 Chshm. 657, 61 Am Dec 528, 27 Miss. 657 (1854).

10) Fayette Subject File, MDAH; "Hinds-Green History," vol. 1, 120; obituary of Mary A. Hinds, *Greenville Times,* 15 June 1895.

11) Frances Preston Mills, ed., "Diary of Susan Sillers Darden," *The History of the Descendants of the Jersey Settlers of Adams County, Mississippi* (Jackson: Hederman Brothers, 1981), 606.

12) Ibid, 607.

13) Harris Dickson Papers, MDAH, Z-28, Box 5.

14) Ibid.

15) Harris Dickson, "Holt Collier, Negro, Soldier of the Confederacy," Box 11; Harris Dickson Papers, MDAH. In 1929 Harris Dickson described Holt Collier's temperance, "Unlike many grown men the child had learned from his experience with others, and until this good day at eighty three, he does not know the taste of whiskey. Never through a long life, enduring four years of hardship in the Civil War, with sixty years exposure at bear hunting, has Holt taken a single drink. In hundreds of bear camps where his white friends caroused, where everything was free, he declined their invitations."

16) Ibid.

17) Harris Dickson, "The Bearslayer," 14.

18) Cemetery records compiled by Gordon Cotton, Hinds Subject File, MDAH.

## CHAPTER THREE: A Primeval Wilderness

1) James C. Cobb, *The Most Southern Place on Earth: The Mississippi Delta and the Roots of Regional Identity* (New York: Oxford University Press, 1992), vii.

Notes to Pages 26-34 • 225

2) David L. Cohn, *Where I Was Born and Raised*, (Boston: Houghton, Mifflin, 1948), 12; Cobb, *Most Southern Place*, vii.

3) John M. Barry, *Rising Tide: The Great Mississippi Flood of 1927 and How It Changed America* (New York: Simon and Schuster, 1997), 97. Roosevelt, "Louisiana Canebrakes," 47.

4) Roosevelt, "Louisiana Canebrakes," 48.

5) Cobb, *Most Southern Place*, 13,14.

6) Arthell Kelley, "The Geography," in McLemore, *History of Mississippi*, vol. 1: 8.

7) Henry T. Ireys, "A Boy's Recollections," in William D. McCain and Charlotte Capers, eds., *Memoirs of Henry Tillinghast Ireys, Papers of the Washington County Historical Society, 1910-1915*, (Jackson: Mississippi Department of Archives and History and the Mississippi Historical Society, 1954), 63.

8) Ibid., 64.

9) Mrs. W. R. Trigg, "In Memory of Mrs. Myra Smith," McCain and Capers, *Memoirs*, 165.

10) Ireys, "Boy's Recollections," in McCain and Capers, *Memoirs*, 64.

11) McCain and Capers, *Memoirs*, 171.

12) Ireys, "Boy's Recollections," in McCain and Capers, *Memoirs*, 65. Henry Ireys, rather than mention Hinds by name, refers to "Plum Ridge." Other planters were named personally. This account was written in 1912 when the Hinds name was, among those who knew its postwar history, considered unspeakable.

13) W. W. Stone, "Some Post-War Recollections," in McCain and Capers, *Memoirs*, 280.

14) John N. Dunn, "A Backward Glance At Washington County," in McCain and Capers, *Memoirs*, 98.

15) Mrs. H. B. Theobald, "Reminiscences of Greenville," in McCain and Capers, *Memoirs*, 52.

16) A. J. Paxton, "Recollections of Deer Creek," in McCain and Capers, *Memoirs*, 104.

17) Orland Kay Armstrong, "He Tracked Bear for Roosevelt," *New York Herald Tribune*, 3 January 1932, 4.

18) "Slave Narratives", WPA, MDAH, also found in "Mississippi Narratives," part 2 of vol. 7 of *The American Slave: A Composite Autobiography*, (Westport, Conn.: Greenwood, 1977), 447-479.

19) Dickson, "Bearslayer," 15.

20) Armstrong, "Tracked Bear for Roosevelt," 4.

21) Harris Dickson Papers, box 5, file 15.

22) Sam Worthington, "Ante-Bellum Slave-Holding Aristocracy of Washington County," in McCain and Capers, *Memoirs*, 351.

23) Seventh United States Census, 1850. Cobb, *Most Southern Place*, 8.

24) Harris Dickson Papers, box 5, file 15. The Saratoga and Brighton Beach referred to by Collier in his interviews are presumably in New York, Saratoga in upstate, and Brighton Beach now a part of New York City. Collier also claims that as a child he was taken to Niagra Falls.

25) Ibid.

26) *American Slave*, 449.

27) Ibid., 458.

28) Harris Dickson Papers. The institution of slavery was often dependent the lash. Any conclusions drawn from Holt Collier's idyllic description of plantation life may be considered suspect. It is certainly possible that his memory of life as a slave was clouded by age and the longing of things past. However, because so many of his statements are corroborated by other sources, it is far more likely that he was in an elite class for a servant, and his existence was exceptionally blessed.

## CHAPTER FOUR: From Greenville to Pittsburg Landing

1) Percy L. Rainwater, *Mississippi: Storm Center of Secession*, (Baton Rouge: O. Claitor, 1938), 221. For a thorough examination of the conditions and causes of the secession movement, see: William Barney, *The Secession Impulse: Alabama and Mississippi*, (Princeton: Princeton University Press, 1974).

2) Strode, *Jefferson Davis, American Patriot*, 401. The *Natchez Courier* on February 16, 1861 reported that there was no rejoicing in Natchez over secession and that Davis' selection as President of the Confederacy was received in Natchez with regret. The *Courier* went on to deride Davis, "Neither in character nor in politics, has he any hold upon the confidence of the people. He has at last attained that for which he has been struggling for ten years past–a Presidency. We may admire the ingenuity with which he has attained his object, and yet despise the tricks by which he has crawled to it."

3) "Declaration of Secession," Mississippi Convention on Secession (Jackson: Mississippian, 1861). "A Declaration of the Immediate Causes Which Induce and Justify the Secession of the State of Mississippi from the Federal Union," in *Confederate Military History, Extended Edition, Mississippi*, (1899, Reprint, Wilmington, N. C.: Broadfoot, 1987), 8.

4) Compiled Service Records of Howell Hinds, MDAH.

5) Compiled Service Records of Thomas Hinds, MDAH.

6) Harris Dickson Papers.

7) Dickson, "Bearslayer," 15.

8) Letter from Provost Marshal A. K. Farrar to Governor John J. Pettus, 17 July 1862, Governor's Papers, MDAH; Winthrop D. Jordan, *Tumult and Silence at Second Creek: An Inquiry Into a Civil War Slave Conspiracy*, (Baton Rouge: Louisiana State University Press, 1993), 323.

9) Letter from Hinds to Pettus, 14 May 1861," Governor's Papers, MDAH; Jordan, *Tumult and Silence*, 308-309.

Notes to Pages 40-51 • 227

10) Howell Hinds Subject File, MDAH.
11) Confederate War Records, National Archives RG 109, Telegrams Received by Confederate Secretary of War, No. 2151.
12) Dunbar Rowland, *Military History of Mississippi, 1803-1898*, in *The Official and Statistical Register of the State of Mississippi*, 1908, (Spartanburg, S. C.: The Reprint Company, 1978), 480.
13) Harris Dickson Papers, MDAH, box 5, file 15.
14) Ibid.
15) *American Slave*, 449-451.
16) Dickson, "Bearslayer," 15.
17) Harris Dickson Papers, MDAH, box 5, file 15.
18) Ibid.
19) Ibid.
20) Ibid., box 11.
21) Ibid., Dickson, "Holt Collier," 3.
22) Harris Dickson Papers; *American Slave*, 449-451.
23) Dickson, "Bearslayer," 46.
24) Compiled Service Records of Confederate Soldiers Who Served in Organizations from the State of Mississippi, National Archives, (Washington, General Services Administration, 1959), also MDAH.
25) William Preston Johnston, *The Life of General Albert Sidney Johnston*, (New York: D. Appleton, 1878), 291-306.
26) Ibid, 306-318.
27) Rowland, *Military History of Mississippi*, 480; "Mississippi;" Dunbar Rowland, *Confederate Military History*, Extended Edition, Vol. 9, (1899; Reprint, Wilmington, N. C. : Broadfoot Publishing Col, 1987), 336; Howell Hinds Subject File, MDAH.
28) Compiled Records of Howell Hinds, MDAH. Howell had served as inspector of the First Brigade, Second Division of the Mississippi State Militia under Clark during the 1840's.
29) Letter from Mississippi Department of Archives and History to Lynda Crist, Editor, 13 January 1986, The Papers of Jefferson Davis, Rice University. Compiled Records of Howell Hinds, MDAH.
30) Harris Dickson Papers; Holt Collier Subject File, MDAH.
31) Dickson, "Bearslayer," 46.
32) Dickson, "Holt Collier," 4.
33) Confederate War Records, National Archives RG 109, Letters received by Confederate Secretary of War H, 159.
34) Johnston, *General Albert Sidney Johnston*, 484-500; Maj. Gen. Lew Wallace, "The Capture of Fort Donelson," in Robert Underwood Johnson and Clarence Clough Buel, eds., *Battles and Leaders of the Civil War*, vol. 1,(New York: The Century Co., 1887), 398.

35) Johnston, *General Albert Sidney Johnston,* 523-537; Col. William Preston Johnston, "Albert Sidney Johnston at Shiloh," in Robert Underwood Johnson and Clarence Clough Buel, eds., *Battles and Leaders of the Civil War,* vol. 1, (New York: The Century Co., 1887), 540. For an account of the Battle of Shiloh see, James Lee McDonough, *Shiloh–In Hell Before Night,* (Knoxville: University of Tennessee Press, 1977).

36) Gen. G. T. Beauregard, "The Campaign of Shiloh," in Robert Underwood Johnson and Clarence Clough Buel, eds., *Battles and Leaders of the Civil War,* vol. 1, (New York: The Century Co., 1887), 583.

37) Brig. Gen. Thomas Jordan, "Notes of a Confederate Staff-Officer at Shiloh," in Robert Underwood Johnson and Clarence Clough Buel, eds., *Battles and Leaders of the Civil War,* vol. 1, (New York: The Century Co., 1887), 599; Johnston, "Albert Sidney Johnston at Shiloh," 564.

38) Gen. Ulysses S. Grant, "The Battle of Shiloh," in Robert Underwood Johnson and Clarence Clough Buel, eds., *Battles and Leaders of the Civil War,* vol. 1, (New York: The Century Co., 1887), 465-486.

39) Johnston, *General Albert Sidney Johnston,* 590.

40) Ibid., 596.

41) *War of the Rebellion; A Compilation of the Official Records of the Union and Confederate Armies,* (OR), (Washington, D.C., 1880-1901), Series 1, vol. 10, 415.

42) Ibid., 612; McDonough, *Shiloh,* 152-153.

43) *American Slave,* 468.

44) Dickson, "Bearslayer," 47.

45) Beauregard, "Campaign for Shiloh," 591; Jordan, "Notes of a Staff Officer," 603.

46) Johnston, *General Albert Sidney Johnston,* 654.

47) OR, Series 1, vol. 10, 112, 396, 398; "The Opposing Forces at Shiloh," in *Battles and Leaders of the Civil War,* vol. 1, 537.

48) Ulysses S. Grant, *Personal Memoirs of U. S. Grant, Selected Letters 1839-1865,* (New York: Library of America, 1990), p.238.

49) Stanley F. Horn, *The Army of Tennessee,* (Norman: University of Oklahoma Press, 1952), 148. If the mortality rate from battle were not enough, the retreating Confederates at Corinth became ravaged with the perils of disease. "Citizens of Corinth were horrified at the ghastly spectacle as the trains of army wagons lumbered in from the battlefield, dripping blood from their heaped-up piles of groaning, suffering wounded. Maimed and suffering men lay everywhere–on porches, on sidewalks, on platforms of railroad stations." Horn, *Army of Tennessee,* 148. One Confederate private wrote of his experience while at Corinth, "We became starved skeletons; naked and ragged rebels. The chronic diarrhea became the scourge of the army. Corinth became one vast hospital. Almost the whole army attended the sick call every morning. All the water courses went dry, and we used water out of filthy pools." Sam R. Watkins, *'Co. Aych',* (New York: Macmillan Publishing Co., 1962), 49.

50) Grant, *Memoirs,* 248.

51) Compiled Service Records of Thomas Hinds, MDAH.

52) Ibid.

53) Ibid.

## CHAPTER FIVE:  Ninth Texas Cavalry

1) Robert G. Hartje, *Van Dorn: The Life and Times of a Confederate General* (Nashville: Vanderbilt University Press, 1967), 175, 189.

2) Ibid., 182.

3) Homer L. Kerr, ed., *Lieut. George L. Griscom: Fighting With Ross' Texas Calvary Brigade*, C. S. A. (Hillsboro, Tex.: Hill Junior College Press, 1976), vii, 1-15.

4) Griscom, *Texas Cavalry Brigade*, 2, Muster Rolls, Apendix A, 209.

5) Martha L. Crabb, *All Afire To Fight: The Untold Tale of the Civil War's Ninth Texas Cavalry,* (New York:  Post Road, 2000), 14.

6) A. W. Sparks, *The War Between the States As I Saw It*, (1901, reprint, Longview, Texas: D & D Publishing, 1987), 68.

7) Ibid., 370.

8) Ibid., 15, 16.

9) Griscom, *Texas Cavalry Brigade*, 38.

10) Hartje, *Van Dorn*, 182.

11) John Allan Wyeth, *That Devil Forrest*, (1899, reprint, Baton Rouge: Louisiana State University Press, 1959), 68.  Forrest had been badly wounded in retreat at Monterey, a short distance from the Shiloh battlefield, and required six weeks' convalescence at his home in Memphis. When restored to command, he was immediately returned to the field.

12) Griscom, *Texas Cavalry Brigade*, 40.

13) Jefferson Davis Papers, Louisiana Historical Association Collection, Tulane University.

14) Letter from Howell Hinds to Jefferson Davis, 11 October 1863, Davis Papers; Dunbar Rowland, *Jefferson Davis, Constitutionalist: His Letters, Papers and Speeches* (Jackson: MDAH, 1923), 59.

15) OR, Series 1, vol. 15, 805.

16) Sparks, *War Between the States*, 257.

17) Ibid., 20, 21.

18) *American Slave,* 466.  There is another account given by Collier that differs from that given in the "Slave Narratives," and other sources. On one of his hunts with President Roosevelt he told of being given his freedom by young Thomas Hinds at the outbreak of the war. According to John Parker, a companion on the hunt, "As Holt told the story tears filled his eyes.  He related how 'Marse Tom' called him into the house one evening and said...I am going to leave now to go to war, and I may never see you again, but here is a paper that I want to give you because it makes you a free man, and you can go anywhere with this paper and be free the balance of your days, and never worry

about anything." Relating to the time he ran away from home to follow the Hinds's into war, Parker wrote that Holt had told him: "I took my freedom papers and went out and just cried myself sick, and didn't say nothing to nobody about it, but I slipped off and got on that boat." John Parker Papers, University of Louisiana at Lafayette.

19) Dickson, "Bearslayer," 47.

20) Griscom, *Texas Cavalry Brigade*, 43.

21) Hartje, *Van Dorn*, 217.

22) Griscom, *Texas Cavalry Brigade*, 44.

23) Ibid., 45, 46.

24) Ibid., 47.

25) Ibid., 48.

26) Ibid., 49.

27) Hartje, *Van Dorn*, 248, fn. 2. One observation of Van Dorn reflected directly on his character. "I would say that General Van Dorn has sadly lost caste in this State by a course of life in private that gives no promise of a successfully conducted campaign against our enemies in this department...his name is sadly handled for intemperance and other vices. I do hope these charges are unfounded, but from all the light before me I fear they are too true." (letter from Robert H. Read).

28) Hartje, *Van Dorn*, 248.

29) Sparks, *War Between the States*, 60, 61.

30) Ibid., 61.

31) Victor M. Rose, *Ross' Texas Brigade*, (1881, reprinted, Kennesaw, Georgia: Continental Book Company, 1960), 84.

32) Ibid., 86, 87.

33) Ibid., 86, 87.

34) Ibid., 88.

35) Griscom, *Texas Cavalry Brigade*, 51, 52.


## CHAPTER SIX: Boots and Saddles

1) Edwin Cole Bearss, *The Campaign for Vicksburg*, vol.1, (Dayton, Ohio: Morningside, 1985), 307-334.

2) Ibid., 324, 325. Rose, *Ross' Texas Brigade*, 91.

3) Griscom, *Texas Cavalry Brigade*, 53; Bearss, *Campaign for Vicksburg*, vol. 1: 336, 337.

4) Bearss, *Campaign for Vicksburg*, vol. 1: 335-347.

5) Ibid., 347; OR, Series 1, vol. 17, pt. 1: 516.

6) Griscom, *Texas Cavalry Brigade*, 56.

7) Rose, *Ross' Texas Brigade*, 92.

8) Hartje, *Van Dorn*, 275.

9) Griscom, *Texas Cavalry Brigade*, 58.
10) Rose, *Ross' Texas Brigade*, 93. Col. Dudley Jones's official report of the battle and the involvement of the Ninth Texas Cavalry appears at OR, Series 1, vol. 23: 123.
11) Hartje, *Van Dorn*, 288; OR, Series 1, vol. 23, pt. 1: 120.
12) Griscom, *Texas Cavalry Brigade*, 60, 61.
13) Hartje, *Van Dorn*, 291.
14) Sparks, *War Between the States*, 68.
15) Hartje, *Van Dorn*, 313.
16) Griscom, *Texas Cavalry Brigade*, 68, 69.

## CHAPTER SEVEN: Vicksburg

1) "Opposing Forces in the Vicksburg Campaign," *Battles and Leaders of the Civil War*, vol. 3: 549.
2) Bearss, *Campaign for Vicksburg*, vol. 3: 752.
3) Ibid., vol. 1, 717, fn 9; vol. 3: 1152.
4) Griscom, *Texas Cavalry Brigade*, 71.
5) Compiled Service Records of Thomas Hinds, MDAH.
6) Ibid; Compiled Service Records of Howell Hinds, MDAH; Howell Hinds Subject File, MDAH. Apparently the Hinds' were more industrious at protecting their valuables than they reported. According to the Last Will and Testament of Alice Hinds Fallon, heirlooms that remained in the family after the Civil War included the ceremonial sword presented to General Thomas Hinds by the Mississippi General Assembly, an engraved gold-headed hickory cane which was a present to General Thomas Hinds from President Andrew Jackson, two oil portraits of General Hinds, and a dozen silver julep cups. According to her will, the hard assets were preserved by "burying them in a field on my grandfather's Mississippi plantation." Alice Hinds Fallon was the daughter of Howell Hinds, Jr. (born to Howell and Mary Ann in 1858). Estate of Alice Hinds Fallon, Norfolk County Probate Court, Commonwealth of Massachusetts, File Number 175,148 (1967).
7) OR, Series 1, vol 24, pt. 1: 289-292, 313.
8) Ibid., 292.
9) OR, Series 1, vol. 15, 805.
10) Rowland, *Mississippi*, vol. 3: 25. Wirt Adams was so well regarded that when the Confederate government was created, President Davis offered him the cabinet level position of postmaster general, a position he declined for a field commission. He was promoted to the rank of brigadier general in September 1863 and survived the war to become a lawyer and planter in the Mississippi Delta. He served as state revenue agent for many years. In 1882 he married the daughter of William Swann Yerger. On May 1, 1888, he was involved in a public duel with John Martin, the editor for the *Clarion* newspaper. At the intersection of President and Amite streets in Jackson, Adams called Martin out for an offensive newspaper article. Both men were armed with pistols. When the smoke cleared, both men lay in the street dead or mortally wounded.

11) Bearss, *Campaign for Vicksburg*, vol. 3: 1090.
12) Rowland, *Military History of Mississippi*, 384-91.
13) Dickson, "Holt Collier," 4.
14) Ibid., 5; Harris Dickson Papers, also, *American Slave*, 467.
15) *American Slave*, 467.
16) Edwin C. Bearss and Warren Gragau, *The Battle of Jackson*, (Baltimore: Gateway, 1981), 89. It is believed by the authors to be the passage known as Sherman's famous quote: "War is hell." For a review of the personality and tactics of Sherman, see: John F. Marszalek, *Sherman: A Soldier's Passion for Order*, (New York: Free Press, 1993).
17) Dunbar Rowland, *Jefferson Davis Constitutionalist: His Letters, Papers and Speeches* (Jackson: Mississippi Department of Archives and History, 1923), vol. 6: 59.

## CHAPTER EIGHT: Delta Rangers

1) Grant, *Memoirs*, 384; Bearss, *Campaign for Vicksburg*, vol. 3: 1279, 1301.
2) Henry Steele Commager, *The Blue and Gray: The Story of the Civil War as Told by Participants* (Indianapolis: Bobbs-Merrill, 1950), vol. 2: 677.
3) Griscom, *Texas Cavalry Brigade*, 72-76.
4) Ibid., 76-80.
5) Ibid., 83.
6) Ibid., 103, 104.
7) Rose, *Ross' Texas Brigade*, 104.
8) Margie Riddle Bearss, *Sherman's Forgotten Campaign, The Meridian Expedition*, (Baltimore: Gateway Press, Inc., 1987), 26.
9) Griscom, *Texas Cavalry Brigade*, 106-111, 140.
10) J. C. Burrus, "Island 76," in McCain and Capers, *Memoirs*, 375.
11) U. S. Army Corp of Engineers, Mississippi River Navigation Maps, Map No. 24, 56th Ed., 1988.
12) Burrus, "Island 76," in McCain and Capers, *Memoirs*, 376. J. C. Burrus served with Evans' Scouts along with his teenage son, Archie Clement Burrus, Howell Hinds and Holt Collier.
13) Ibid., 377; also, MDAH, WPA, RG-60, Box 429, J. C. Burrus, *Outlaw Days, Tragedy of the River, Story of the Robberies of Coe who Held Forth On Island 76 During the War*.
14) Ibid., 377.
15) Ibid., 378; also: OR, Series 1, vol. 32: 2.
16) Ibid.
17) OR, Series 1, vol. 32, part 1: 175-177.
18) Margie Riddle Bearss, *Sherman's Forgotten Campaign*, 247-278.
19) Sparks, *War Between the States*, 371; Griscom, Texas Cavalry Brigade, 140.

Notes to Pages 96-103 • 233

20) "Burrus Recollections," Eunice Stockwell Papers, MDAH, 3.
21) William Alexander Percy, *Lanterns on the Levee* (Baton Rouge: Louisiana State University Press, 1941), 344.
22) Mamie Bowen Warfield, "Recollections of Childhood," in McCain and Capers, *Memoirs*, 385.
23) Worthington, "Ante-Bellum Aristocracy," in McCain and Capers, *Memoirs*, 362.
24) Stevenson Archer, "Captain Evans and His Texas Scouts," McCain and Capers, *Memoirs*, 223. J. A. Fowler, originally from Company F was graciously listed as "killed" in the official muster rolls of the regiment. Compiled Service Records of Confederate Soldiers Who Served in Organizations from the State of Texas, National Archives.
25) Deposition of Dr. O. M. Blanton, Commission of Claims, 28 July 1874. From the personal collection of Georgie Blanton Cooper, great-granddaughter of O. M. Blanton.
26) *American Slave*, 463. Harris Dickson Papers; Dickson, "Holt Collier."
27) Rowland, *Mississippi*, vol. 3: 97. Goodspeed, Biographical and Historical Memoirs of Mississippi, vol. 1 (Chicago, Goodspeed, 1891), 468.
28) *American Slave*, 464.
29) Ibid., 468.
30) *Fayette Chronicle*, 28 December 1894, from a letter by "Richlieu" to the Jackson *Clarion* in December 1864 reporting the killing of Lt. Earl in the streets of Fayette on 2 December 1864.
31) OR, Series 1, vol. 31: 501. Also, "Hinds-Green History," vol. 1: 51.
32) *Fayette Chronicle*, 28 December 1894. Harris Dickson made a note that Holt Collier acknowledged being accused by the authorities as the person responsible for killing Lieutenant Earl. There is no corroboration for this. In the newspaper account, written thirty years after the fact, Earl's assailant is mentioned as being a Confederate sergeant and if true, Collier would be excluded as a suspect. Harris Dickson Papers, Box 5, file 15.
33) *American Slave*, 468.

## CHAPTER NINE: Occupation and Court-Martial

1) *The History of Jasper County, Iowa*, (Chicago: Western Historical Company, 1878). 559-60; Robert Y. Kerr, " The Wittemberg Manuel Labor College," Benjamin F. Shambaugh, ed., *Iowa Journal of History and Politics*, 1926, vol. 24: 291-304.
2) Wittemberg Manual Labor College Collection, Iowa Historical Society. For the history of the manual labor movement see: Jane Reister, "Mechanical Institutes and Manual Labor Colleges in Iowa," 1970, Collections of the Iowa Historical Society, Iowa City, Iowa.
3) Plat of Wittemberg, Office of the Jasper County Recorder, Unnumbered book, 57,58.

4) "Minutes of the Manual Labor College, 1856-1859", Collections of the Iowa Historical Society.

5) Obituary of John King, *Newton Journal*, 18 April 1888. King was an integral part of the college even in death. Both shared the same declining years, and in the year of King's death, the old college building long neglected was demolished.

6) *Roster and Record of Iowa Soldiers in the War of the Rebellion, 1861-1866* (Des Moines, Iowa: Emory English, 1908), vol. 1: 729.

7) Ibid., vol. 1: 675.

8) Ibid., vol. 1: 676.

9) Ibid., vol. 1: 676.

10) Ibid., vol. 1: 679.

11) Bearss, *Campaign for Vicksburg*, vol. 1: 479-87.

12) Andrew F. Sperry, *History of the 33d Iowa Infantry Volunteer Regiment, 1863-66* (Fayetteville: University of Arkansas Press, 1999), 11.

13) Bearss, *Campaign for Vicksburg*, vol. 1: 507.

14) Sperry, *33d Iowa*, 22.

15) Grant's and Porter's naval landing at Bruinsburg in 1863 was the largest naval transport of men and material until D-Day, 1944.

16) Joseph T. Glatthaar, *Forged in Battle, the Civil War Alliance of Black Soldiers and White Officers* (New York: Free Press, 1990), 132-135.

17) Dickson, "Holt Collier," 6.

18) Harris Dickson Papers, MDAH.

19) Dickson, "Bearslayer," 48.

20) The Freedmen's Bureau was a social agency created by an act of Congress as a Bureau of Refugees, Freedmen, and Abandoned Lands. It was an agency of the War Department by congressional act of 3 March 1865; 13 Stat. 507. In essence the government of the unreconstructed South was placed in the hands of the Freedman's Bureau. It "made laws, executed them and interpreted them; it laid and collected taxes, defined and punished crime, maintained and used military force, and dictated such measures as it thought necessary. The very name of the Bureau stood for a thing in the South which for two centuries and better men had refused even to argue–that life amid free Negroes was simply unthinkable, the maddest of experiments." W. E. Burghardt DuBois, *The Souls of Black Folk*, (Chicago: A. C. McClurg, 1903), 27-28.

21) Rembert W. Patrick, *The Reconstruction of the Nation*, (New York: Oxford University Press, 1967), 34-41. Also see, William C. Harris, *The Day of the Carpetbagger*, (Baton Rouge: Louisiana State University Press, 1979).

22) Dickson, "Holt Collier," 47.

23) *American Slave*, 452. Also, Des Moines Daily State Register, 5 February 1867.

24) *Daily State Register*, 5 February 1867.

25) Ibid.

26) Records of the Bureau of Refugees, Freedmen, and Abandoned Lands (Record Group 105), Records of the Assistant Commissioner for the State of Mississippi, MDAH, M-826. Roll 6.
27) Ibid.
28) Ibid, Roll 29.
29) Ibid. "W. C." refers to Washington County.
30) Lewis Baker, *The Percys of Mississippi* (Baton Rouge, Louisiana State University Press, 1983), 5-7. Also, for a exhaustive and detailed history on the Percy family, see: Bertram Wyatt-Brown, *The House of Percy*, (New York: Oxford University Press, 1994).
31) Harris Dickson Papers, MDAH, box 5, file 15.
32) Ibid.
33) Dickson, "The Bearslayer," 48.

## CHAPTER TEN: To Texas and a Distant Farewell

1) Harris Dickson, "Bear Stories," *The Saturday Evening Post*, 10 April 1909; 20, 21, 52.
2) William Elsey Connelley, *Quantrill and the Border Wars*, (Cedar Rapids, Iowa: Torch Press, 1910), 457. Tom Evans, identified by Holt Collier as the brother of Perry Evans, is listed as one of the guerrillas who fought in Kentucky with Quantrill.
3) *Hart v. Hinds,* Case No. 459, Chancery Court Records of Washington County, Mississippi. Also see letter from MDAH, Michael F. Beard to Lynda Crist, editor of The Papers of Jefferson Davis, 13 January 1986, Howell Hinds Subject File, MDAH.
4) *Mississippi v. Richardson,* Case No. 241, Records of the Washington County Circuit Court, Minute Book 3, page 315, 18 December 1867.
5) *Mississippi v. Hinds,* Case No. 279, Records of the Washington County Circuit Court, Minute Book 3, Page 346, 18 December 1867.
6) Deposition of Dr. O. M. Blanton, Commission of Claims, 28 July 1874, personal collection of Georgie Blanton Cooper, great-granddaughter of O. M. Blanton. Also, Blanton Family Papers, University of Mississippi.
7) Howell Hinds Subject File, Special Order No. 5, Records of the Headquarters, 4th Military District of Mississippi, MDAH.
8) Eunice Stockwell Collection, MDAH. Also, Vicksburg *Times and Republican,* 17 August 1872.
9) Blanton Deposition.
10) Letter from Jean Smith to Martha R. Blanton, 12 January 1870, personal collection of Georgie Blanton Cooper and Blanton Family Papers.
11) Dickson, "Bearslayer," 48.
12) Ibid.
13) Washington County Records, MDAH, 137.

14) Ninth Census of the United States, 1870. By 1870, because of Collier's independence and Thomas's devotion to his sister, it can be presumed that Holt's association with Thomas Hinds had evolved into a familial relationship. There is no question that they were devoted to each other.

15) *Hart v. Hinds.*

16) Vicksburg *Times and Republican,* 17 August 1872.

17) William C. Harris, "The Reconstruction of the Commonwealth: 1865-1870, in McLemore, *History of Mississippi,* vol. 1: 569. Governor's Papers, MDAH, Papers of Ridgely C. Powers, RG 27, vol. 84, 1872.

18) Ibid., 544. Governor's Papers of Ridgely C. Powers, MDAH.

19) O. M. Blanton Subject File, MDAH.

20) Harris Dickson Papers, MDAH.

21) Eric Foner, *Reconstruction: America's Unfinished Revolution, 1863-1877* (New York: Harper & Row, 1988), 537-544.

22) Cobb, *Most Southern Place,* 72. For a study on the transition of slaves to sharecroppers, see Sydney Nathans, "Gotta Mind to Move, A Mind to Settle Down: Afro-Americans and the Plantation Frontier," in William J. Cooper et al., *A Master's Due: Essays in Honor of David Herbert Donald* (Baton Rouge: Louisiana State University Press, 1985).


## CHAPTER ELEVEN: The Hunter

1) Dickson, "Bearslayer," 47. For a thorough examination of the 1875 Mississippi election, see: William C. Harris, *The Day of the Carpetbagger,* (Baton Rouge: Louisiana State University Press, 1979), 650-712.

2) Harris Dickson Papers, box 13, folder no. 4, MDAH.

3) James Gordon, "A Camp Hunt in Mississippi," *Outing,* October, 1885, 64-70.

4) James Gordon, "Bear-Hunting in the South: Tunica County, Mississippi," *Scribner's,* October, 1881, 857-863.

5) Theodore Roosevelt, "Louisiana Canebrakes," 47-60.

6) Gordon, "Bear Hunting," 857.

7) Dickson, "Bear Stories," 20.

8) Gordon, "Bear-Hunting," 857.

9) Ibid.

10) Dickson, "Bear Stories," 20.

11) Gordon, "Bear Hunting," 857.

12) Mrs. H. B. Theobald, "Reminiscences of Greenville," in McCain and Capers, Memoirs, 52.

13) *Greenville Times,* 25 August 1877, "Quite an interesting game of baseball was played Tuesday afternoon between Holt Collier's Club from Deer Creek and Harvey Scott's Club of Greenville."

14) Harris Dickson Papers, MDAH; Dickson, "Bear Stories," 20.

Notes to Pages 140-150 • 237

15) Dickson, "Holt Collier," MDAH. The year of this episode is unknown.
16) Dickson, "Bear Stories," 20.
17) Dickson, "Holt Collier," MDAH.
18) Ibid.
19) Paul Schullery, *The Bear Hunter's Century*, (Harrisburg: Stackpole Books, 1988), 207.
20) Harris Dickson, "When the President Hunts," *Saturday Evening Post*, 8 August 1908, 3, 4, 23, 24.
21) Harris Dickson Papers, box 13, folder 4, MDAH.
22) Tenth Census of the United States, 1880. Rose is listed as "wife" of Holt Collier.
23) Ibid. We know that Augusta Collier was Holt's sister. The Census of 1870 listed her as living with Harrison and Daphne. She was referred to then as 'Gusta.' Though they were listed as Hinds' in the 1880 census, Anna, Earnest, Robb and Evie were referred to as Colliers in the 1870 census.
24) The details of this affray are compiled from: *Quachita Telegraph* [Monroe, La.], 3 June 1881, from reports in the *Lake Providence Herald*. Also, *Monroe Bulletin*, [Monore, La.], 1 June 1881; *New Orleans Democrat*, 15 June 1881. Sheriff's Book, West Carroll Parish, Louisiana, 30 September 1886, 385.
25) *Greenville Times*, 9 July 1881. Also, Holt Collier Subject File, MDAH. *American Slave*, 461. *The Comet* of Jackson, a local newspaper with limited circulation, also reported the incident: "July 6, — A white man was shot and killed this morning on Bogue Phalia, twenty miles from Greenville, by Holt Collier, colored, for resisting arrest. The man is suppose to be Sage, the murderer of the Lott boys, at Floyd, Louisiana." Miscellaneous Newspapers Collection, 1845-1900, MDAH.
26) Eleventh Census of the United States, 1890; Marriage Records of Washington County, MDAH.
27) Clive Metcalfe Papers, Southern Historical Collection, University of North Carolina at Chapel Hill.
28) *Weekly Democrat*, 24 November 1898.
29) "Hinds-Green History," vol. 1: 56; "Death Notices," *Greenville Times* (1878-1906); Eunice Stockwell Papers, MDAH. Mary Ann Hinds surviving daughters were Mrs. C. M. Currell, Greenville, Mississippi, Mrs. Ben Von Phul, St. Louis, Missouri, Mrs. Godfrey M. Fogg, Nashville, Tennessee, and Mrs. Kate Coleman Duck, St. Louis, Missouri
30) "Death Notices," *Greenville Times* (1878-1906); Eunice Stockwell Papers, MDAH. Howell Hinds Jr. ultimately settled in Cleveland, Ohio and married Nellie Price. Eventually he came into possession of family heirlooms that included the ceremonial sword presented to his grandfather by the Mississippi General Assembly and a gold handle walking cane given to his grandfather by President Andrew Jackson. These heirlooms were buried by Howell Hinds during the Civil War. These items were in turn passed on to Howell Jr's daughter, Alice Hinds. Alice Hinds married Robert M. Fallon of Cleveland, Ohio, but the last sixteen years of her life she lived in Milton, Massachusetts. She died there in 1967. Although she treasured her family

238 • *Notes to Pages 151-157*

pieces, upon her death she made a very unusual directive to the executor of her estate to "destroy all family portraits other than the portraits of my great grandfather, [General] Thomas Hinds." It can only be surmised that she was aware that her first cousins in Mississippi were of mixed blood, and she wanted no part of it. That may also explain why the heirlooms that would clearly have been treasured by Mississippi archivists were instead donated to the Western Reserve Historical Society of Cleveland, Ohio, only to be sold at auction in 2001. Estate of Alice Hinds Fallon.

## CHAPTER TWELVE: The Great White Hunter

1) Gregory C. Wilson, "How The Teddy Bear Got His Name," *Potomac Magazine*, 30 November 1969; 33-36. Wilson was curator of the Roosevelt Collection at Harvard.

2) Scullery, *Bear Hunter's Century*, 134.

3) After the initial action was taken by Wheeler in Cuba, he was heard to shout, "We've got the Yankees on the run." John P. Dyer, *From Shiloh to San Juan, The Life of "Fighting Joe" Wheeler*, (Baton Rouge: Louisiana State University Press, 1941), 230. Roosevelt considered Wheeler "a regular game-cock." Edumund Morris, *The Rise of Theodore Roosevelt*, (New York: Ballantine Books, 1979), 639.

4) Edmund Morris, *The Rise of Theodore Roosevelt*, (New York: Ballantine Books, 1979), 698-734. For a detailed account of the inauguration of Roosevelt, see: Edmund Morris, *Theodore Rex*, (New York: Random House, 2001), 3-19.

5) Morris, *Rise of Theodore Roosevelt*, 35, 43, 49.

6) Ibid., 384. The Boone & Crockett Club was founded by Roosevelt to preserve game in the wild. It's efforts largely contributed to the passage of the Forest Reserve Act and the establishment of the National Park system.

7) Nannie Pitts McLemore, "The Progressive Era," McLemore, *History of Mississippi*, vol. 2, 29-38.

8) Lindsay Denison, "President Roosevelt's Mississippi Bear Hunt," *Outing*, February, 1903; 603-610.

9) Goodspeed, *Memoirs of Mississippi*, 900.

10) Shelby Foote, conversation with the author, 20 November 1998.

11) Theodore Roosevelt Papers, Library of Congress, Series 14, General Correspondence, Letter from Roosevelt to Fish, 6 November 1902. Microfilm collection at W. D. McCain Library, University of Southern Mississippi, Hattiesburg.

12) Theodore Roosevelt Papers, Letter from Roosevelt to Parker, 6 November 1902.

13) Theodore Roosevelt Papers, Letter from Chief John E. Wilkie to George Cortelyou, Secretary to the President, 7 November 1902. Assigned to protect the President on the trip were operatives Tyree, Walsh, and Connell.

14) Denison, "Roosevelt's Mississippi Bear Hunt," 603.

*Notes to Pages 157-164 • 239*

15) Jacob McGavock Dickinson Papers, Tennessee Library and Archives, Nashville, Scrapbook 4.
16) J. L. Burt, "Holt Collier," *The Pica,* 23 January 1934, 3,5, [publication of the Greenville High School], MDAH, microfilm roll A-2273.
17) Letter from one hundred-year-old Willie Claiborne Brown to Mayersville postmaster Herbert Herman dated 27 October 1972, *Deer Creek Pilot,* [Rolling Fork, Miss.], March, 1972. Brown was a local familiar with the events of the hunt. He wrote of the Roosevelt's request on Sunday for a dinner of possum. Freeman Wallace left the camp and rode to the home of Mack Karson who "took old Rover, his trained possum dog, and made the dream come true." On Sunday the 16th, Swint Pope cooked the possum and served it with sweet potatoes and turnip greens "and they all ate and sang."
18) Letter from John Parker, 26 November 1902, Theodore Roosevelt Papers.
19) Dickson, "Bear Stories," 21.
20) Wilson, "Teddy Bear Got His Name," 34.
21) Armstrong, "Tracked Bear for Roosevelt," 5.
22) "President Speeds Toward Bruin Land," Cincinnati, Ohio, November 13, 1902; "President Hunts Bear," Memphis, Tennessee, November 13, 1902; "In the Mississippi Canebrake," Memphis, Tennessee, November 13, 1902; "President Ready to Meet a Bear," Smedes, Mississippi. Taken from miscellaneous newspaper accounts on file at the Roosevelt Collection, Harvard University.
23) "President Ready to Meet a Bear," Smedes, Mississippi.
24) Jacob M. Dickinson, "Stories and Reminiscences: "Theodore Roosevelt's Mississippi Bear Hunt," *Outdoor America,* April, 1924; 5, 6, 60.
25) Morris, *Rise of Theodore Roosevelt,* 21.
26) Armstrong, "Tracked Bear for Roosevelt," 5.
27) "President Ready To Meet a Bear," taken from miscellaneous newspaper accounts on file at the Roosevelt Collection, Harvard University.
28) Denison, "Roosevelt's Mississippi Bear Hunt," 607. It was reported that two correspondents tried to get into camp only to be stopped by Freeman Wallace. Complaining that the guards had "no legal right to stop us," Wallace responded by tapping his shotgun and saying "This is the only law we know." When a bribe of twenty-five dollars was attempted on another guard, the correspondents were told, "I wouldn't take you out there for a million dollars. Mistah Mangum told us any of us who took white men there would be shot or hung, and I ain't goin' to take no chances." *New York Times,* 15 November 1902.
29) Denison, "Roosevelt's Mississippi Bear Hunt," 607-8.
30) Dickinson, "Stories and Reminiscences," 5; Denison, "Roosevelt's Mississippi Bear Hunt," 608. Roosevelt was "satisfied at the simplicity of the arrangements." His tent contained "four cots which were occupied...by himself, Mr. Fish, Mr. Dickinson, and Secretary Cortelyou. The negroes slept on blankets under an open tent fly." *New York Times,* 15 November 1902.

240 • *Notes to Pages 165-172*

## CHAPTER THIRTEEN: The "Picnic"

1) Dickinson, "Stories and Reminiscences," 60. This poem titled "The Hunt" is five verses. The author is unknown, described only as a "local poet." This poem was discovered in the papers of Jacob Dickinson along with several other documents relating to the 1902 Mississippi bear hunt. It is likely that the poem was written in camp and read around the campfire. Jacob McGavock Dickinson Papers.

2) Dickson, "Bear Stories," 21.

3) Ibid.

4) Ibid. Mangum's "indisposition" is thought to have been from too much drink and a late night around the campfire. Roosevelt saw little amusement at having such fun on a hunt. While hunting he never partook of tobacco or alcohol, nor would he hunt on a Sunday. It is likely that the only men on this expedition that would not drink were the president and Collier. John Parker writing of Roosevelt said, "In all of our various trips he never once tasted intoxicants of any kind or used tobacco in any form, and in addition I never once heard him tell a smutty story." John Parker Collection.

5) Denison, "Roosevelt's Mississippi Bear Hunt," 608.

6) Ibid.; Dickinson, "Stories and Reminiscences," 6. Courtelou and Lung went on a deer hunt, and the others are believed to have remained at the camp.

7) Dickson, "Bear Stories," 21.

8) Harris Dickson Papers, MDAH.

9) Harris Dickson Papers, MDAH.

10) Denison, "Roosevelt's Mississippi Bear Hunt," 609.

11) Dickson, "Bear Stories," 52.

12) Dickson, "Bear Stories," 52.

13) *American Slave*, 455. It should be noted that of the many interviews given by Collier, this is the only reference in which he took credit for discouraging Roosevelt from killing the bear.

14) Dickson, "Bear Stories," 52.

15) Ibid.

16) Theodore Roosevelt Papers, Library of Congress, Series 1, Letters Received, Memorandum dated 14 November 1902. To this inventory was added "Female bear. Weight 180 pounds. Measured 5 feet 4 inches" and "Large female bear — 220 lbs. Killed 2 days after the other."

17) *American Slave*, 456. John Parker wrote an account of this episode in 1924 that provides additional information. He remembered that they had fifty four dogs on the hunt and that the conditions were very hard and dry, so much so that "after the first day, their feet were very raw and they did not hunt as effectively as we had hoped." After Roosevelt refused to kill the bear he dispatched Parker to finish the beast off. Parker wrote: "I distinctly remember his throwing a knife which had been sent him by the Emperor of Japan, a wonderful steel object about the thickness of a paper cutter, telling me that I had been at the head of the chase and to kill him. I declined to use that knife, but John McIlhenny threw his hunting knife, and I used that, sticking

the bear under the ribs while the dogs were at him in front." Letter from John Parker to Judge J. M. Dickinson, Chicago, Ill., 26 February 1924. John Parker Collection.

18) *American Slave,* 456.

19) Dickson, "Bearslayer," 15; *American Slave,* 457; Armstrong, "Tracked Bear for Roosevelt," 4.

20) Dickinson, "Stories and Reminiscences," 5. The final tally of kills attributed to Robert Eager Bobo, also a Mississippian, is not known. It is estimated that by the end of his hunting career, Holt Collier's bear kills were in excess of three thousand.

21) Denison, "Roosevelt's Mississippi Bear Hunt," 610.

22) Ibid.

23) Dickson, "Holt Collier," Box 11, page 8, MDAH. This is the only documented account in which Holt Collier ever acknowledged having any offspring.

24) Dickinson, "Stories and Reminiscences," 5. One can only speculate to what extent Roosevelt went to elicit Collier's admission. Unfortunately, the details were never reduced to writing.

25) Denison, "Roosevelt's Mississippi Bear Hunt," 610.

26) *New York Times,* 15 November 1902.

27) Ibid.

28) Theodore Roosevelt Papers, Library of Congress, Series 1, Letters Received, Letter from Parker to Roosevelt, 26 November 1902.

29) Elting E. Morison, *The Letters of Theodore Roosevelt,* (Cambridge, Mass.: Harvard University Press, 1951), 378.

30) Denison, "Roosevelt's Mississippi Bear Hunt," 603.

31) The best explanation of the caption is made by Edmund Morris who attributes this to a comment by Dr. Booker T. Washington, who had earlier declared Theodore Roosevelt's opposition to any further "drawing of the color line" in southern politics. Edmund Morris, *Theodore Rex,* (New York: Random House, 2001), 172.

32) Wilson, "Teddy Bear Got His Name," 34.

## CHAPTER FOURTEEN: In the Louisiana Canebrakes

1) William Faulkner, *Go Down Moses* (New York: Random House, 1940), 170.

2) In January, 1903, the Columbian chargé at Washington signed the Hay-Herran Treaty leasing the land for the Panama Canal to the United States for 100 years. In February the Department of Commerce and Labor was created with George B. Cortelyou, a 1902 hunt participant, its first secretary.

3) Author's interviews and oral histories taken from Holt's neighbors, Luella Anderson (b. 1910) and Nathan Wilson (b. 1918). Ms. Anderson claims that Toots was a stepchild. Mr. Wilson believes him to have been Collier's son, and that he was born about 1905.

4) Mississippi Laws, Chapter 73, Acts of 1900. The Confederate Pension Act of 1900 had been passed to provide for indigent servants, soldiers and sailors of the Confederacy.

5) Eunice Stockwell Papers, MDAH.

6) Confederate Pensions, MDAH.

7) Seymour Eaton, *The Roosevelt Bears, Their Travels and Adventures*, illus. V. Floyd Campbell, (Philadelphia: Edward Stern & Co., 1906). The bears depicted in this popular work were "Teddy-B" and "Teddy-G," often thought of as "boy-girl," "bad-good," and "black-grey." The volume contains poetry, prose, and delightful illustrations.

8) William F. Holmes, *The White Chief: James Kimble Vardaman*, (Baton Rouge: Louisiana State University Press, 1970). 105-111, citing *Greenwood Commonwealth*, 10 January, 7 February, 21 March, and 22 August 1903. See Albert D. Kirwan, *Revolt of the Rednecks: Mississippi Politics, 1876-1925* (New York: Harper & Row, 1951), 155-160.

9) Theodore Roosevelt Papers, Library of Congress, Series 1, Letters Received, Campaign flier titled "To the White Voters and the Wives and Daughters of Richmond.".

10) Stamboul, Louisiana was re-named 'Roosevelt' in 1907 in honor of the president.

11) Dickson, "When the President Hunts," 3. Two months prior to joining the President on this hunt a brief newspaper article announced that S. S. Brown, Walter Blacle, Louis Suton, Harley Metcalfe and Holt Collier, "whose fame as a bear killer is even known at the [W]hite [H]ouse," departed on a four day hunt with twenty-two dogs "a majority of which were curs of this city picked up on the street." *Greenville Times*, 31 August 1907.

12) Schullery, *Bear Hunter's Century*, 185. Lilly was described by John Parker as "a man of 55 years of age who had never taken a smoke, chew or drink in his life, and did not use either tea or coffee. He never swore, and under no conditions, hunted or permitted his dogs to hunt on Sundays. The best description of his physique is illustrated by the fact that he could take three flour barrels, and, at his age, could go forward and backward, jumping in and out with the greatest ease." John Parker Collection.

13) Roosevelt, "Louisiana Canebrakes," 48.

14) Ibid.

15) Dickson, "When the President Hunts," 4. The misspelling of "Metcalfe" is Dickson's error.

16) Roosevelt, "Louisiana Canebrakes," 49. The misspelling of "Metcalfe" and "Lilly" are Roosevelt's error.

17) Dickson, "When the President Hunts," 4. It was observed by John Parker after this experience that: "Men who are fond of hunting represent, as a rule, those who love the open life, who love their fellow-men and who are fearless. Theodore Roosevelt possessed all of these qualities to the superlative degree, and bore hardships of every kind which are necessarily one of the adjuncts of hunting, without the slightest complaint of any kind or character, and in addition thereto, deservedly earned the affection and absolute confidence of those

who were with him on these trips....On one particular occasion when we were camping on the Tensas River and moved down about fifteen miles to a lower and better hunting ground, in some way the commissary department got lost in the woods, and when the bunch of hungry men pulled up in camp after a long hard ride, the entire food of any kind or character was represented by one piece of salt meat and a sack of meal, which had been brought along for dog bread. The nearest approach to cooking utensils was an old frying pan, and it immediately eased any murmurings on the part of the others to see first the meat fry and then the corn bread patted into corn cakes or tortillos, and to hear the Colonel say 'After our long ride, this is just bully.'" John Parker Collection.

18) Douglas C. Wynn, "Remarks at Dedication of Theodore Roosevelt Monument, Bear Lake, Madison Parish, La., 14 October 1960. This work is unpublished and was found among the private collection of Jane Weathers. Wynn related this moment to a passage from Kipling: "But there is neither East nor West nor border nor breed nor birth / When two strong men stand face to face though they come from the ends of the earth."

19) Dickson, "When the President Hunts," 24.

20) Ibid.

21) Roosevelt, "Louisiana Canebrakes," 56-8.

22) R. L. Wilson, *Theodore Roosevelt Outdoorsman* (Agoura, California: Trophy Room Books, 1994), 210. On each gun was a silver plate engraved with the name of the recipient, the year 1907, and the fact that it was presented by President Theodore Roosevelt. *Delta Review*, Autumn Issue, 1964.

23) Theodore Roosevelt, *Theodore Roosevelt: An Autobiography* (New York: Macmillan, 1913), 332.

24) Dickson, "Bear Stories," 52.

## CHAPTER FIFTEEN: Pensioner

1) Faulkner, *Go Down Moses*, 335.

2) Author's interviews and oral histories from Jane Metcalfe Weathers, daughter of Harley and "Sallie" Metcalfe, 9 May 1992. "Miss Jane" told the author that the cub was a family pet enjoyed by her and brothers, Harley Jr., Frederick, and Edmund.

3) Eunice Stockwell Collection, MDAH.

4) Percy, *Lanterns*, 128.

5) Ibid., 230.

6) Armstrong, "Tracked Bear for Roosevelt," 4.

7) Harris Dickson Papers, MDAH. Dickson's works were published in New York, Philadelphia, Indianapolis, and London. Among them were: *She That Hesitates, The Ravanels, Duke of Devil-May-Care, Gabrielle Transgressor, The Black Wolf's Breed,* and *Old Reliable.* He also wrote many short stories.

8) Dickson, "Holt Collier," box 11, page 7, MDAH.

9) Ibid.

10) Land Records of the Washington County Chancery Clerk, Book 114, page 157.
11) *American Slave*, 448.
12) Author's interviews and oral histories with Peter Johnson, 14 December 1992, Nathan Wilson, 14 December 1992, and Luella Anderson, 20 June 1992.
13) Undated newspaper article, Holt Collier Subject File, MDAH. In the 1990's Thomas 'Pete' Johnson returned to Mississippi promoting the memory of Holt Collier. Because of his efforts, a highway marker recognizing Collier was dedicated at the Live Oak Cemetery in Greenville in 1996.
14) Noel Workman, "The Colorful Willa Johnson," *Delta Review*, Holiday, 1964.
15) Burt, "Holt Collier," 3,5.
16) *American Slave*, 447.
17) Barry, *Rising Tide*, 305.
18) Percy, *Lanterns*, 250.
19) Approximately fifty percent of the African Americans of Washington County migrated north after the 1927 flood. Marvin E. Goodwin, *Black Migration in America from 1915-1960* (New York: Lewiston, 1990).
20) Author's interviews and oral histories of Jane Weathers, 9 May 1992, Leila C. Wynn, Harley Metcalfe III, and John Adams, 2 October 1996.
21) Eddie LaFoe and John Johnson conversations with Hank Burdine provided to author, 11 February 1998.
22) Confederate Pension Records, MDAH.
23) Percy, *Lanterns*, 270.
24) Land Records of the Washington County Chancery Clerk, Deed Book 221, page 116.
25) Author's interviews and oral history of Peter Johnson, E. B. LaFoe Jr., and Harley Metcalfe III. During prohibition several of the town's gentlemen relied upon Holt to supply them with bootleg or 'corn' whiskey.

## **CHAPTER SIXTEEN: End of the Hunt**

1) Faulkner, *Go Down Moses*, 247.
2) Author's interview and oral history of Pete Johnson, 14 December 1992.
3) Armstrong, "Tracked Bear for Roosevelt," 21.
4) Harris Dickson Papers, MDAH.
5) *American Slave*, 463.
6) Harris Dickson Papers, MDAH. Holt had not attended school himself. He had been left temporarily at Bardstown to be a juvenile valet to Alice Crozier's son.
7) Mrs. Holcombe had an interest in Collier and visited him often. She gathered considerable information on him and, like Harris Dickson, planned a work on his life. *The American Slave*, 462. Holt's home was located (and remains standing today) at 304 North Broadway in Greenville, Mississippi. The home of Sarah Williams was located at 507 North Broadway.

*Notes to Pages 214-220* • 245

8) Death Certificate Records, MDAH.

9) Author's interview and oral history of Pete Johnson, 14 December 1992.

10) Obituary, *Daily Democrat Times,* [Greenville, Miss.], 3 August 1936. Author's interview and oral history of Pete Johnson, 14 December 1992.

## EPILOGUE

1) *Daily Democrat Times,* August 10, 1936. Holt Collier Subject File, MDAH.

2) House Bill 951 designating the Teddy bear as the state toy of Mississippi was signed into law by Governor Ronnie Musgrove on March 22, 2002. Although the bill failed to mention or recognize this Mississippi legend by name, it is yet another recognition for Holt Collier's accomplishments.

3) Holt Collier Subject File, MDAH, letter from Laura Harrell to Major Robert E. Greene, U. S. Army Headquarters, Washington, D. C., 20 March 1970. Holt Collier was not the only slave to serve the Confederacy. Though they were not armed combatants, several other Washington County slaves served in various capacities, including Collier's brother, Marshall, who also received a servant's pension following the war. Other African-Americans from Washington County who served the Confederacy in some capacity included: Tom Kennedy, Ed Rankin, John Tolbert, Nat Offutt, Anderson Rice, Dolfus Smith, Tige Crizory, Dick Dixon, Thornton Davis, Dick Cox, Saul Swiney, John Freeman, Joshua Willis, John Mills, John Robb, Wash Nugent, Wash Nelson, Bill Cately, Ike Freeman, Pink Lee, John Warfield, Jake Campbell, Anders Folks, Charles Scott, Alec Byers, Ike Cain, Henry Singleton, Norval Johnson, Sol Kirk, Henry Fisher, Dan Moody, Reuben Holmes, Somerset Hickman, Armstron Davis, Alec Miller, Tom Freeman, Lewis Blanton, Bill Turnbull, John Hull, Bill Finlay, Bawley Frazier, Merdy Nelson, Orville Cately, Jerome McCutchen, Dolph Smith, Bennie Denson, Holt Wallace, Ceasar Scott, Lewis McMickens, and Ned Davis. *Greenville Times,* 28 November 1887.

4) Sparks, *War Between the States,* 371.

5) Randal B. Caldwell, "The Assassination' of Captain King of College Farm, Iowa," (unpublished manuscript, 1991).

6) Ibid.

7) Harris Dickson Papers, MDAH.

8) Tenth Census of the United States, 1880; Author's oral history and interview with Fredrick Smith, Greenville, Mississippi, grandson of Adeline Hinds, listed in Census of 1880 as child of Augusta and Thomas Hinds.

9) Nathan Miller, *Theodore Roosevelt: A Life,* (New York: Morrow, 1992), 496-500. Roosevelt and his son Kermit killed 17 lions, 11 elephants, 20 rhinoceroses, 9 giraffes, 47 gazelles, 8 hippopotamuses, 29 zebras, 9 hyenas, and many others, for a total of 512 kills.

10) Burt, *The Pica,* 3,5.

11) Faulkner, *Go Down Moses,* 167.

12) Ibid, 170.

# INDEX

## A

Abbeville, Mississippi  67, 68
Adams, Colonel Wirt  44, 82, 84-5, 87, 105, 231
Adams, John  208
Adams, John 'Grizzly'  151
Adams' Mississippi Cavalry  90
Adams, Nathan  208
Alligator, Mississippi  161
Amacker, Major,1907 hunt  188
Anderson, Lomax  31
Anderson, Luella  204, 241
Anguilla, Mississippi  161
Archer, Reverend Stevenson  97-8, 233
Arcola, Mississippi  97
Army of Northern Virginia  116
Atlanta, Georgia  96

## B

Baldwin, Mississippi  64
Bardstown, Kentucky  35, 140, 212, 244
Baseball, Holt Collier's Club  139
Battle of Atlanta  96
Battle of Belmont  92
Battle of Corinth  52
Battle of Horseshoe Bend  8
Battle of Iuka  64, 105
Battle of Milliken's Bend  108
Battle of New Orleans  8-9, 11, 23
Battle of Shiloh  40, 51-61, 84, 104, 185
 casualties, 55
Bayou Pierre  3
Bear Creek  75
Bear Lake, Louisiana  191-2
Beauregard, General P. G. T.  51-52, 54, 56, 58, 61, 104
Beck, Dr. Otis H.  214
Belle Air Plantation  125
Belting  64
Benton, Mississippi  90, 92
Berryman, Clifford Kennedy  178-180, 183, 219
Bethesda, Tennessee  77
Big Black River  85, 90, 91
Big Black River Bridge  108
Big Sunflower River  159, 168
Black Bayou  92
Black bear  136-8
Black Hawk War  37, 46

Blanton, Dr. Orville M.  99-100, 125-7, 130
 Full pardon for  130
Blanton family  125-7
Blanton, Lewis  245
Blanton, William C.  125
Blantonia Plantation  125
Bobo, Mississippi  161
Bobo, Robert Eager  151, 172, 241
Boddie, Fay S.  203
Boggy Bayou  30, 216
Bogue Phalia River  92, 198
Bolivar County, Mississippi  79, 92, 114, 198
Bolivar, Mississippi  93
Bolivar, Tennessee  66, 73
Bolivar Troop  92
Bolton, Mississippi  90
Bolton Station  82
Booker, Captain  94
Boone, Daniel  vi, 151
Boone & Crockett Club  153, 238
Booneville, Mississippi  60, 104
Border ruffians  104
Bourbon County, Kentucky  5
Bowen, General John  115
Bowie knives  110, 136
Bowling Green, Kentucky  46, 48-9, 84, 185
Bradley, Sheriff Bill "Wild Cat"  143, 144
Bragg, General Braxton  44, 51, 53, 61, 65, 67-8, 75, 76-8, 88
Brandon, Mississippi  87
Breathitt County, Kentucky  59
Breckenridge, General John C.  44, 51, 56, 155
Brentwood, Tennessee  78
Breton Wildlife Refuge  186
Brighton Beach, New York  22, 32, 34, 140, 226
Brighton Plantation  146
Broadway Street, Greenville  203, 214
Brogden's Springs, Texas  58
Brown, Jeff  31
Brownsville, Mississippi  90
Bruinsburg, Mississippi  6, 81, 84, 107
Buck, Mrs. Kate Coleman  224, 237
Buell, General Don C.  50-1, 54-5, 65
Bureau of Indian Affairs  111
Bureau of Refugees, Freedmen and Abandoned Lands  114, 234, 235

246

Burleson, Alabama 75
Burlington, Iowa 104
Burr, Aaron 6
Burrus, Archie Clement 100
Burrus, John Crawford 93, 95, 100, 185
Bush's Ferry 85
Byers, Alec 245
Byrne, Major Edward P. 54-5, 125, 126-7, 129, 130
Byrne's Artillery 38, 45, 54-5, 61, 185

# C

Cain, Ike 245
Cairo, Illinois 46
Camden, Mississippi 90
Cameron, A. J. 40
Campbell, Jake 245
Camp Boone, Tennessee 44, 47, 48
Camp Dunbar, Mississippi 40
Cane Ridge Church 40
Canton, Mississippi 80, 90
Carpetbagger rule 128, 130, 133
Carrollville, Mississippi 64
Carvelle Saloon 125-6
Cately, Bill 245
Cately, Orville 245
Catfish Row 26
Census of 1880 142, 245
Chalmers, General James 44
Champion Hill, Mississippi 81, 108
Charleston Harbor 106
Chattanooga, Tennessee 65
Chickasaw Bluffs, Mississippi 81
Choctaw Agency 80
Choctaw Bayou 83, 84
Choctaw Nation 12-13, 17
Cincinnati, Ohio 34, 161
Citronelle, Alabama 96
Clark, General Charles 17, 44, 47, 50, 51, 53, 84, 92, 94
  Captain 92
  Governor 44, 148
Clark, George Rogers 3
Clarksdale, Mississippi 161
Clear Creek 104
Clinton, Mississippi 86, 90, 108
Coahoma County, Mississippi 114
Cocks, Drusilla (Sallie) 18
Coe, Milford 92-5
Coffeeville, Mississippi 68
Cold Springs Plantation 146
Coldwater River 106

Coleman, Dr. Frank 18
Coleman, Judge John 18
College Farm, Iowa 103
Collier, Allen 5, 11, 20, 143
Collier, Amanda 20
Collier, Augusta (Gusta) 20, 40, 125, 129, 143, 217
Collier, Coley 142
Collier, Daphne 12, 16, 17-18, 20, 23, 129, 143,
Collier, Effy 142
Collier, Elliot 25
Collier family plot 25
Collier, Frances Parker 184, 207-8, 210-11
Collier, Harrison 11-12, 16, 17-18, 20, 23, 41, 129, 143, 184
Collier, Holt 20, 21-4, 26, 28-36, 38-45, 47-9, 51, 53-4, 59, 61-66, 68-70, 73-76, 80, 82, 84-6, 90-92, 94-97, 100-105, 108-112, 114-117, 119-220
  deputy 145
  early childhood 30-31
  injured by his prey 33
  killed his first bear, age of ten 33
  shooting of conductor 109-110
Collier, J. B. 143
Collier, Joseph 20
Collier, Maggie Collier 142
Collier, Maria 20
Collier, Meriamm 20
Collier, Marimon 143
Collier, Marshall 20, 21, 22, 23, 138, 143, 211, 245
Collier, Mary 20, 129
  grave marker 25
Collier, Rich 112, 116-117
Collier, Rose 142, 146
  wife of Holt Collier 142, 146
Collier, Topp 143
Columbia Pike 76
Columbia, Tennessee 58, 75-77, 79
Columbus, Mississippi 80
Columbus, Ohio 161
Commercial National Bank of Greenville 148, 210
Company 'I', Ninth Texas Cavalry 59-60, 63-66, 89, 91, 96
Confederate hospital 55
Confederate Servant's Pension 185
Confederate States of America 38, 215

248 • *Holt Collier*

Connell, Secret Service operative 238
Cook, Fields xiv
Coon Bayou 163
Cooper's Deerslayer 189
Corinth, Mississippi 51-2, 55-6, 58, 59-62, 64, 67-8, 104, 105, 228
    second battle of 64-68
Cortelyou, George B. 156, 239, 241
    Chairman, Republican National Committee 156
    Postmaster General 156
    Private secretary to Presidents McKinley and Roosevelt 156
    Secretary of Commerce 156
    Secretary of the Treasury 156
Cosby's First Brigade 82
Courtland Plantation 146
Court martial of:
    General Van Dorn 67
    Holt Collier 115-117
Courtney House 126
Cox, Dick 245
Cravat, Rebecca 13
Creek Indians 7-8
    defeated at Talladega 8
    War of 1812 7
Crizory, Tige 245
Crockett, Davy vi, 151
Crouch, J. H. 186
Crozier, Alice 35, 212
Crozier, Edward W. 40
Cumberland Gap 46
Cumberland River 5, 49
Currell, Mrs. C. M. 224, 237

# D

*Daily Democrat Times* 215
Dakota Territory 133
Darden, Putnam 40, 47
Davis, Armstron 245
Davis, Isaac 10
Davis, Jefferson Finis 10-12, 17, 21, 41, 196
    childhood friend of Howell Hinds 10-12, 17
    first letter from Howell Hinds 41
    visitor to Home Hill Plantation 21
    United States Senator 37
    President of CSA 37-8, 49-51, 58, 61-2, 67-9, 82, 87, 226
Davis, Joseph E. 10
Davis' Mill 73, 105
Davis, Ned 245
Davis, Samuel 10
Davis, Thornton 245
Deed of gift of slaves 40
Deer Creek 29, 92, 97, 139, 237
Delta Compress Company 148
Delta Rangers 89-102
Democratic Party 133, 153, 187
Denison, Lindsay 169, 172, 175, 202, 239
Denson, Bennie 245
Dent, Colonel 97
Department of Southern Mississippi 61
Depression of 1929 212
Depression of 1873 131
Devours, Julia 224
Dickinson, Jacob 155, 161, 172, 173, 197, 239, 240
    Asst. U. S. Attorney General 155
    General Counsel for the Illinois Central Railroad 155
    Secretary of War 155
    Tenn. Supreme Court Justice 155
Dickson, Harris 22, 26, 42, 85, 116, 174, 188, 201-2, 205, 212, 217, 220
District of Mississippi 67
District of Vicksburg 114
District of Washington 114
Dixon, Dick 245
Dorsey, Calvin 158, 168, 170
Dorsey, Frank 158, 168, 170
*Drawing the Line in Mississippi* 178-9
Duck Hill, Mississippi 90
Dunbar, a wounded man 47
Dundee, Mississippi 161
Dunn, Samual Reed 29
Durant, Mississippi 90

# E

Earl, Lieutenant I. N. 101
Eaton, Seymour 187
Editorial cartoons 179-182, 219
Edward's Depot 86
Edwards Station 82
Egremont Plantation 155
Egypt Plantation 92
Election of 1875 133
Eleventh Louisiana Colored Infantry 108
Elizabeth, New Jersey 127
Elizabethtown, Kentucky 48
Elkhorn Tavern 58
English, Captain James N. 59

# Index • 249

Enolds, Alec 188, 190, 194, 196
Enolds, Bill 158, 168
Epps, Wyatt, innkeeper 21
Estill, Mississippi 161
Estill, Jack 94-5
Estill, Rhodes 93
Evans, Captain Perry 59-60, 62-4, 73, 80, 85-6, 89, 91-2, 94-100, 121, 124, 216, 220
Evans' Rangers (Texas Scouts) 63-4, 80, 112, 116, 126,185, 232
Evans, Tom 121
Everman, W. W. 185
Execution of slaves, Jesse and Albert 21-22

## F

Farmington, Mississippi 60-61, 77
Fathers, Sam 220
Faulkner's *Go Down Moses* 220
Faulkner, William xi, 205, 211, 220
Fayette, Mississippi 21-2, 101
Fields, Colonel Cristopher 93
Fifth Iowa Infantry 104-108
Finlay, Bill 245
First Mississippi Cavalry Regiment 92
First United States Volunteer Cavalry 152
Fish, Stuyvesant 154-5, 161, 174, 175, 239
Fisher, Henry 245
Flood of 1927 207-8, 225, 244
Florence, Alabama 75
Flournoy, General Thomas 7-10
  attack at Burnt Corn Creek 7
Floyd, Louisiana 143
Fogg, Mrs. Godfrey M. 224, 237
Folks, Anders 245
Foote, Admiral Andrew Hull 46, 49
Foote, Huger Lee 154-5, 161, 166, 168, 170, 173
Foote, Shelby 1655
Fornication of Thomas Hinds 125
Forrest, General Nathan Bedford 44, 50, 61, 63, 72, 74, 76, 77, 78, 84, 96, 98, 152, 229
Fort Donelson 49-50, 227
Fort Henry 49
Fort Mims 7
Fort Mims Massacre 7, 10
Fort Pemberton 106
Fort Stoddert 7
Fort Sumter 38, 51

Fort Worth, Texas 121, 124
Forty-Ninth Infantry Regiment 108
Fourth Iowa Cavalry 85
Fourth Wisconsin Cavalry 101
Fowler, arrest and execution of 98-99, 233
Franklin, Tennessee 78, 96
Frazier, Bawley 245
Free Presbyterian Church 104
Freedmen's Bureau 110, 114, 234
Freeman, Ike 245
Freeman, John 245
Freeman, Tom 245

## G

Gallagher, arrest of 98
Garvin's Ferry 91
General Assembly of the Territory of Mississippi 4
Georgia Assembly 3
Glenbar Plantation 29, 150, 196
Glencoe horses 22
Goat Island 93
Goodman Station 90
Grand Gulf, Mississippi 81
Grand Junction, Tennessee 72, 73, 105
Grand Lake, Arkansas 105
Grant, General Ulysses S. 46, 49-57, 68-71, 72, 75, 80-84, 86-7, 89, 97, 105, 106, 107, 108
Grayson County, Texas 58
Green, Abner 4
Green family 17-18
Green, General Nathaniel 29
Green, Thomas 3-4
Green, Thomas, Jr. 3-5
  father of Leminda Green 5, 25
Green River Bridge, skirmish 47-49
Greenville, Mississippi 19, 28-31, 41, 79, 99, 109, 110, 112, 113-117, 125, 126-7, 130, 148, 155, 159, 185, 188, 199-200, 202, 203-5, 207, 209, 210-212, 214-215, 216, 217, 224
  old Greenville 5, 19, 100, 128, 222
Greenville Compress Company 148
Greenville Landing 31, 43
Greenwood, Mississippi 106, 187
Grenada, Mississippi 68, 69,74, 105
Grierson, Colonel Benjamin F. 72-4, 81, 83
Guerilla outlaws 97
Gulf of Mexico 26

Gunfight at Washburn's Ferry vii
Gwin, Dr. William M. 15, 223

# H

Hamilton, General Schuyler 105
Hampton, Wade 141, 151, 153-4
Handy, W. C. 199
Hard Times, Louisiana 107
Hardee's Division 45
Hardee, General William 51, 90, 155
Harper, William L. 40
Hatchie Bridge 66
Hatchie River 66
Havana Harbor 152
Headquarters, District of Mississippi 67
Helena, Arkansas 106
Helena Hills 107
Helm, Major George M. 140, 143, 145, 154-5, 157, 161, 166, 174, 177, 186
Hermitage, home of Andrew Jackson 11
Hicksman, Somerset 245
Hill, William 85
Hinds, Alice 18-19, 109, 143, 150, 231
Hinds, Cameron Howell 17, 19, 20-24, 28, 30, 31, 32, 34, 35, 36, 37, 38, 39, 40-50, 51, 53-61, 63, 65, 82-88, 92, 94-5, 98, 100-102, 104, 108-112, 212, 214
    married Drusilla (Sallie) Cocks 18
    visits the Hermitage 11
    Mississippi General Assembly 17
    childhood friend of Jeff Davis 11, 17
    Adjutant Inspector 17
Hinds, Carrie 25
Hinds, Coleman 18, 223, 224
Hinds County, Mississippi 13, 90
Hinds, Ernest 143
Hinds, Evie 143
Hinds family 4, 17-23
    pilgrimages north into Kentucky 33-4
Hinds family plot 24-5
Hinds, Floyd 143
Hinds, General Thomas vii, 7-16, 32, 34, 40, 44, 47-50, 54, 56, 65, 82, 92, 100, 109, 111-113, 124-5, 128-30, 143, 154, 185, 217-18, 229
    appointment as Brigadier General 10
    campaign for Governor 13-14
    descendants of 142-3
    died at Home Hill 16
    inability to serve 56
    Mississippi General Assembly 13, 16
    Justice of the Orphan's Court 7
    service on commission 10-12
    sought appointment as United States Marshall 15
    State Militia 7
    Treaty of Doak's Stand 13
Hinds, Geraldine (Adeline) 217
Hinds, Howell Jr. 150
Hinds, James 4
Hinds, John 4-5
    flatboat captain 4
    grave marker 25
Hinds, John, (son of Howell) 19, 150
Hinds, Leminda Green 7, 11, 12, 25
Hinds, Maria Crozier 18
Hinds, Mary Ann Coleman Lape 18, 129, 130, 150
Hinds Mississippi Dragoons 7-8
Hinds, Richard 25
Hinds, Robb 143
Hinds, Tulley 143
Hinton, M., overseer 224
Hitler, Adolph 219
Hobart, Vice President Garret A. 152
Holcombe, Mrs. T. A. 214, 244
Holly Springs, Mississippi 64, 66, 68-74, 81, 104, 105
    Van Dorn's raid 69-71
Holmes, Governor David 7-8
Holmes, Reuben 245
Holt Collier's Club 139
Home Hill Plantation 5, 12, 14, 15-16, 17, 19-23, 63, 82-4, 87, 124, 130, 218, 224
Hopkinsville, Kentucky 10
Hotel Greenville 148
House servants xiii, 17-18
Hull, John 245
Hunt, D. F. 185-6
Hushpuckena, Mississippi 161

# I

Ideal Toy Corporation 183
Illinois Central Railroad 154
Indian Bayou 91, 99
Indian boy 63
Indian hunters xv

Index • 251

Institution of slavery xiv, 38, 226
Ireys Plantation 98, 224
Island 76 vii, 93-5
Issaquena County, Mississippi 146
Iuka, Mississippi 61, 64, 105

## J

Jackson, Brutus 196
Jackson, General Andrew 3-6, 8-9 11, 13-16, 130, 223
Jackson, General Thomas J. 'Stonewall' 57
Jackson, General William H. 79
Jackson, Mississippi 13, 65, 67, 82, 84, 86-7, 90, 108
    Siege of Jackson 86
Jackson, President Andrew 3-6, 8-9, 11, 13-16, 130, 223
Jackson, Rachel 11
Jackson, Tennessee 65
Jackson, William H. 79
James, Frank 124
Jefferson City, Missouri 104
Jefferson County, Mississippi 18, 21-2, 23-4, 36, 38, 41, 42, 61-2, 83, 84, 87, 98, 124
    early documented events 17-18
Jefferson Flying Artillery 38, 40, 41, 45, 47
Jeffersonian Republicans 12
Jefferson, President Thomas 6, 187
Joe's Bayou 193
Johnson, Ben 158, 162
Johnson, Jack xv
Johnson, Lieutenant, execution of 98
Johnson, Norval 245
Johnson, Peter 204-5, 220, 244
Johnson, President Andrew 223
Johnson, Willa 205
Johnston, General Albert Sidney 45-6, 49-54, 57-8, 59
    death of 53-4
    retreat to Murfreesboro, 49
Johnston, General Joseph E. 80, 81-2, 87, 89-90
Jones, Colonel Dudley 58, 59, 61, 63, 66, 70, 231
Jones, Henry 23
Judge Advocate General Lowry 98
Judge John Coleman 18
Justice O'Bannon 146

## K

Keep, Major, of Mayersville 31
Kelso Plantation 159, 163, 177
Kennard's Bridge 77
Kennedy, Tom 245
Kentucky Brigade 54-5
Key, A. M. 146
Killingsworth, W., death of 21
King, Captain James A. 103-8, 110-17, 217
    murder of 112-17, 128, 175, 196, 201, 215, 216
King, Elizabeth 103-4
King, Elizabeth Meyer 104
King, John 103-4, 234
Kirk, Sol 245
Kosciusko, Mississippi 80, 90

## L

LaFoe, E. B., Sr. 210, 244
LaGrange, Alabama 75
Lake Bolivar 93
Lake Village, Arkansas 31
Lake Washington 28, 155
Lambert, Dr. Alexander 188, 195
Lape, C. C. 18
Lape, Ellie A. 18
Lape, Martha W. 18
Lape, Mary E. 18
Lape, William 18
Lattimore, William 13
Lawrence, Major, of Louisville, Kentucky 31
Lee, Bob 94, 95
Lee, Fitzhugh 197
Lee, General Robert E. 116
Lee, General S. D. 90
Lee, Pink 245
LeFleur, Louis 13
Le Fleur's Bluff 13
Leland, Mississippi 161, 196
Lewisburg, Tennessee 77
Lexington, Alabama 75
Lexington, Kentucky 34
Lexington, Mississippi 74, 90
Lick Creek 52
Lilly, Ben 151, 189-91, 197, 242
Lincoln, President Abraham 37, 38, 89, 115, 152, 218, 223
Litigation 21, 125
    Fornication, Thomas Hinds 125
Little Sunflower camp 162

Little Sunflower River  139, 159, 163, 167, 171-2, 177
Live Oak Cemetery  214, 215, 244
Lobdell Estate  92
Locks Mills, Tennessee  73
Long Beach, New York  32
Longino, Governor Andrew H.  153
Longstreet, General James  57
Lott, Colonel Hiram R.  143-4
Lott, Jesse  143-5
Lott, Richard  143-5
Louisiana Black Bear  136-8
Louisville, Kentucky  161
Louisville, Mississippi  80
Lowry, Judge Advocate General  98
Lucy, pet bear  198, 199
Lula, Mississippi  161
Lumpkin's Mill  66, 105
Lung, Dr. George Augustus  156, 173
Lynnville, Tennessee  75

# M

Madison Station  90
Maine disaster  152
Mangum, E. C., 154, 159, 161, 166, 173, 176, 239, 240
Marmore, gunboat  93
Marshall County, Mississippi  21
Marshall, Tom  116
Martin, John  231
Masonville, Alabama  75
Matthies, Colonel C. L.  105
Maury, General Dabney  67
Maury Institute  58
Mayersville, Mississippi  31
Mays, Willie  xv
McAllister, Major  30
McCardle, W. H.  83
McCulloch, General Henry E.  108
McCutchen, Jerome  245
McDougall, Thomas  156, 177
McIlhenny, John A.  156, 161, 171, 188-9, 192, 193
    Civil Service Commission  156
    Rough Riders  156
McKinley, President William  152, 156, 187
McKinley's assassination  152
McMickens, Lewis  245
McPherson, General James B.  74
Meadock (Medock)  49, 63
Memphis and Charleston Railroad  105

Memphis *Scimitar*  187
Memphis, Tennessee  34, 41, 44, 45, 58, 82, 105, 109, 112, 161, 196, 229
Memphis Zoo  vi, 198
Merdy, Nelson  245
Meridian Expedition  95-6
Meridian, Mississippi  79, 95-6
Messenger's Ferry  86
Metclafe, Albert Gallatin  198-9, 200
Metcalfe, Clive  29, 146, 148-50, 184, 186, 190-200, 211
    diary entries  148-150
Metcalfe family  148, 205
Metcalfe, Frederick Augustus  148, 199
Metcalfe, Harley  146, 148-50, 184, 190-7, 199, 242
Metcalfe, Harley, Jr.  210
Mexican War  37, 46
Meyers, Lieutenant John  112
Meyers, W. S.  113-114
Michtom, Morris  183
Miller, Alec  245
Miller, Dr. Hugh  188
Miller, Martha Priscilla  148
Milliken's Bend  107, 108
Mills, John  245
Mississippi Delta  xiii, 19, 27-8, 39, 92, 110, 131, 139, 148, 161, 200-1, 207-8, 211, 220
Mississippi bear hunt  xv, 151-164
Mississippi Cavalry Regiment  105
Mississippi Central Railroad  65, 66
Mississippi City, Mississippi  40
Mississippi Department of Archives and History  215
Mississippi Dragoons  6, 8
Mississippi General Assembly  13, 16, 17, 237
Mississippi River  4, 6, 12, 13, 20, 26, 57, 68, 89, 91, 93, 100, 104, 106, 107, 113, 143, 207-8
Mississippi Supreme Court  130
Mississippi Valley  26, 141
Mobile, Alabama  40
Mobile & Ohio Railroad  74
Monterey, Tennessee  229
Montgomery, Alabama  37-8
Moody, Dan  245
Moore's Bluff, Mississippi  90
Mooresville, Mississippi  61
Morgan, John Hunt  77, 84
Moscow, Tennessee  73, 105

Mound Bayou, Mississippi 161
Mounds Landing, Mississippi 207
Mount Holly Plantation 155
Mount Horeb Church 214
Mount Pleasant, Tennessee 59, 77
Mount Pleasant, Texas 59
Mulattos, children of Thomas Hinds 143, 217
Mulvilhill, Kentucky 48
Murphy, Colonel Robert C. 72, 74
Mussolini, Benito 219
Myers, Lieutenant John 112

# N

Nashville and Decatur Railroad 76
Nashville, Tennessee 11, 47, 49, 75, 76, 224
Natchez District 3-8, 28
Natchez, Mississppi 4-5, 88, 101, 222
Natchez Trace 5
National Progressive Party 154
National publications 202-3
Negro baiting 187-8
Negro hunters xv
Negro service in Confederate Army 185, 208, 209, 215, 221
Negro soldier 105, 108
Nehi soda 204
Nelson, Wash 245
New Albany, Mississippi 69,73
New Mexico Territory 224
New Orleans Board of Trade 154
New Orleans Cotton Exchange 154
New Orleans, Louisiana 89, 112, 140, 154, 177, 199, 221
Newman, Doctor 110
Newstead Plantation 146, 196, 198, 199, 200, 204
Newton County, Iowa 103, 215
Newton, Iowa 103, 104
New York City, New York 32, 183, 201, 205
New York Herald Tribune 32
Niagara Falls 32, 226
Ninth Texas Cavalry 57-71, 73-80, 82, 85, 90-92, 96, 104, 208, 220
  casualty list 90-91
  cavalry regiments 58
  organization 58
Nitta Yuma, Mississippi 161
Nugent, Wash 245

# O

O'Bannon, Justice 146
Obituary, death of Holt Collier 245
Offutt, Nat 245
Ohio River 93
Onward Store 215
Ord, General Edward 66
Osborn, Ichabod 192, 194
Osborn, John 197
Osborn, Tom 192, 194, 197
*Outing* Magazine 202
Owl Creek 52
Oxford, Mississippi 68, 105

# P

Panther Burn, Mississippi 161
Parker, John M. 154, 156, 161, 168, 169, 171-73, 175, 176-77, 179, 188-9, 192-3, 197, 230, 240
Passenger pigeon 36
Paternalistic servitude, slaveowner xiv, 23-4
Patton, James 13
Pea Ridge, Arkansas 58, 65
Peabody Hotel 26
Pearl River 90
Pelahatchie, Mississippi 90
Pelahatchie Station 86
Pelican Island 186
Pemberton, General John 67, 75, 82-4
Percy, Col. William Alexander Percy 115-116, 141, 155, 185-6, 200, 208
  Father of LeRoy Percy 208-9
  'Gray Eagle' of the Delta 115, 208
Percy, Camille 208
Percy, LeRoy 141, 148, 154-5, 166, 174, 196, 200, 201-2, 208-210, 217
  Carnegie and Rockefeller Foundations 155
  Federal Reserve Bank 155
  U. S. Senator 155, 200
Percy, W. A. 115-116, 141, 155, 185-6, 200, 208
Perkin's Landing 107
Peters, Dr. George B. 79
Peters, Mrs. George B. 79
Pettus, Governor J. J. 39, 49
Phelan, Senator James 67
Pickett, William 151
Pierce, President Franklin 37
Pigeon hunts 36
Pinckney Treaty 3

Pittsburg Landing 50, 51
Platners Fork 6
Plum Ridge Plantation 17, 19-20, 23, 28, 30-36, 39, 43, 63, 82, 92, 97, 99, 108-9, 111-112, 124, 129, 130, 143, 214, 218, 224
Plum Ridge Street 217
Polk, Dr. Thomas G. 125, 129
Polk, General Leonidas 46, 51, 95, 155
    Episcopal Bishop of Louisiana 46
Polk, President James K. 218
Pontotoc, Mississippi 69, 75
Pope, Swint 158, 173-4, 239
Port Gibson, Mississippi 57, 81, 84, 108
Port Hudson, Louisiana 89
Porter, Admiral David 96, 106
Postwar Mississippi 109-111
Powers, Governor R. C. 130
Prentiss, General Benjamin M. 52-53
Presbyterian Church 104
Preston, A. W., Adjutant General 114
Price, General Sterling 65, 67, 105
Princeton, Mississippi 29
Prohibition 208
Provost Marshall 62
Pulaski, Tennessee 75
Pulitzer Prize 178
Pushmataha, Choctaw chief 12

# Q

Quail matches 31
Quantrill, William Clarke 124

# R

Railroad commissaries 159
Rankin, Ed 245
Ratliffe's Ferry 90
Rattlesnake Bayou 19, 28, 30, 32, 97
Raymond, Mississippi 81, 108
Red River 83
Redleaf Plantation 97
Refuge Plantation 98
Republican National Convention 152
Rescue Plantation 188
Rice, Anderson 245
Richardson, Henry 125, 173
Richmond, Virginia 80, 88
Ripley, Mississippi 64, 65, 73
Rixey, Dr. 188, 192
    Surgeon-General of the United States Navy 188

Robb, J. H. 185-6
Robb, John 245
Rocky Ford, Mississippi 72
Rodney, Mississippi 83
Rolling Fork, Mississippi 161
*Roosevelt Bears, The* 187
Roosevelt, Kermit 245
Roosevelt, President Franklin D. 219
Roosevelt, President Theodore vi-vii, xi, 136-7, 151-183, 184, 186-198, 201-204, 206-7, 212, 239
    African safari 218
Rosecrans, General William S. 64, 66, 77
Ross, General Lawrence Sullivan 'Sul' 58, 61, 92, 98, 121
Ross, Jewish merchant 43
Ross' Texas Brigade 58, 63, 66, 92, 96, 98, 231
Rough Riders 152, 156
Russellville, Alabama 75
Ryan, Major W. L. 114

# S

Sacred Heart Convent 18
Sage, Travis Elmore 143, 144-6
    also known as Stacks 145
St. James Episcopal Church 148
St. Louis, Missouri 34, 46, 104, 129, 140, 199, 224
St. Thomas Boy's School 10
Salem Road 71
San Antonio, Texas 152
Santa Fe, Tennessee 75, 76
Saratoga, New York 22, 32, 34, 140, 226
Satartia, Mississippi 82
*Saturday Evening Post* 202
Scorched Earth Policy 95
Scott, Ceasar 245
Scott, Charles 245
*Scribner's* Magazine 202
Second Creek Massacre 39
Sharecropping 131-2
Sharkey County, Mississippi 146, 154, 159, 160, 163, 167, 173, 177, 215
Sharkey, William Lewis 130
Sharpsburg, Maryland 67
Sharp's Mill, Mississippi 60
Sheriff Bill "Wild Cat" Bradley 143, 144
Sheriff George Helm 145

Sherman, General William Tecumseh 52-53, 81, 86-7, 90, 95-6, 153, 232
Sherman, Texas 124
Shields, Leo 196
Shiloh, Battle of 40, 51-61, 84, 104, 185, 228
  casualties 55
Shiloh Church 55
Shiloh Meeting House 51
Ship Island 40, 41
Sillers, William 93, 95
Sims Plantation 97
Singleton, Henry 245
Sixth Cavalry 58
Sixth Kentucky Regiment 55
Skipwith's Landing 97
Skirmish at Bear Creek near Canton 90
Skirmish at Bolton 90
Skirmish at Clinton 90
Skirmish at Edwards Station 90
Skirmish at Jones and Messinger Fords 90
Skirmish between Clinton and Jackson 90
Skirmish near Bolton 90
Skirmish near Canton 90
Skirmish near Clinton 90
Skirmish near Jackson 90
Skunk River 103
Slave honor xiv
Slaves in the Mississippi Delta 19, 26-8, 34
Slaves to serve the Confederacy 245
Smedes Plantation 162, 163
Smedes Station 159, 161-162
Smith, Alf 94, 95
Smith, Dolph 245
Smith, Dolfus 245
Smith, General Kirby 102
Snyder, Jeff 201
Snyder's Bluff 106
Somerville, Tennessee 73
Sonora, Mexico 150
Southern Railroad 82, 86
Spanish-American War 152, 153
Spanish Rule over Natchez Region 3
Springfield, Kentucky 10
Springfield Mansion 4
Springfield Plantation 5-6
Spring Hill, Tennessee 75-79
Stamboul, Louisiana 188
Star of the West 106

State University at Oxford, later to become 'Ole Miss" 20
State's Rights 59
Stewart, Philip Bathell 177
Stoneville, Mississippi 129, 130, 140, 155
Stone, W. W. 30
Sugar Creek 75
Sullivan County, Tennessee 103
Sullivan, Victoria 125
Sunflower County, Mississippi 114, 146
Sunflower River 91, 163, 177
Sutler, a trading boat 94
Swan, Mat 61
Swiftwater Plantation 98, 99, 150
Swiney, Saul 245

## T

Tabasco® Sauce 156
Tallahatchie River 67, 106
Taylor's Springs, Tennessee 77
Teddy Bear vi, 180, 183, 187, 215, 219
Teddy Bear Dinner 197
Tennessee River 49, 50-52, 75
Tensas River 188, 201-2, 243
Texas, Constitutional Convention 59
Texas cowboy 117, 121-124
Theobald, Mrs. Harriet B. 30, 125, 127, 130
Third Cavalry regiments 58
Third Mississippi Infantry Battalion 52
Thirty Third Iowa Regiment 106
Thomastown, Mississippi 80
Thompson's Station, Tennessee 76-78
Tilghman, General Lloyd 67
Tishomingo Hotel 56
Titus Grays 59-60, 64, 73
Tolbert, John 245
Tombigbee River 95
Trans Mississippi Department 80, 91
Trans-Mississippi District 57
Treaty of Doak's Stand 12-13, 17
Tunica, Mississippi 161
Tupelo, Mississippi 61, 75
Turnbull, Bill 245
Twenty Seventh Cavalry Regiment 58
Tyree, secret service operative 238

## U

U. S. Engineers 40
Uncle Tom's Cabin 27

## U

Union Bayou 28
United Confederate Veterans 185, 209
United States Congress 4, 14, 15
   Hinds conducted a campaign 14-15
   Hinds elected to 15
United States District Court 129
United States Fleet 93
United States Military Academy 37, 46, 57, 78, 223

## V

Vaiden, Mississippi 90
Van Buren, Arkansas 51, 58
Van Dorn, General Earl 51, 57-8, 61, 65-7, 68, 72-9, 105, 152, 230
Van Dorn, Peter A. 13, 57, 223
Vardaman, James K. 153, 187, 196, 200
*Vernon*, steamer 44
Vernon, Texas 90
*Vicksburg*, steamer 45
Vicksburg, Mississippi 64, 65, 68, 71, 72, 74-5, 80-90, 95, 107, 108, 113, 115-116, 188, 201
   surrendered 89
Vicksburg National Military Park 196
Villeré Plantation 8
Von Dresser, William 212-213, 220
Von Phul, Mrs. Ben 224, 237

## W

Wallace, Freeman 158, 162, 239
Wallace, Holt 245
Walnut Ridge Plantation 141
Walsh, Secret Service operative 238
Warfield, John 245
Warfield, Mamie Bowen 97
Warren County Courthouse 115, 196
Warrenton, Mississippi 81
Washburn's Ferry 145-6
Washington, Booker T. 187, 241
Washington County Board of Supervisors 188
Washington County Building and Loan Association 210
Washington County Home Guard 148
Washington County, Mississippi 28, 32, 34, 38, 40, 50, 82, 92, 97, 114, 116, 133, 146-7, 150, 155, 201, 205, 208, 211-212
Washington D. C. (City) 104, 159, 174, 193, 202
Washington, General George 29, 187
Washington, Mississippi 6, 15, 19, 222
*Washington Post* 178, 180
Waterproof, Louisiana 83
Waters, Wilburn 151
Water Valley, Mississippi 68
Wayside Plantation 97
West Carroll Parish, Louisiana 143
West, Cato 4
West Point Military Academy 37, 46, 57, 78, 223
Wheeler, General 'Fighting' Joe 76, 77, 84, 152
Whitfield's Texas Brigade 58
Wichita Mountains, Oklahoma 186
Wilkinson County, Mississippi 10
Williams Bayou 28
Williams, Sarah 214, 244
Williamsport, Tennessee 75, 76
Willis, Joshua 245
Wilkerson, Eliza 85-86
Wilson, Nathan 204, 241
Winchester xii, 145, 161, 197, 206, 212
Winterville, Mississippi 98
Wittemberg Cemetery 103, 216, 217
Wittemberg Community, Iowa 113
Wittemberg Manual Labor College 103
Worthington, Sam 34, 89, 97-99
Wright, William 151

## Y

Yazoo and Tallahatchie Rivers, confluence of 107
Yazoo City, Mississippi 85, 90, 96, 98
   Expedition to and capture of 90
Yazoo County, Mississippi 85
Yazoo-Mississippi Delta 26
Yazoo Pass Expedition 105-106
Yazoo Pass Levee 106
Yazoo River 82, 96, 106, 163, 168
Yazoo River Basin 19, 26, 28, 68, 81, 91
Yazoo River Campaign, Expedition 96
Yellow Fever 27, 33
Yerger, Captain William Swann 84-5, 231
Yocona Creek 105